D1231502

Reeling with Laughter

American Film Comedies— From Anarchy to Mockumentary

Michael V. Tueth

THE SCARECROW PRESS, INC.
Lanham • Toronto • Plymouth, UK
2012

Published by Scarecrow Press, Inc.
A wholly owned subsidary of The Rowman & Littlefield Publishing Group, Inc.
4501 Forbes Boulevard, Suite 200, Lanham, Maryland 20706
www.rowman.com

10 Thornbury Road, Plymouth PL6 7PP, United Kingdom

British Library Cataloguing in Publication Information Available

Library of Congress Cataloging-in-Publication Data

Tueth, Michael.
  Reeling with laughter : American film comedies—from anarchy to mockumentary /
Michael V. Tueth.
       p. cm.
  "Introduction—Anarchic comedy: Duck soup—Romantic comedy: It happened one night—Screwball comedy: Bringing up baby and What's up, doc?—Musical comedy: Singin' in the rain—Sex farce: Some like it hot—Satire: Dr. Strangelove—Parody: Young Frankenstein—Neurotic comedy: Annie Hall—Dionysian comedy: Animal house—Mockumentary: Waiting for Guffman—Animated: South Park: bigger longer & uncut."
  Includes bibliographical references and index.
  ISBN 978-0-8108-8367-3 (hardback : alk. paper)—ISBN 978-0-8108-8368-0 (ebook)
  1. Comedy films—United States—History and criticism. I. Title.
PN1995.9.C55T83 2012
791.43'617—dc23   2012000155

∞™ The paper used in this publication meets the minimum requirements of American National Standard for Information Sciences—Permanence of Paper for Printed Library Materials, ANSI/NISO Z39.48-1992.

Printed in the United States of America

Contents

Acknowledgments

I wish to thank the many people involved in the creation of this book. First, I owe much gratitude to my colleagues at Fordham University for their support and advice during the process: Dr. Amy Aronson, Dr. Jennifer Clark, Dr. Brian Rose, Dr. James Van Oosting, and Dr. Jonathan Gray, whose expertise in film studies, narrative, and social change has constantly inspired and encouraged me. I also owe a considerable debt to Ms. Linza Mostert, our department secretary; Lindsay Karp and John Scott in the Faculty Technology Center at Fordham University; and Rev. James Martin, S.J., and Rev. Mark Luedtke, S.J., all of whom have offered me both technical assistance and moral support in my research and writing. Finally, I am deeply grateful for the personnel and resources of the Gerald M. Quinn Library and the Walsh Family Library at Fordham University, as well as the Bobst Library at New York University, for the wealth of information they have provided.

Introduction

This book has emerged from many years of teaching about comic literature at Regis University in Denver, comedy and religion at Loyola University in Chicago, and American film comedy at Fordham University in New York City, exploring the rich vein of comic theory, scholarly criticism, and popular appreciation to share with my students. This study attempts to offer a survey of film comedy according to various subgenres that have sustained their popularity and quality over the years and strives to find its own particular niche in film studies. A substantial amount of criticism has been published focusing on individual comedians, directors, and screenwriters. Many studies have focused on specific genres of film comedy: romantic comedy, screwball comedy, parody, musical comedy, and so on. There have also been wide-ranging collections of the "greatest film comedies," which usually offer only a brief description and analysis of each film. I would like to think that this work situates itself somewhere in the middle, dealing with one classic example of each genre with a more detailed description of each film's production and more extensive analysis of each film's achievement.

This survey does not include certain groups of great film comedies. First, the list of films is limited to the era of sound movies, since the two decades of silent film comedy seem to have received thorough treatment over time. Now that sound film has filled our screens for more than eighty years, there is more than enough material to observe. Second, certain genres, such as "road pictures" and "buddy movies," are not studied as separate genres, since they do not seem to have generated their own formulas and, instead, offer variations on the more inclusive frameworks of musical comedy, screwball comedy, parody, sex farce, and anarchic comedy. Some excellent comedies seem to defy neat categorizations or combine genres. Where does one place *Auntie Mame* in the spectrum of Hollywood comedy? Is *Tootsie* a satire on gender issues, a sex farce involving multiple deception and drag performance, or a rather sophisticated romantic comedy—or all three? Is *The Apartment* really that funny? And what about the "comedian comedy" of such stalwarts as Danny Kaye, Bob Hope, Lily Tomlin, or Robin Williams, whose performances have not been limited to any specific genre?

American comedy, like the American version of the English language, offers so many riches because it has inherited considerable comic wealth from all that has gone before it. Even before any formal drama emerged, primeval cultures celebrated life with ceremonies that combined playfulness with religious experience, fertility rites, or seasonal change. Satire was one of the earliest forms of comedy in the often lewd and raucous plays of Aristophanes. The trials and triumphs of romantic love began to get comic attention in the New Comedy of Plautus and Terence and persisted as standard material in the witty social commentary of Moliere and the satires and sentimental comedy of Restoration comedy. The religious drama of the Middle Ages often included portrayals of St. Peter as a buffoon or the Devil as a ridiculous, albeit terrifying, figure. Commedia dell'arte combined slapstick routines with satirical stereotypes of the foolish, the deceptive, the lascivious, and the senile, among others. Meanwhile, true to America's immigrant history, other countries have sent some of their best comic talent to Hollywood: Ernst Lubitch and Billy Wilder from Germany, and Charlie Chaplin, Peter Sellers, Cary Grant, and John Cleese from England. Audrey Hepburn came from Belgium by way of England. Even Sweden's Greta Garbo famously deigned to laugh in *Ninotchka*. I hope that the study of each of the films in this book pays homage to the rich and diverse tradition of its respective genre.

Meanwhile, my analysis of each film varies chapter by chapter. Certain films are studied in a somewhat deductive approach as early examples of what developed into a standard formula (*It Happened One Night* as romantic comedy or *Bringing Up Baby* as screwball comedy). The analysis of other films includes a substantial amount of external critical commentary because the particular works have attracted so much academic attention (*Annie Hall, Singin' in the Rain,* or *Dr. Strangelove*). The study of some films attempts to highlight features that tend to get relatively little attention (the precise narrative structure of *Some Like It Hot* or the extensive literary tradition behind *Young Frankenstein*). Other films are significant because they broke relatively new ground in film comedy (the revolutionary place of *National Lampoon's Animal House* as the first "college comedy" to present student life as a major countercultural experience or *South Park: Bigger, Longer & Uncut* as a notably more transgressive use of film animation). Finally, a certain set of films is studied to promote their cause in one way or another (*Duck Soup* as the best of the Marx Brothers' films, *Waiting for Guffman* as the most subtle of the relatively new genre of mockumentaries, or *What's Up, Doc?* as deserving of more critical respect than it has thus far received).

Finally, there is an episode in *National Lampoon's Animal House* that illustrates, by way of contrast, my approach to these particular films. In the only scene that takes place in an actual classroom setting, the burned-out and cynical English professor, Dave Jennings (Donald Sutherland), is trying to provoke some discussion on *Paradise Lost* in a large lecture hall filled with disinterested students. He begins his presentation somewhat defensively, saying, "It's a long poem. It was written a long time ago. And I'm sure that a lot of you have trouble understanding what he was trying to say." Noticing the students' utter unresponsiveness, he sighs and confesses, "Okay. . . . Don't write this down, but I find Milton probably as boring as you find Milton. He's a little bit long-winded, he doesn't translate very well into our generation, and his jokes are terrible." The bell rings, and, as the students rush out of the classroom, he calls after them, saying, "But that does not relieve you of your responsibility for this material! I'm not joking! This is my job!"

As a college teacher, I can understand that *Paradise Lost* was probably a required section of the course syllabus in the liberal arts curriculum of Faber College in 1962. Fortunately, no such requirement governs the choice of material in this book. There seems to be general agreement that each of these twelve films is a gem. Although some of them were released "a long time ago" (starting with 1933), they are not boring, long-winded, or unable to "translate very well into our generation." Each one has been a joy for me to watch and to study. I hope that you experience the same joy as you read this book. I am not joking. This is my job.

CHAPTER 1

Anarchic Comedy

DUCK SOUP (1933)

In his treatment of the Marx Brothers as the "anarchists" of film comedy, Gerald Mast calls them the "legitimate descendants of the American iconoclastic tradition" of Mack Sennett, Charlie Chaplin, and Buster Keaton. Like their distinguished predecessors from the silent era, the Marx Brothers "made films that ridiculed the sweet, the nice, the polite, the acceptable" and proceeded to "hurl comic mud at the gleaming marble pillars of the American temple."[1]

However, unlike Chaplin and the others, the Marx Brothers (even Harpo) were anything but silent. In fact, they came to Hollywood precisely because of the arrival of sound. The success of *The Jazz Singer* in 1927 sent Hollywood into a panic as the moguls realized that audiences would demand films with synchronized dialogue. Comedy, in particular, could no longer rely on slapstick physical humor or exaggerated or even subtle (in the case of Chaplin) facial expressions and bodily gestures. Film comedy needed words, and the Marx Brothers, especially with the assistance of skillful Broadway scribes, were an answer to Hollywood's prayers.

The Marx Brothers could also bring Broadway star power to Hollywood. Their many years of vaudeville performances, beginning in 1907 and including frequent appearances as headliners at the Palace Theater, eventually led to their leading roles in the 1924 Broadway revue *I'll Say She Is* and finally to major theatrical success in the 1925 hit comedy *The Cocoanuts*, with a book by George S. Kaufman and music by Irving Berlin, followed by *Animal Crackers*, also written by Kaufman, with music and lyrics by the equally respected songwriters Bert Kalmar and Harry Ruby, in 1928. Both of these shows also enjoyed national tours. It had taken more than twenty years, but by the time they went to Hollywood, the Marx Brothers were major stars.

In the search for comic writers, Hollywood was frantically raiding Broadway, looking for playwrights, songwriters, and performers. The Marx Brothers

Rufus T. Firefly (Groucho), Pinky (Harpo), Chicolini (Chico), and Rob Roland (Zeppo) in full battle mode while their headquarters collapses around them in the Marx Brothers' *Duck Soup* (1933).

had a special affinity for comic dialogue. Mast describes each of the brothers' "individual relationships to talk," writing the following:

> Groucho talks so much, so rapidly, and so belligerently that talk becomes a kind of weapon. . . . Groucho's ceaseless talk leads the listener in intellectual circles, swallowing us in a verbal maze, eventually depositing us back at the starting point without knowing where we have been or how we got there. . . . Chico's relationship to talk also substitutes sound for sense and the appearance of meaning for meaning. To Chico, "viaduct" sounds like "why a duck". . . "sanity clause" like "Santa Claus." . . . He alone can puncture Groucho's verbal spirals by stopping the speeding train of words and forcing Groucho to respond to his own erroneous intrusions. . . . The substitution of sound for sense reaches its perfection in Harpo, who makes only sounds. Harpo substitutes whistling and beeps on his horn for talk. Ironically, he communicates in the films as well as anybody.[2]

Duck Soup (1933) was the Marx Brothers' fifth film for Paramount Studios in as many years. The studio had enjoyed great success with its film versions of their Broadway hits *The Cocoanuts* (1929) and *Animal Crackers* (1930) and followed them up with two more box-office successes, *Monkey Business* (1931) and *Horse Feathers* (1932). In fact, *Horse Feathers* had been Paramount's highest-grossing film the previous year. Nevertheless, the studio was dealing with some financial issues in general (and with the Marx Brothers in particular), and *Duck Soup* would turn out to be the brothers' last project with Paramount.

In spite of their problems, the studio heads indicated their sincere commitment to the film. First, they assigned Leo McCarey to direct. McCarey had already directed a startling total of more than ninety films in ten years, beginning with his days at Hal Roach Studios, where he had worked on the *Our Gang* comedies and had been responsible for the pairing of Stan Laurel and Oliver Hardy. By the early 1930s, he was directing major projects with such top Hollywood stars as Eddie Cantor and Gloria Swanson. Allan Eyles goes so far as to say that *Duck Soup* stands out as the "only occasion that the team was guided by a director with a real genius for comedy."[3] The studio also chose Bert Kalmar and Harry Ruby, the songwriters behind the brothers' third Broadway hit and second film for Paramount, *Animal Crackers*, to write the screenplay and songs for the film. In their development of the story, it is highly likely, as several critics have suggested, that Kalmar and Ruby were influenced by the success of the Broadway smash hit of 1931, *Of Thee I Sing* by the Marx Brothers' other playwright, George S. Kaufman. It had already been rumored that the Marx Brothers would make a film version of Kaufman's musical satire of the American presidency and the election process, which had been taken seriously enough to be awarded a Pulitzer Prize, the first musical to do so.[4] *Duck Soup*'s art director, Hans Dreier, was another established veteran, with sixty films already to his credit, including *An American Tragedy* (1931), *Dr. Jekyll and Mr. Hyde* (1932), *A Farewell to Arms* (1932), and the first Academy Award winner, *Wings* (1927); and he would go on to contribute to *The Lady Eve* (1941), *A Foreign Affair* (1948), and *Sunset Boulevard* (1950) among the total of 500 films in his lifetime. In terms of money and talent, *Duck Soup* was an important project of the Hollywood establishment.

And yet *Duck Soup* would prove to be the Marx Brothers' most outrageous attack on the establishment, especially governmental and military folly. The film's title sets the tone of absurdity. At various points in the planning, the film had the working titles of *Ooh-La-La, Cracked Ice,* and *Grasshoppers.* Reportedly, McCarey finally suggested the title *Duck Soup*, which would be consistent with the "animal" names of the brothers' three previous films. The film's titles and opening credits are displayed over the footage of ducks floating in a large soup kettle—the first and (almost) only reference to ducks in the entire film. The phrase is basically a slang expression describing something that is easy to accomplish, suggesting that any fool can run a country or lead a nation into war. And Groucho, as the newly appointed president of Freedonia, Rufus T. Firefly, is just the idiot to do it.

The timing of a film that mocked the political realm is significant. Franklin Roosevelt had been inaugurated president on March 4, 1933, and *Duck Soup* was released on November 17 of that year. At his first public appearance as president, Firefly sings:

> The last man nearly ruined this place,
> He didn't know what to do with it,
> If you think this country's bad off now—
> Just wait till I get through with it.

The allusion to the disastrous consequences of Herbert Hoover's administration and the daring initiatives of Roosevelt's "first 100 days" could hardly be lost on the 1933 movie audience. In the same song, Firefly also announces that the "laws of my administration" will outlaw smoking, telling dirty jokes, whistling, and chewing gum (all of which behavior he blatantly exhibits himself) and declares, "if any form of pleasure is exhibited, report to me and it shall be prohibited," obviously referencing the hypocrisy and bluestocking attitudes of the Prohibition era, which Roosevelt had only recently brought to an end. The target of the film's satire, however, is not any particular politician or policy, but the very institution of government in general, rife with egotism, greed, deception, hypocrisy, and particularly enamored of war. As Mast observes, the "target of *Duck Soup* is democracy and government itself; grandiose political ceremonies, the law courts, and war are reduced to the absurd." At the same time, its parody of the "serious" genres of European kingdom films, according to Mast, implies that the "sanctified institution is as hollow and dead as the cinematic cliché."[5] In its substitution of nonsense for political order and its mockery of Hollywood's attempts at aristocratic elegance, the film is genuinely anarchic.

The story takes place in the mythical republic of Freedonia. Eyles points out that as the "only Marx Brothers' film to have a completely mythical background," its setting serves the following two comic purposes:

> It creates an ideal world in which the Marxes—especially Groucho as president—can operate. While the setting is different, there is no real attempt to create an entirely different society. The Marxes appear in traditional costume. Margaret Dumont, as the wealthiest widow in the land, is unchanged in manner. . . . Her name, Gloria Teasdale, is hardly "Freedonian," and other names, like Trentino and Vera Marcal, are just roughly European. The Lemonade Seller could have come from the Coney Island boardwalk, as could Chico and Harpo's peanut stall.[6]

Meanwhile, "while it might seem absurd if Groucho were president of the United States," Eyles remarks, "there is no difficulty in accepting him as the leader of a mythical country."[7]

Governmental Folly

The most prominent source of humor in the film is its political satire. The film's opening sequence introduces the Marx Brothers' anarchic viewpoint. Freedonia is facing financial collapse. When the country's president approaches the philanthropic Mrs. Teasdale for another loan of twenty million dollars, she announces that she will lend the money only on the condition that the current president resign and hand the government over to a "progressive, fearless leader" (à la FDR?), Rufus T. Firefly, with whom she appears to be smitten. Her request is granted. The following scene—with its expansive and elaborate art deco setting and wardrobe and its symmetrical presentation of the singing chorus, ballet dancers, and military guard—might be seen as a parody of MGM's and Paramount's own costume dramas of the period (*Morocco* [1930], *Rasputin and the Empress* [1932], *Sign of the Cross* [1932], *Queen Christina* [1933], and so forth). In this grandiose setting, the elite of the land—including the "Honorable Secretary of Finance and Parking"—gather to greet their new president.

With an overblown musical introduction—including the national anthem, "Hail Freedonia"—the assembled crowd continues to await him, while Firefly is discovered asleep, although fully clothed underneath his nightshirt and with a cigar in his mouth. Hearing an alarm, which resembles a firehouse bell, he slides down the firehouse pole and arrives unseen at the ceremony. When Mrs. Teasdale recognizes and greets him, the standard Groucho-Dumont interchange follows, featuring his combination of outrageous flirtation and insult and an introduction to the vivacious Vera Marcal, who is a spy for the enemy country, Sylvania. (The country's name manages to suggest both the electronics company familiar to American consumers by the 1930s and the sinister Eastern European setting for the 1931 horror film *Dracula*.) When asked of his plans for the country, Firefly sings his inaugural address, "These Are the Laws of My Administration," a list of his plans to raise taxes, engage in graft, and reward adultery, among other things. Eyles's account of the number illustrates the anarchic character of Groucho's declaration:

> Groucho is at great pains to dispel any idea that he will be a mature and responsible leader. His ideas for running the country, expressed in song, are tyrannical, chaos-inducing, and self-interested. They express the Marx (and anarchic) view that authority means abuse and corruption. When power is placed in Groucho's hands, he expresses this view to an extreme, here in words, later in the war he causes. This time he is fighting authority from the inside, by *his own* misuse of it. He attacks the idea, whereas normally he attacks the people that have the power instead of being one of them himself.[8]

Firefly's irresponsibility, along with the film's satire of governmental ineptitude in general, continues as he meets with his Council of Deputies. His nonsequitur responses to their questions and proposals prompt the secretary of war to resign. When Firefly spots a peanut vendor, Chicolini (Chico Marx), in front of the palace, he offers to hire him for a "soft government job" as a way to "scare the cabinet." Unaware that Chicolini is a spy, he appoints him secretary of war. Chicolini suggests that they create a standing army because "then we save money on chairs."

Chicolini and Firefly's driver, Pinky (Harpo Marx), are both spying on behalf of Trentino (Louis Calhern), the ambassador from nearby Sylvania who is plotting to take over Freedonia. When Firefly's secretary (Zeppo Marx) finds evidence of this plot, he advises Firefly to find a way to insult the ambassador, who would then strike President Firefly, giving them grounds to banish him from Freedonia. From this deceptive bit of diplomatic manipulation—and Firefly's own impetuosity and overactive imagination—matters will eventually escalate into full-scale war between the two countries. History provides examples of many actual wars that have originated from similarly slender or deceptive rationales.

At Mrs. Teasdale's tea party, Firefly attempts to carry out the plan by gratuitously insulting Trentino, but instead, when Trentino responds by calling him an "upstart," it is Firefly who strikes the first blow, striking the ambassador with his glove, an action that Trentino declares "may plunge our countries into war." The display of political foolishness continues when, shortly afterward, Trentino informs Mrs. Teasdale that his president has called him back to Sylvania, thus eliminating the need for Firefly to force him out of the country. Trentino now wants to reconcile with Firefly and avoid the need to go to war. Mrs. Teasdale invites Firefly to come to her home for the reconciliation. When she telephones him, he is once again in bed, this time eating crackers, putting a lie to Mrs. Teasdale's remark, "I know that you're very busy." When he arrives, Firefly gives her his plans for war, which she has not even requested. Firefly once again strikes the ambassador, and war is declared. Firefly's eagerness for warfare is fairly obvious. At one point, he confesses, "There must be a war—I've paid a month's rent on the battlefield," alluding to the self-interests of many a politician, weapons manufacturer, or others who stand to benefit from military adventures.

The judicial branch and diplomatic corps are also mocked in the sequence in which Chicolini is put on trial for treason because he tried to steal the war plans. President Firefly, serving as both judge and defense attorney, continually interrupts the trial with nonsensical remarks, turning the judicial system on its ear. The trial is brought to a standstill by the news that Sylvania's troops are "about to land on Freedonia's soil." Mrs. Teasdale arrives in the courtroom, "on behalf of the women of Freedonia, to make one final effort to prevent war." Firefly replies that he will gladly do everything in his power to "keep our Freedonia at peace with the world." He offers to extend a hand of friendship to Ambassador Trentino. Then he imagines that Trentino will refuse his offer of peace and works himself up into a fit of indignation, so that when Trentino actually arrives, Firefly immediately accuses him of not accepting his gesture of reconciliation and slaps him again. Trentino once again declares war, and the last opportunity to avoid conflict is lost.

The Fog of War

The film moves into an outrageous satire on the folly of war, especially among European nations. Americans in the early 1930s harbored a great deal of antiwar sentiment. The universal shock at the horrors of World War I, which had ended only fourteen years earlier, combined with the long-standing American policy of noninvolvement in European affairs, prompted a strong isolationist sentiment in the country, exhibited in Congress's vote against joining the League of Nations, increased tariffs on imports, and immigration quotas. A significant wave of pacifist sentiment had also developed in the United States with the founding of groups such as the Women's International League for Peace and Freedom in 1919 and the War Resisters League in 1923. Such attitudes toward military ventures would linger even into the early years of World War II. It is important in this context to recall that as late as 1939, when Britain and France declared war on Germany, President Roosevelt responded by issuing a statement of U.S. neutrality. It would take the attack on Pearl Harbor, more than two years later, to convince the United States to join the battle. So the Marx Brothers were probably treading on fairly safe ideological territory in their mockery of the military mind.

The satire on militarism begins with a lavish musical number, "We're Going to War," which, as one critic has pointed out, is the only instance when all four of the brothers performed a musical number on screen. They are joined by a huge chorus of the politicians and common people expressing the universal excitement and glory of a nation's entry into battle, in a sequence that, as Mast points out, parodies the "way movies, plays, and musical comedies turn the serious business of war into operetta fare."[9] Harpo marches into the ballroom limping and twirling a large baton, followed by a military drum corps. As the military band lines up behind the presidential cabinet, the brothers play on the soldiers' helmets as if they were xylophones. They then lead the entire assembly in a minstrel show chorus of "hi-de-hi-de-ho," followed by a variation on a Negro spiritual, "We got guns; they got guns; all God chillun got guns," and all four brothers strumming on banjos, singing, "Oh, Freedonia, don't you cry for me," prompting everyone to dance to "Turkey in the Straw" and finally break forth in a frenzy of general jubilation. Anyone with an ounce of antiwar sentiment would grasp the irony of such a celebration of the upcoming violence.

The musical number morphs into the longest sustained sequence of the film, a ten-minute parody of warfare throughout U.S. history that brings the film to its anarchic conclusion. It is worth noting that almost all the references to war are U.S. conflicts, although the film's battle is presumably being fought in Europe, focusing the satire considerably. The first episode in the series begins with the brothers in a tableau of Revolutionary War soldiers, which leads into a hilarious depiction of Harpo as Paul Revere, who keeps interrupting his ride to engage in sexual dalliance with ladies along the way.

The scene then moves to the World War I-style military headquarters of President Firefly, where anarchy reigns. Firefly wears a series of costumes throughout the sequence: Civil War caps, both Union and Confederate; some sort of elaborate Prussian grenadier's feathered hat; a World War I helmet; a coonskin cap; a large bandage tied to create rabbit ears; and finally a large water jug with his face drawn on it. As commander in chief, he commandeers a machine gun (from a violin case), only to be told that he is shooting at his own men. He bribes his secretary to keep that information under his hat, then he keeps the money, saying, "Never mind, I'll keep it under my hat." He sends messages by telegraph—collect—reporting that two hills have been attacked, putting thirteen hillbillies out of work, and that some snipers invaded their machine-gun nest and laid an egg. He prefers to buy trenches rather than have soldiers dig them. He complains about too many messages from the front and asks why they never get messages from the side. When he is told that a general has reported experiencing gas attacks, he suggests that he take a "teaspoon of bicarbonate of soda and a half a glass of water."

Any acts of chivalry or heroism are mocked. When Mrs. Teasdale begs Firefly to come over to her location to protect her, he arrives only to proceed directly to gorge on her food supply. He then moves to the window to fight "for this woman's honor, which is probably more than she ever did." When Harpo is chosen to "have the rare privilege of risking his life for his country" by running through enemy lines, Firefly encourages him by saying, "While you're out there risking life and limb through shot and shell, we'll be in here thinking what a sucker you are." When his gun falls out the window, he asks Mrs. Teasdale to "run out and get it for me like a good girl." When they finally win the battle, and Mrs. Teasdale breaks into the national anthem, the brothers respond by throwing fruit at her.

Throughout this sequence, Harpo alternates between being the innocent but dim-witted factotum and a randy little devil easily distracted by his sexual urges. As the innocent helper, he is sent out to "comb the countryside for volunteers" by wearing a sandwich board that reads, "Join the Army and see the Navy." When he hears someone say that "we must have help," he cheerfully puts a "Help Wanted" sign on the headquarters' front door. When he is chosen to run through enemy lines, he ends up locked in an ammunition supply closet, where he lights up and throws away a cigar, igniting all the ammunition. As mentioned earlier, his midnight ride is interrupted twice. He sees a woman undressing in front of her window; he dismounts, slaps a feed bag on his horse, and proceeds to seduce the woman, only to be interrupted by the arrival of her husband. Even more inappropriate behavior ensues when the husband insists on taking a bath right away, only to discover that, in his naked state, he is sitting on Harpo, who is hiding in the bathwater. Harpo responds to another young lady's invitation to her bedroom, only this time the lady ends up in one bed, while Harpo sleeps in the other—with his horse. Adultery is one sort of transgressive activity; bestiality is quite another. When Firefly telegraphs for reinforcements and reports that there are "three men and a one woman trapped in a building. Send help at once. If you can't send help, send two more women," Harpo, smiling wickedly and holding up his fingers, suggests three more women. When Mrs. Teasdale joins them in trying to hold up a wall, Harpo steps behind them and fondles her derriere.

Chico is ever the opportunist, even in battle. Firefly sends him to "clean out" an enemy machine-gun nest, he replies, "All right. I'll tell the janitor." When Firefly wonders where his secretary of war is, Chicolini shows up and punches the time clock to report for work. When told that Freedonia is facing disastrous defeat, he replies that he has done something about it—he has changed sides. He explains to Firefly that he has come to Freedonia's headquarters, however, because the "food is better over here." Firefly urges him to come and work for him again with the promise of a vacation, and he easily switches sides. He fixes the selection process for the volunteer to run through enemy lines so that he is not chosen. So much for patriotic selflessness.

Through it all, the coverage of the battle is interrupted by documentary footage of actual army tanks and other machinery in operation. When it is announced that "help is on the way," the film presents an incongruous montage of assistants rushing to the scene: fire engines, police motorcycles, marathon runners, swimmers, crew rowers, monkeys, elephant herds, and a flock of dolphins. None of the help actually arrives, of course.

Victory is won when Trentino gets his head trapped in a hole in the wall as he tries to break into headquarters. As the brothers pelt him with apples instead of ammunition, he surrenders. As Eyles observes, the "ultimate weapon that brings the enemy to surrender is not an atom bomb but hard cooking apples."[10] As they throw the remaining apples at Mrs. Teasdale, the film comes to an abrupt end. Mast compares this to similar endings in some of their other Paramount films, saying that they are "perfect Marx Brothers endings because they don't really end anything. They are deliberately sloppy contrivances to finish a film that has no logical finish and that was not really going anywhere anyway."[11]

Incompetence, bribery, opportunism, sexual adventurism, dereliction of duty, reversal of loyalties, "friendly fire" and accidents with ammunition, naive heroism that translates into being a "sucker"—the battle sequence of *Duck Soup* stands as an extensive catalog of the ignoble, foolish, and downright dishonest activities of military officers and enlisted men throughout U.S. history. War is presented as an anarchic activity, with victories achieved through stupidity and blind luck, a bleakly comic piece of political theater. It is no wonder that the conquered leader Trentino and Mrs. Teasdale as the muse of battle—like the female figures of Columbia in World War I and "Liberty Leading the People" in the iconography of the French Revolution—are pelted with fruit, the traditional response to a lousy vaudeville performance.

Eyles observes that the film's blatant mockery of war was not missed by certain powerful leaders, writing the following:

> War has become an absurd farce: without meaning, without logic. . . . The end of *Duck Soup* is a comment on all wars: that they are pointless, tending to arise from trivialities, to be rejoiced in by men as a kind of super-game, and won by chance and luck. . . . The film's implications are pacifist, and it may be of interest to recall that *Duck Soup* was banned in the Italy of Mussolini.[12]

Standard Marxism

Duck Soup, however, can be enjoyed for other reasons besides its satire on governmental and military folly. It contains a rich collection of standard Marx Brothers material that audiences had already been enjoying for twenty-five years. Groucho continues his mind-boggling conversations, replete with puns and double entendres, eager to confound any serious situation. He takes his job as president lightly, catching up on his sleep whenever he can. Besides, when he discovers that Mrs. Teasdale is an extremely wealthy widow, his attention is far more focused on winning her hand in marriage than on running her country. He repeatedly combines expressions of devotion to her and a string of insulting comments. Mast proposes that this is simply another Marx Brothers attack on society, in this case, the idealization of romance. "Why does the rich maiden put up with so much abuse? Perhaps the fact that this question has no sensible answer is one more element in the film's parody."[13]

His first encounter with the wealthy widow, as chairwoman of his Welcoming Committee, contains some of his quickest and most hostile sallies. When she tells him that she sponsored his appointment because she considers him the "most able statesman in all of Freedonia," he remarks, "That covers a lot of ground. Say, you cover a lot of ground yourself. You better beat it. I hear they're going to tear you down and put up an office building where you're standing." Undeterred, Mrs. Teasdale continues her welcome address, until Firefly observes that she talks so much she "must have been vaccinated with a phonograph needle." Their conversation proceeds as follows, with Firefly deflating each one of Mrs. Teasdale's romantic declarations with hostile commentary until his true motives are revealed:

> Firefly: Where is your husband?
>
> Teasdale: Why, he's dead.
>
> Firefly: I'll bet he's using that as an excuse.
>
> Teasdale: I was with him to the very end.
>
> Firefly: No wonder he passed away.
>
> Teasdale: I held him in my arms and kissed him.
>
> Firefly: I see. Then it was murder. Will you marry me? Did he leave you any money? Answer the second question first.
>
> Teasdale: He left me his entire fortune.
>
> Firefly: Is that so? Can't you see I'm trying to tell you that I love you?

Harpo also provides his familiar shtick. Maurice Charney draws a succinct description of his persona as "always the perpetual child, impulsive and happy-go-lucky," full of "childlike mischievousness."[14] In his silence, he communicates mainly with his face and the assortment of automobile horns stuck in his belt. In one telephone conversation early in the film, for example, he apparently manages—thanks to the film's sound track—to answer all the caller's questions by various honks on his several horns, with different intonations communicating "hello," "no," "what?," "ooohh," laughter, and a final angry "good-bye."

Always wearing his innocent smile, Harpo interferes with everyone's attempts to conduct normal business. One example should suffice. In his first major appearance in the film, Pinky (Harpo) joins Chicolini (Chico) for a meeting at Trentino's office to report on their spying assignments. After the ambassador's secretary lets them in the door, they rush to his desk to answer his ringing telephone. After several attempts, they realize that the ringing is coming from the large alarm clock in Pinky's pocket. When Trentino asks them to be seated, Pinky sits in the ambassador's chair and pulls him onto his lap. He lights his and Trentino's cigar with a blowtorch, and then, behind Trentino's back, he cuts off most of his cigar. When asked for Firefly's "record," he, of course, pulls a phonograph record out of his coat. When Trentino tosses it in the air in frustration, Harpo pulls a pistol out of his pocket and shoots the flying record. Chico rings a bell, pulls another cigar out of Trentino's desk humidor, shouting, "And the boy gets a cigar," and then slams the humidor lid on Trentino's fingers. As the ambassador doggedly gives the two spies further instructions, Pinky, pulling scissors out of his prolific coat, cuts off some of Trentino's hair and trims the tails off his morning coat. As they depart, Pinky brushes glue onto Trentino's derriere and manages to encase the ambassador's fingers in a mousetrap, all of this with a grin on his face, a gleam in his eye, and malice toward no one. Harpo's antics are pure playfulness; in the context, they also end up challenging authority and order. To focus too much on his actions as rebellion, however, would endow Harpo with too much intentionality. As Frank Krutnik observes, "There is no attempt to motivate much of his eccentric behavior, such as cutting off ties, bisecting cigars, burning up hats, offering up an exposed leg, and so on. He just *does* these things."[15] Such motiveless mischief intensifies the general atmosphere of anarchy.

Harpo's invasion of personal space is best demonstrated in the two "peanut vendor/lemonade stand" sequences, which, by doing nothing to further the film's plot, also contribute nicely to its anarchic message. As soon as he shows up at Chicolini's peanut stand, Harpo/Pinky proceeds to his standard tricks. He steals peanuts, uses his scissors to cut off Chicolini's pretzel stick, swings his thigh up into Chicolini's hand, and, pretending to box with Chicolini, kicks him in the derriere. The two of them move closer to an adjacent lemonade vendor (Edgar Kennedy), and Pinky immediately reaches down into one of the customers' pants while simultaneously pulling out the lemonade vendor's pocket, which he cuts off to make a bag for his stolen peanuts. He moves in so close to the lemonade man that he sets off the horn that Pinky keeps in his pants. He will later fill the horn bag with lemonade like a rubber bulb syringe and squirt the vendor in the face with his own beverage. Both Pinky and Chicolini mess with the vendor's mind by switching their three hats (Kennedy's derby, Harpo's top hat, and Chico's conical Italian cap), during the course of which Pinky manages to slide his thigh into the peanut vendor's hand and conclude with his trademark "googie" expression of crossed eyes, puffed cheeks, and a stuck-out tongue. Finally, as the vendor resumes arguing with Chicolini, Pinky grabs the vendor's derby and sets in on fire with the gas jet in the peanut cart.

His second encounter with the lemonade man is more aggressive. Pinky has been left in charge of the peanut stand. The lemonade vendor approaches wearing a straw hat. He starts to terrorize Pinky by taking a bag of peanuts and smearing mustard on Pinky's hands. Pinky responds by wiping his hands on the towel attached to the vendor's belt, cutting off a piece of the towel, and then knocking the bag of peanuts out of his hand. While the vendor is bent over picking up his peanut bag, Pinky sticks the straw hat in the peanut cart fire. The vendor takes revenge by pushing over the peanut stand, but Pinky responds by climbing barefoot into the large lemonade container, scaring away all the customers. Mast observes that "this intimate physical contact is violently antisocial, violating social codes of distance, propriety, and masculinity."[16]

These two sequences, with their roots in commedia dell'arte by way of the circus and vaudeville stage, are filmed in front of a stationary camera, resulting in nothing very cinematic but, fortunately, a priceless record of the Marx Brothers' typical stage comedy. They both come close to silent film comedy, providing delightful relief from the verbal gymnastics that characterize the rest of the film. Another running gag features Harpo/Pinky as Firefly's driver. "His Excellency's car" consists of a motorcycle and a sidecar. Twice in the film Firefly jumps in the sidecar and orders Pinky to drive, and Pinky drives off in the motorcycle, leaving Firefly motionless in the sidecar. The third time he takes a drive, Firefly insists that he will not be fooled more than twice and insists on sitting on the motorcycle with Pinky in the sidecar. Of course, Pinky drives off in the sidecar, leaving Firefly stranded again.

Beyond his childlike behavior and aggressive mischief, Harpo also displays a lively sexual appetite. As Mast describes Harpo, "He is pure satyr. He makes no pretenses about his drives or his intentions, for he is a man of nature."[17] He chases Trentino's secretary, and, encountering Vera Marcal in Mrs. Teasdale's home, he immediately grabs her and starts dancing with her. His participation in the war involves the previously described dalliances that interrupt his midnight ride, his request for more women at the headquarters, and the liberties he takes with Mrs. Teasdale's backside. His trangressive behavior violates major taboos when, first, he is discovered hiding in the bathwater in which an almost cuckolded husband (who happens to be the lemonade vendor from earlier in the film) is sitting, inviting the viewers to imagine extremely intimate physical contact between the two men. In his second respite from his ride, he ends up in bed with his horse, who has taken the trouble to remove his/her shoes, prompting more than one critic to suggest that some commentary was being made about the newly issued Motion Picture Production Code's restrictions on depictions of sexual behavior. Harpo's use of his scissors to cut plumes off of military helmets, the long plume of the president's official pen, Chicolini's pretzel stick, the lemonade vendor's pocket, Trentino's morning coat tails and cigar, and other items suggests castration, while his habit of placing his thigh in other men's hands carries another threat of homosexual flirtation. At one point, revealing his tattoos to Firefly, he makes the image of a dancing girl on his forearm wiggle and displays her telephone number on his stomach. For Harpo, sexuality can be either playful or aggressive or sometimes both at once.

One of Harpo's best sequences builds on the contrast between his silence and the comic possibilities of sound. After he and Chicolini have broken into

Mrs. Teasdale's house to steal the war plans that Firefly has given her, they are instructed by fellow spy Vera Marcal that they must not make a sound. This would seem to be a natural assignment for the silent Pinky. Yet in the course of his search for the plans, he manages to set off the chimes of a grandfather clock and the melody of a music box (in the shape of a duck, it should be noted), plays a harp melody on the strings of a grand piano, and then suffers (in silence) as Chicolini drops the lid of the piano on Pinky's fingers. Later, after he acquires the combination to Mrs. Teasdale's safe, he sets off the safe's alarm, which plays "Stars and Stripes Forever," and finally smashes the safe to pieces and tosses it out the window. Harpo, the silent one, manages to create quite a bit of noise.

Chico may be the most effective of the brothers in creating a mood of surrealism; his puns, malapropisms, nonsequiturs, and oblique replies to questions make mincemeat out of linguistic logic. His Italian accent only heightens the incongruity. His "full, detailed report" to Trentino on his and Pinky's spying is a good example of his defiance of all logic in word and action:

> Chicolini: All right. I tell you. Monday, we watch Firefly's house. But he no come out. He wasn't home. Tuesday, we go to the ball game. But he fool us. He no show up. Wednesday he go to the ball game. But we fool him. We no show up. Thursday was a doubleheader. Nobody show up. Friday, it rained all day. There was no ball game. So we stayed home; we listened to it over the radio.
>
> Trentino: Then you didn't shadow Firefly?
>
> Chicolini: Sure we shadow Firefly. We shadow him all day.
>
> Trentino: What day was that?
>
> Chicolini: "Shadowday. That's-a some joke, huh, boss?"
>
> Trentino: Now will you tell me what happened on Saturday?
>
> Chicolini: I'm glad you asked. We follow this man down to a road house. At this road house he meet a married lady.
>
> Trentino: A married lady?
>
> Chicolini: I think it was his wife.
>
> Trentino: Firefly has no wife!
>
> Chicolini: No? Then you know what I think, boss? I think we follow the wrong man.

Chico's other display of his peculiar logic occurs, appropriately, in a court of law where the "truth and nothing but the truth" is supposed to prevail. Chico is forced to answer questions from both the prosecuting attorney and Firefly, who, violating all protocol, intervenes to serve as his defense attorney. At first, Firefly, presiding as judge, says to Chicolini, "I bet you eight to one we find you guilty." Chicolini responds, saying, "Atsa no good. I can get ten to one in the barbershop." When asked by the prosecutor when he was born, he answers, "I don't remember. I was just a little baby." The prosecutor asks, "Isn't it true you tried to sell Freedonia's secret war code and plans?" Chicolini responds, "Sure, I sold the code and two pair of plans." He laughs and turns to Firefly with his usual boast, "That's-a some joke, huh, boss?" When Firefly starts questioning him, he turns the tables and offers his own question, saying, "What is it has a trunk but no key, weighs 2,000 pounds, and lives in a circus?" The prosecutor interrupts, shouting, "That's irrelevant!," and Chicolini responds, "Hey, that's the answer! There's a whole lot of relephants in a circus." Another court official cries out, "That sort of testimony we can eliminate," to which Chicolini replies, "That's a-fine. I'll take some . . . eliminate. A nice cold glass of eliminate." When Firefly suggests that "we give him ten years in Leavenworth, or eleven years in Twelveworth," Chicolini counters, "I'll take five and ten in Woolworth." And so it goes until the trial is interrupted with the news that Sylvanian troops are about to land on Freedonian soil, and "this means war!" Of course, this ends the court proceedings, since Chicolini is supposed to be the secretary of war, which is complicated by the fact that he serves as a spy for the enemy. Absurdity rules!

By this point in the Marx Brothers' career, Zeppo serves practically no comic function, except as occasional straight man for Groucho. This would, in fact, be his last appearance as one of the brothers; he left the group when they moved to MGM. His very stiffness and dullness, however, combined with his unquestioning cooperation with his brothers' mayhem, enhance the surrealistic mood. Margaret Dumont as Mrs. Gloria Teasdale serves a similar but more significant role in her consistent attempts at normal behavior. She first tries to save Freedonia by removing the incompetent president and replacing him with Firefly. She strives for dignity in her welcome ceremony for the new president. She attempts to broker a truce between Freedonia and Sylvania, hoping to avoid warfare. She breaks into singing in a burst of patriotic fervor when Freedonia achieves victory. She even responds to Firefly's flattery in hopes of experiencing a romantic relationship or even marriage. All of these attempts at normalcy are, of course, sabotaged by the lunacy of the Marx Brothers. This is as it must be, since she epitomizes, not only in her exaggerated refinement but simply in her femininity, the tension that Krutnik examines in his treatment of comedian comedy. He writes the following:

> Within the genre, women tend to signify the demands of integration and responsibility for the male . . . a not uncommon final frisson that explicitly presents the woman as the target of the male comedian's

revolt against order. A famous example is the final shot of *Duck Soup*, where the Marx Brothers' pelting of Margaret Dumont provides a parting testimonial to the comedians' characteristic "anarchy." The woman embodies everything that has to be assaulted to maintain their independence.[18]

Such lunacy reaches something of a pinnacle when, late in the film, all three of the brothers, dressed as Groucho/Firefly, perform the famous "mirror scene." It is supremely surrealistic comedy, illustrating why Salvador Dali admired them so much. Groucho/Firefly, hearing all the noise Harpo/Pinky is making in his destruction of the safe in Mrs. Teasdale's living room, comes down the stairs to investigate. Harpo, who is dressed to look like Groucho in a white sleeping gown and nightcap, as well as sporting a painted moustache and glasses, tries to escape but crashes into a floor-to-ceiling mirror, smashing it to pieces and revealing another room behind it. As Groucho enters the room, Harpo's only "escape" is to pretend to be Groucho's reflection in the mirror that used to fill the frame. As Groucho sees Harpo, looking like him in the broken mirror's now-empty space, he engages in an elaborate sequence of gestures and movements in interaction with his "reflection" too intricate to be described in detail. All of Groucho's movements are matched by Harpo. Finally, when Chico, also dressed as Groucho, also steps into the frame on Harpo's side, the game is over.

However, on closer inspection, the illusion is apparently being deliberately sustained by Harpo/Pinky and Groucho/Firefly (and the film's director) to test how long they can maintain the game or to see how one can trip up the other one. Near the end of the routine, Groucho, walking out of the doorway frame, signals to the audience that he has come up with a way to challenge his opponent. They both reappear, one with a black top hat behind his back, the other with a light-colored Panama hat behind his. As they trade sides across the mirror divide and simultaneously place their hats on their heads, the top hat is transformed into another Panama straw. When one of them drops his hat, the other reaches through the mirror divide again to grasp the hat and give it back to its owner. All logic and verisimilitude are thereby constantly threatened and finally crumble as Chico enters the frame and brings it all to its illogical conclusion.

In *Duck Soup*, the anarchy of the Marx Brothers came close to becoming true satire in its presentation of the political chicanery and military blundering that have thrived throughout human history and had only recently been more than amply demonstrated in the first three decades of the twentieth century. But the mayhem of their routines was also rooted in their own experiences of a hardscrabble childhood and their frantic attempts to please their vaudeville audiences by any means necessary until they made it to Broadway and Hollywood; however, it would be wrong to characterize their work, even *Duck Soup*, as deep satire. The surrealism of their work is timeless, not a statement about their particular era. And much of the film's criticism of politicians and the military gets blunted by the childishness of the farcical routines and lack of any sincere anger in the brothers' gleeful performances.

Not everyone enjoyed their approach. Leo McCarey himself, the renowned director of the film, finally confessed many years later to his difficulty in working with them, saying, "The most surprising thing about this film was that I succeeded in not going crazy, for I really did not want to work with them: They were completely mad. . . . They were the four battiest people I ever met."[19]

Yet their comedy lives on, well beyond their glory years in the 1930s, to enter the pantheon of film comedy. They invite all of us to take up the weapons of anarchy against the deadening systems of any era. It is not too audacious of us to honor them, as Eyles does, as the "most heroic of all the screen comedians. They tackle a world that obstructs them and brings it to submission." They live on as "heroes to everyone who has suffered from other people's hypocrisy, pomposity, pendantism, and patronage. They settle for none of it. The Marxes assume that we join them on their comic crusade."[20] And year after year, generation after generation, we gladly do.

A Sampling of Anarchic Comedies

You Can't Take It with You (1938)
It's a Mad, Mad, Mad, Mad World (1963)
A Hard Day's Night (1964)
Help! (1965)
Harold and Maude (1971)
Monty Python's The Meaning of Life (1983)
Good Morning, Vietnam (1987)
A Fish Called Wanda (1988)
Team America: World Police (2004)
Borat: Cultural Learnings of America for Make Benefit Glorious Nation of Kazakhstan (2006)

Notes

1. Gerald Mast, *The Comic Mind: Comedy and the Movies*, 2nd ed. (Chicago: University of Chicago Press, 1979), 281.
2. Mast, *The Comic Mind*, 282–83.
3. Allan Eyles, *The Marx Brothers: Their World of Comedy* (New York: Paperback Library, 1969), 95.

4. Simon Louvish, *Monkey Business: The Lives and Legends of the Marx Brothers* (New York: St. Martin's Press, 1999), 231.

5. Mast, *The Comic Mind*, 281–82.

6. Eyles, *The Marx Brothers*, 95.

7. Eyles, *The Marx Brothers*, 95.

8. Eyles, *The Marx Brothers*, 96.

9. Mast, *The Comic Mind*, 285.

10. Eyles, *The Marx Brothers*, 109.

11. Mast, *The Comic Mind*, 286–87.

12. Eyles, *The Marx Brothers*, 109–10.

13. Mast, *The Comic Mind*, 283.

14. Maurice Charney, *The Comic World of the Marx Brothers' Movies* (Teaneck, N.J.: Fairleigh Dickinson University Press, 2007), 45.

15. Frank Krutnik, "Genre, Narrative, and the Hollywood Comedian." In *Classical Hollywood Comedy*, Kristine Brunovska Karnick and Henry Jenkins, eds. (New York: Routledge, 1995), 27.

16. Mast, *The Comic Mind*, 284.

17. Mast, *The Comic Mind*, 284.

18. Krutnik, "Genre, Narrative, and the Hollywood Comedian," 37.

19. Louvish, *Monkey Business*, 270.

20. Eyles, *The Marx Brothers*, 7.

CHAPTER 2

Romantic Comedy

IT HAPPENED ONE NIGHT (1934)

Romantic comedy is the hardiest perennial in the Hollywood conservatory, for both the producer and the consumer of the product. The genre is a particularly congenial environment for performances by likeable, attractive actors of limited dramatic range or without any outstanding gift for comedy (think Matthew McConaughey or Jennifer Lopez) whose box-office appeal usually guarantees a film's financial success. Meanwhile, it is a reliable candidate for a "date movie." While often relegated to the ranks of "chick flicks," certain romantic comedies, if they feature the right actress (anyone from Marilyn Monroe to Cameron Diaz), can also bring a male audience to the multiplex. While these two factors render romantic comedies attractive to both filmmakers and audiences, the genre is often critically dismissed for its predictable plots and mildness of the comic performances.

It was not always thus. Especially during the 1930s and 1940s, many romantic comedies featured some unforgettable performances by the studios' most prestigious actors (Cary Grant, Katharine Hepburn, Carole Lombard, Jean Arthur, Jimmy Stewart, Irene Dunne, Spencer Tracy, Olivia de Havilland, Myrna Loy, Loretta Young, William Powell, and so forth) working with sophisticated screenwriters (Robert Riskin, Billy Wilder, Garson Kanin, Robert Sherwood, Norman Krasna, S. N. Behrman, Charles Brackett, and so on) and top-flight directors (Frank Capra, Howard Hawks, Leo McCarey, Ernst Lubitsch, George Cukor, George Stevens, and so forth). And history can point to one moment, at least, when a romantic comedy succeeded well enough to enter the record books.

It Happened One Night (1934) staked its claim in Hollywood lore on the night of February 27, 1935, when it became the first film to capture all five of the top prizes at the Academy Awards: Best Picture; Best Director, Frank Capra; Best Screenplay, Robert Riskin; Best Actor, Clark Gable; and Best Actress, Claudette Colbert. It held that record for forty years, until *One Flew over the Cuckoo's*

Runaway heiress Ellie Andrews (Claudette Colbert) has serious misgivings about traveling with newspaper reporter Peter Warne (Clark Gable) in *It Happened One Night* (1934).

Nest earned the same five awards in 1975. The stories about the making of the film and the awards competition are legendary (although not always reliable), and the success of the film is remarkable considering the impressive list of other nominees that year. The twelve nominees for Best Picture included such memorable films as Cecil B. DeMille's *Cleopatra*; the first Fred Astaire–Ginger Rogers musical, *The Gay Divorcee*; *The Thin Man*; *The Barretts of Wimpole Street*; Ernst Lubitsch's *The Merry Widow*; and *Imitation of Life*. Only ten comedies have ever won the Best Picture Oscar.[1] On hindsight, one critic's sour prediction now seems deliciously ironic. Elizabeth Yeaman wrote in the *Hollywood Citizen-News*, "In the years to come, I hardly think that critics or the public will regard *It Happened One Night* as a great picture."[2]

But by then the critics and the public had already made up their mind. When the film premiered at Radio City Music Hall in February 1934, it only lasted a week. Columbia Pictures apparently had low expectations for it and had not conducted much of a marketing and advertising campaign. But the critical reviews and word of mouth were so positive that the film was booked back into Radio City later in the year, along with multiple bookings in smaller movie houses throughout the country. It turned into a blockbuster success by the end of the year and was soon regarded as a leading contender in the 1934 Oscar race.

The happy coincidence of motives and personalities that led up to the making of the film adds to its charm. The screenplay had solid credentials. Robert Riskin based his script on a magazine story, "Night Bus," written by the successful writer Samuel Hopkins Adams, who had begun as a muckraking journalist for the *New York Sun* and various magazines early in the twentieth century and then became a chronicler of the Jazz Age in a couple of frank novels, *Flaming Youth* and *Unforbidden Fruit*, in the 1920s. Eventually turning to screenwriting, Adams turned his two Jazz Age novels into films; one of them, retitled *The Wild Party* (1929), was a major showcase for the free-spirited "flapper" Clara Bow. Riskin had begun his long collaboration with Frank Capra writing dialogue for Jean Harlow's 1931 hit, *Platinum Blonde*, which Capra directed. The following year, he worked with Capra on the Pat O'Brien melodrama *American Madness*. He then continued to work with Capra on one of his most popular weepies, *Lady for A Day*, in 1933. Buoyed by their successful collaboration (which would continue throughout the rest of the decade with such Capra classics as *Mr. Deeds Goes to Town* [1936], *You Can't Take It with You* [1938], and *Mr. Smith Goes to Washington* [1939]), Capra and Riskin moved on to their next project, *It Happened One Night*.

The film, as they say, almost didn't happen. Louis B. Mayer at MGM turned it down, so Harry Cohn bought it for Columbia Pictures, a far less prestigious studio. The casting process was rocky. After several actors turned down the part, Mayer agreed to loan out Clark Gable to Columbia to do the film. Some accounts claim that Mayer arranged the deal as a punishment for Gable's prima donna behavior at MGM, refusing to accept certain roles offered him and reportedly calling in sick much too often, when Mayer had good reason to suspect that the star was either too drunk or too hungover to report for duty. Other explanations are that MGM actually did not have a project ready for Gable at the time, and, since they were paying him $2,000 a week under his contract whether or not he was working, Mayer loaned him out to Columbia for $2,500 a week, making a nice profit on the deal.

By 1934, Gable was MGM's number one male star. Having begun his career playing villains, gangsters, and he-man roles, Gable started getting major fan attention by the beginning of the 1930s. The studio finally realized what they had in Gable and cast him in no fewer than thirteen films released in 1931, pairing him with their biggest female stars, including Norma Shearer, Greta Garbo, and Joan Crawford (who had specifically requested Gable for her leading man). The following year, Gable clinched his sex-symbol status when he starred with Jean Harlow in the smoldering *Red Dust*. By 1933, he was back with Joan Crawford in *Dancing Lady*. It has been said that, having become accustomed to star treatment, Gable was not pleased with Mayer's loaning him to Columbia Pictures, and he showed up for his first meeting with Capra in an inebriated condition.[3]

Claudette Colbert was no more eager than Gable to work on the picture. She had been quite busy as well, having starred in two major productions that were also released in 1934—the Cecil B. DeMille epic *Cleopatra* and the melodrama *Imitation of Life*—and she was looking forward to spending a long Christmas vacation in Sun Valley. She was not very interested in doing a comedy, anyway. Born in France and raised in New York City, Colbert came to Hollywood after several years of leading roles on Broadway and had developed an impressive resume of more than twenty films playing in glamorous roles opposite such sophisticated leading men as Fredric March and Maurice Chevalier. As the decadent Empress Poppea in Cecil B. DeMille's 1932 pre–Motion Picture Production Code depiction of Roman sensuality, *The Sign of the Cross*, Colbert appeared bathing in a marble pool filled with asses' milk. Her persona was built around elegance and continental sophistication, with just enough sensuousness to keep her interesting and quite popular. (Both *Cleopatra* and *Imitation of Life* ended up competing with Capra's film for the Best Picture Oscar.) Understandably, a role in a screwball Frank Capra comedy would not seem beneficial to the image she was so carefully developing; however, after Columbia Pictures offered her a salary of $50,000 and promised that the film would be shot in four weeks so that she could go on that long-desired vacation, she took the part of spoiled heiress Ellie Andrews.

The casting of Gable and Colbert, two actors who had been given little previous opportunity to display their comedic talents on film, reveals one of the secrets of the genre's success. Gable and Colbert were not great comedians in their own right and, in fact, were better known for more serious roles. Tina Olsin Lent points out that, in the screwball comedies of the 1930s, "for the first time the romantic leads were also the comic leads."[4] The pattern of combining romantic and comic behavior has continued, particularly in the romantic comedy genre up to the present day. Many the stars of romantic comedies are not character comedians identified with particular comic characteristics, like Charlie Chaplin, Mae West, or the Marx Brothers. Their roles seldom involve any slapstick pratfalls or physically dangerous stunts, à la Buster Keaton, Jerry Lewis, or Jim Carrey. They are not required to be particularly witty or clever, like Bob Hope or Danny Kaye. They need not have risen through the ranks of stand-up comedy, as did Steve Martin, Woody Allen, or Robin Williams, or sketch comedy, as have Lily Tomlin, Eddie Murphy, Mike Myers, Will Ferrell, and so many of the graduates of *Saturday Night Live.* They need only play their lovable characters in conformity with the traditional built-in conflict of the romantic comedy formula, succinctly defined by one critic in describing the lead characters: "These two could hardly be less suited to one another—although, of course, from the titles on, everyone in the theater knows better."[5]

Romantic comedy offers opportunities for a range of actors. Over the years, many highly respected actors who have made their reputation in more serious roles (Meryl Streep, Robert De Niro, Dustin Hoffman, and Audrey Hepburn) have occasionally dipped their toes in the romantic comedy pool. It also helps if an actor is particularly good looking, like Matthew McConaughey, Kate Hudson, Ashton Kutcher, Julia Roberts, or Cameron Diaz. Gable and Colbert met both requirements.

It Happened One Night offers many pleasures. It has been labeled (inaccurately, in my opinion) as one of the first great screwball comedies, with its mix of hostile dialogue between the romantic leads and their physical antics. Lent, for instance, refers to it as the "archetype of the screwball comedy genre," and several other critics place the film in the same category.[6] It also qualifies as something of a "road picture," since the major portion of the story takes place during Ellie and Peter's bus ride from Florida to New York, during which they manage to learn a few things about the real world, fall in love, and change the direction of their lives forever. Kathrina Glitre quotes *Variety*'s review of the film as "another long-distance bus story."[7] Meanwhile, it manages to be rather sexually titillating, with the suggestiveness of the word *it* in its title; the mild display of flesh in Gable's "striptease" and Colbert's display of some leg; the portrayal of an unmarried man and woman spending the night together in a motel room separated only by the "walls of Jericho"; and the several coded innuendos in Colbert and Gable's flirtatious conversations, with references to Peter's "trumpet," the "stiffness" of the raw carrots they eat, Ellie's conclusion that, in hitchhiking at least, "the [female] limb is mightier than the [male] thumb," and so on.

It had its social ramifications for Depression-era audiences as well, featuring a romance between an heiress and a working-class journalist who, in fact, had just been fired. Their relationship could be seen as a symbol of "any kind of reconciliation—between the classes, the genders, the generations; between Depression anxiety and happy-go-lucky optimism."[8] Wes D. Gehring observes that these "more class-conciliatory screwball and romantic comedies" carried an "implosive" artistic and political message:

> Film theorist and later director Andrew Bergman has termed the mid-1930s attempt of screwball comedy (and for our purposes, romantic comedy) to pull things together—"implosive." It is an apt expression, for one might define the first years of the Depression as *explosive* in two ways. First, in the early 1930s the extreme political left was actually encouraging class warfare. Second, this volatile period was paralleled in cinema by such anarchistic edgy personality comedians as the Marx Brothers and W. C. Fields. Indeed the Marx's *Duck Soup* (1933), under the masterful direction of Leo McCarey, showcases both satirically violent politics and dark comedy in an inspired story where Groucho is leader of a country! . . . These more class-conciliatory screwball and romantic comedies came along at a time when President Franklin Delano Roosevelt's new administration was attempting to orchestrate

its own version of "implosive" politics in all walks of American life. Not surprisingly, some Marxist period critics ludicrously suggested Hollywood's then new love affair with come-together romantic comedy was the result of a White House directive.[9]

Nevertheless, while never advocating rebellion or anarchy, there was a touch of class conflict in Capra's vision. *It Happened One Night* offered several portrayals of the common man and woman as good-hearted, generous, and optimistic victims of the country's bad economic times. This affection for ordinary folk fit in with what Tamar Jeffers McDonald labeled the "reverse class snobbery" of Depression-era movie audiences that considered "poverty as morally superior to wealth."[10]

Finally, the story reflects the new level of sexual equality in the country at the time. American women had won the right to vote, and many of them were going on to college and/or entering the working world. Throughout the 1920s and even the early years of the Great Depression, many were indulging in a new identity as fun-loving, cigarette-smoking, cocktail-sipping "flappers." Both men and women flocked to see the various vamps, femme fatales, and "it" girls presented at their local movie palaces. The image of the "modern woman" was changing, and Lent considers *It Happened One Night* and other 1930s comedies as the "most in-depth exposition on the Hollywood screen" of the era's "thoroughgoing exploration and reconceptualization of the ideal love relationship between men and women."[11] Romantic comedy has continued in this vein up to the present, portraying the battle of the sexes as a contest between equally matched opponents who are destined, of course, to arrive at mutual surrender in the fabled arena where love conquers all.

A brief synopsis of the plot may be helpful. *It Happened One Night* begins as Ellie Andrews (Colbert), a spoiled and temperamental heiress, has rebelled against her condition by marrying King Westley (Jameson Thomas), an upper-class aviator playboy whom her father (Walter Connolly) despises. Her father has imprisoned her on the family yacht, promising to have the marriage annulled. Undeterred, Ellie dives off the yacht and swims ashore to begin her escape to New York City, where Westley awaits her. She boards a "night bus" in Miami and ends up sitting next to a smart-aleck reporter, Peter Warne (Gable). Originally hostile to one another, they form a tentative alliance when they see the newspaper stories about her with her picture plastered on the front page. During one of the bus's rest stops, Peter offers to accompany her to New York City if he can have exclusive rights to the story of her reunion with Westley. Since her suitcase and almost all of her money were stolen at the previous rest stop and the bus has left without her, she agrees to the arrangement.

They spend their first night of the trip in an inexpensive auto-camp in a rather unconventional but innocent arrangement of separate beds separated by a blanket hung on a clothesline, which Peter dubs the "walls of Jericho." The next morning, when they realize that another passenger has caught on to her secret, they abandon the bus and proceed to hitchhike to New York City.

The two spend their second night together in the open air, with Ellie sleeping on a pile of hay, while they both begin to realize that they are attracted to one another. On the third and final night of their trip, they choose to stay in a motel outside Philadelphia instead of trying to make it to New York City. As they both lie awake, Ellie leaves her bed and steps through the "walls of Jericho" to confess to Peter that she has fallen in love with him. He resists taking advantage of the situation, reminding her that she is technically still a married woman.

However, through a series of mishaps and missed signals, Ellie and Peter get separated before they reach New York City. Ellie, thinking that her profession of love scared Peter away, decides to "remarry" Westley in a church ceremony. On the day of the wedding, however, Ellie confesses to her father that she is still in love with Peter, and Peter reluctantly tells the father of his love for Ellie. Peter, with the father's help, wins Ellie back in enough time to save her from the marriage to Westley and takes her away to get married somewhere on the road. The couple then enjoys their honeymoon night in another motel.

Contrary to considerable critical opinion, *It Happened One Night* is far more successful as a romantic film than a screwball comedy. While Lent's illuminating study of the film insists on describing the film as a screwball comedy, Gehring disagrees, offering an outline of the basic differences between the two genres and positioning *It Happened One Night* solidly in the romantic comedy category.[12] He identifies five points that distinguish the two genres.

"First," writes Gehring, the "screwball variety places its emphasis on 'funny,' while the more traditional romantic comedy accents 'love.' The screwball genre relies on physical comedy and ludicrous events, while romantic comedy is more reality based with little or no slapstick." Gehring compares the lunatic activity and eccentric characters of *Bringing Up Baby* (1938) to the "realistically human" coworkers-in-love in *The Shop around the Corner* (1940). This certainly describes *It Happened One Night*'s more realistic narrative, in which the characters are quite recognizable, with normal reactions to their situations and very little physical shenanigans, like Cary Grant's chasing through the woods to find an escaped leopard in *Bringing Up Baby*.

Second, screwball comedy "spoofs the romantic process; love comes across as hardly more significant than a board game" for the married egotists in *Twentieth Century* (1934) or the dueling newspaper couple in *His Girl Friday* (1940), whereas the "romantic genre frequently embraces sentimental and/or melodramatic story developments completely alien to screwball comedy." Think of the instances of heartbreak, sickness, hopelessness, and other serious problems of the main characters in *Sabrina* (1954), *Annie Hall* (1977), *Moonstruck* (1987), or *Pretty Woman* (1990). *It Happened One Night* likewise pauses every now and then for some soft-focus romantic moments, for example, in the moonlit open field when Ellie is frightened or the couple's intimate conversation in the motel room on the last night of the trip. And, Capra being Capra, there is the sequence with the boy on the bus whose out-of-work mother has fainted from hunger, as well as the common-man camaraderie of the bus passengers as they join in singing "The Daring Young Man on the Flying Trapeze." Plenty of melodrama and sentimentality find their way into this comedy.

Third, the characters in screwball comedy—the leads as well as the supporting characters—are almost all eccentric. In the jailhouse scene near the end of *Bringing Up Baby* or the courtroom scene in the final moments of *What's Up, Doc?*, every character, even the representatives of law and order, is obsessed or emotionally out of control. The main characters in romantic comedy, however, are "decidedly less controlling, more serious." In addition, in romantic comedy the "supporting characters . . . also tend to be more funny than flakey." Think of the professional colleagues of Spencer Tracy and Katharine Hepburn in their series of comedies or the various supportive friends in *Sleepless in Seattle* (1993) or *You've Got Mail* (1998). Similarly, even the authority figures in *It Happened One Night*—Ellie's millionaire father and Peter's newspaper editor—are not presented as the tyrannical and irrational blocking characters of Shakespeare or Moliere, but they clearly have good reason to be upset with the situation. Everyone is relatively normal in the midst of their comic predicaments.

Fourth, Gehring contrasts the mating ritual in the two genres. In screwball comedy, the "eccentric heroine frequently finds herself in a triangle with the sought-after male and his life-smothering fiancée." Again, *Bringing Up Baby* serves as the template for this pattern, as the audience roots for Susan (Katharine Hepburn) in her crusade to release her beloved David (Cary Grant) from the grip of the uptight Miss Swallow. In romantic comedy, however, while there may be a third party in the equation, Gehring explains, "conflict for this genre is more apt to occur over [the romantic leads'] character differences rather than over another character." It becomes something of a rule of romantic comedy that the boy and girl who are "meant for each other" are polar opposites: the control freak versus the free spirit, the professional versus the ne'er-do-well slacker, the shy nerd versus the popular beauty, the jock versus the brain, the spoiled rich girl versus the hardworking poor guy, and so on. Their first meeting is usually unpleasant; their initial interaction is frequently hostile, often compounded by issues of gender, ideology, or social class. Their romantic involvement will, of course, eventually dissolve these obstacles.

In this vein, Ted Sennett describes the relationship of Peter and Ellie as the "simple story of romance between . . . a charming, albeit spoiled and headstrong rich girl who could thumb a ride, dunk a doughnut, and fall for a plainspeaking man who didn't wear undershirts."[13] This particular contrast proved immensely popular for quite some time. "For the rest of the 1930s and even into the 1940s," writes Sennett, the "screen was overrun with willful heiresses fleeing stuffy marriages, or rich young men and women mingling incognito with the common folk to learn humility and understanding, and—more often than not—finding true love in the bargain."[14]

The fifth difference that Gehring points out is the plot pacing. "Screwball comedy escalates near the close." They invariably come to their conclusion with frantic chase scenes, slamming doors, colliding vehicles, mounting arguments or cross-purpose conversations, revelations of deceptions or disguises—or all of the above—adding up to lunatic frenzy. Think of the frantic conclusions of *Arsenic and Old Lace* (1944), *Some Like It Hot* (1959), *What's Up, Doc?* (1972), and *Victor, Victoria* (1982). "Contrastingly," says Gehring, "romantic comedy slows to a turtle's pace at the close, as the audience agonizes over whether the couple will ultimately get together." Gehring offers the example of Billy Crystal slowly coming to his senses and reconnecting with Meg Ryan for a kiss at the stroke of midnight on New Year's Eve at the conclusion of *When Harry Met Sally* (1989). Capra, on his part, puts the audience through twenty minutes of emotional torture near the end of the story before Peter and Ellie manage to clear up the misunderstandings that have driven them apart and finally admit that they are in love and are right for one another. Even Ellie and her father's march down the wedding aisle maintains the suspense. Ellie does make a mad dash out of the ceremony rather than repeat her vows, but no one chases her. Then, after everybody gets what they want, the film ends with the quiet lowering of the "walls of Jericho"—a turtle's pace indeed!

Gehring concludes that *It Happened One Night* "fits much more comfortably under the five-point romantic comedy umbrella . . . especially with regard to an accent on reality and love over pure eccentricity."[15] He refers his readers to the opinion of genre expert Jim Leach, who agrees that

> Capra's vision is not really screwball at all . . . whereas the only positive strategy in screwball comedy is to accept the all-pervasive craziness, the populist comedy argues that what society regards as crazy (Mr. Deeds's attempt to give away his fortune) is really a manifestation of the normal human values with which society has lost touch.[16]

All this being said, *It Happened One Night* succeeds so brilliantly as a romantic comedy because it presents a fully rounded story of two adults separated by class, money, and gender, who find one another and, to some extent, their deeper selves by a series of role-playing and other ludic adventures, including some sexual games, to escape their dead-end or imprisoning situations and achieve the freedom that Northrop Frye insists is the goal of comic drama, what he has called the "mythos of Spring."[17] Each of these elements deserves closer examination.

Several critics have pointed to the differences between the two lovers. In her summary of the film's narrative, McDonald emphasizes the class conflict found in so many films of the period, observing that *It Happened One Night* exemplifies "reverse class snobbery as a trope." It begins with Ellie's "imprisonment" on her father's yacht but develops as the education of the spoiled heiress in the ways of the "real world":

> Ellie's naivety, assuming she can make her way with limited funds, is exposed as a rich person's malaise: She is forced very quickly to learn the true value of money in Depression-era America. . . . The phoniness of rich people is mocked, and cozy proletarian values are celebrated instead; the scene on the bus where everyone is singing together acts as a counterbalance to the moments where we see Ellie's father shouting at his minions. Harmony can only prevail where everyone is prepared to join in, the film seems to suggest; while there may be problems . . . these can be faced better as a community. The rich man and his daughter, before her alternative education begins, are morally bankrupt, while the poor people lack only money, not heart.
>
> *It Happened One Night* removes the audience for a time from its own experiences, to expose the arid upper-class world of privileged Ellie, but then brings her down to earth, and back to contemporary reality. . . . The experience enriches her spiritually and emotionally, and she grows as a person from her time spent without money.[18]

In line with McDonald's analysis of the story as the education of a naive rich girl, Ellie is first shown bedecked in a satin dressing gown (the sort of attire that audiences were, in fact, accustomed to seeing Colbert wearing in her other films), furiously smoking (a sure sign of upper-class decadence) while she paces around her stateroom "prison" on the family yacht. She has clearly terrorized the ship's staff, who cower before her as they deliver to her the steak dinner her father has ordered to make her end the fast she has been keeping as a protest against her imprisonment. She talks back to her imperious father, defying his command that she eat something, finally knocking over the entire serving tray (a scandalous and insensitive waste of food when many of her countrymen at the time were standing in breadlines).

Her behavior on the bus is in keeping with her expectations of privileged treatment and sense of the social superiority and power that her moneyed position gives her. As Thomas E. Wartenberg observes, "For all her rejection of her father, she shares his confidence that the world revolves around the needs of the rich."[19] When she reimburses a kindly older woman for buying her bus ticket, thus avoiding unwanted attention, Ellie surprises the woman by adding the customary generous tip for her services. In her first encounter with the wisecracking

Peter, she responds to all of his remarks with silent, haughty glares and later patronizingly addresses him as "young man." When the bus makes a thirty-minute stop for breakfast, she heads off to a hotel, confident that the bus will not leave without her. When she returns, she cannot believe that the bus has indeed departed. Then, worried that Peter is going to report her to her father, she offers to pay him for his silence. Peter responds, saying the following:

> You know, I had you pegged right from the start. You're the spoiled brat of a rich father. The only way you can get anything is to buy it. Now you're in a jam, and all you can think of is your money. It never fails, does it? Ever hear of the word *humility*? No, you wouldn't. I guess it never occurred to you just to say, "Please, Mister, I'm in trouble, will you help me?" No, that'd bring you down off your high horse for a minute.

However, after the theft of her money and suitcase, Ellie begins to experience what life is like when one has little or no financial resources or any of the privileges that come with them. At one of the stops on the bus's route, she spends the time, as she later describes it, "running in and out of doorways, trying to keep out of the rain." When, as they continue on to New York City on the next bus, she starts to buy some candy, Peter prevents the purchase, reminding her that they are on a budget. They spend their first night of the trip in the same room of an auto-camp to save money. When Ellie prances up to the door of the camp's communal shower the next morning, she is laughed at and told to get in line with the rest of the women. When a girl in the line sticks her tongue out at her, Ellie sticks out her own tongue in response and then chuckles to herself, as she begins to discover that the company of the common folk is rather enjoyable. For her breakfast, Peter tells her that their budget allows her only one egg. She is then introduced to the joys of dunking doughnuts and, later that day, the fun of piggybacking across a creek. When the next night falls, she learns what it feels like to sleep in a haystack rather than a luxurious bed and to be grateful for the carrots that Peter steals from a nearby farm for breakfast. She later discovers that one can make one's way on the road by hitchhiking, as well as by paying for a ride. Her situation is financially limited, but also a lot of fun.

What she is fundamentally experiencing is a freedom that her wealthy girlhood had never provided. She offers a vivid description of her "imprisonment" by her father when, as she eats her single egg and doughnut breakfast, she responds to Peter's characterization of her as a "spoiled brat" by saying the following:

> Perhaps I am, although I don't see how I can be. People who are spoiled are accustomed to having their own way. I never have. On the contrary, I have always been told what to do and how to do it and when and with whom. . . . Nurses, governesses, chaperones. Even

bodyguards. . . . I actually went shopping once without a bodyguard. It was swell! I felt positively immoral.

Her shopping trip ended when, at the sight of the detectives that her father sent after her, Ellie ran out of the store and jumped into the first car she saw, which is how she met King Westley. She says, "We ran around all afternoon. Father was frantic." It becomes obvious that, for Ellie, Westley represents both an experience of freedom and a stroke of revenge on her father. But her current journey is much more liberating. "Ellie's mad flight from her gilded cage," writes Maria di Battista, "teaches her the varieties of social movement possible to an American with heart and spirit enough for the ride."[20] Heart and spirit and the love of an ordinary working Joe, not the money and privilege of a society marriage, will provide a more authentic path to the freedom she had been seeking by her secret marriage to Westley and her dive off her father's yacht.

Wartenberg's study of the film adds another element of conflict, primarily associated with gender roles. Pointing to its "parallel criticisms of class and gender hierarchy," he states that "wealth and masculinist assumptions of superiority based on expertise are represented as forms of pride inimical to the democratic values the film endorses. . . . Peter's masculinist pretensions are subject to as serious and sustained a critique as Ellie's moneyed hauteur."[21] His description of Ellie and Peter's mutual dislike when they first meet recognizes not only her upper-class snobbery but also his sense of masculine superiority:

> For Ellie, Peter is an impudent young man on the make. To keep him in his place, she takes the haughty line the wealthy reserve for their social inferiors. On the other hand, Peter registers Ellie as a spoiled, upper-class brat, a young woman ignorant of life. Because Peter sees himself as a man of the world, someone who knows his way around—a stance authorized by a masculinist inflation of his own capabilities—he has nothing but contempt for her.[22]

The audience's introduction to Peter occurs when he, fairly intoxicated, is being fired over the telephone by his editor for some vaguely unsatisfactory piece of journalism that he has written. His impudent responses to his boss, enhanced by his pretending to be "telling off the boss" after the editor has actually hung up on him, so impress the company of men who appear to be his fellow newspaper writers that they hail him as the "king" and escort him to the bus that will return him to New York. When he takes it upon himself to toss out the window a pile of newspapers resting on the seat that he wants to occupy, he engages in an argument with the bus driver, which includes some threats of physical violence. He thus comes across as a belligerent, fast-talking quasi-windbag faking his way through life while enjoying a few drinks or even the prospect of a fistfight, all qualities that fit the image of the newspaper reporter in the 1930s. According to Wartenberg, it is worth noting that the figure of the newspaper reporter was a staple of the Hollywood comedies of the 1930s,

> because many of the scriptwriters lured to Hollywood by its glamour and good money had been newspaper people, the figure of the cynical and hard-boiled reporter became a means of commenting on their own situation. Like reporters, scriptwriters are generally not free to choose their subjects but produce to meet the demands of a paymaster . . . by heroizing the reporter, scriptwriters were able to assert their own superiority to the circumstance in which they worked.[23]

The reporter-hero is thus endowed with a sense of his own superiority, which the events of the trip and the reactions of his heiress-companion will work to undermine.

Some of Peter's claim to superior knowledge and skill is justified and, in fact, useful. In his verbal sparring with the driver (Ward Bond) when he first boards the bus, Peter mocks the driver's inability to say anything other than "Oh, yeah?," and he then proceeds to win the argument with a tall tale about the time people were able to get the news by reading the newsprint stain on his pants acquired when he sat on a stack of newspapers too long. He comes to Ellie's aid when she is being harassed by the annoying Mr. Shapeley by claiming to be her husband, and he later scares off Shapeley by pretending to be a gangster. He spots the man who steals Ellie's suitcase, although he is unable to catch him. He saves Ellie's bus ticket, which she had left on her seat. He is able to get the pair lodging for the night at the auto-court and arranges an outdoor sleeping area (and a little food) for them on the second night of their trip. And, of course, he teaches Ellie how to properly dunk a doughnut.

However, some of his vaunted worldly wisdom gets deflated as he tries to instruct Ellie. His demonstration of the way a man undresses to go to bed and his doughnut instructions are overblown, especially when he half-jokingly announces that he's thinking of writing a book on the subject of dunking. When he boastfully attempts to demonstrate the best use of one's thumb for hitchhiking, again informing Ellie that he is thinking of writing a book on that topic as well, Ellie mockingly replies, "There's no end to your accomplishments!" After his various methods to hail a passing car fail, Ellie, stepping up and lifting her skirt, accomplishes the deed in no time at all, which, she says later, has "proved once and for all that the leg is mightier than the thumb." Thus, Peter's sense of superior knowledge is diminished as effectively as Ellie's dependence on her wealth and social position.

Meanwhile, as Ellie liberates herself from her previous lifestyle, Peter's resentment of rich people is simultaneously deflated. He grows to admire Ellie's resourcefulness in the hitchhiking episode and other moments. He is obviously moved by her honest expression of love during their last night together. Finally, he enjoys a man-to-man conversation with Ellie's Wall Street mogul father.

Most of all, as he succumbs to his own love for Ellie, he gains a new self-understanding. When Ellie's father asks him, "Do you love my daughter?" Peter replies, "Any guy that'd fall in love with your daughter should have his head examined. A normal human being couldn't live under the same roof with her, without going nutty." When the father asks him the question once again, Peter shouts, "Yes, but don't hold that against me. I'm a little screwy myself." As Wartenberg observes,

> Pushed into a corner, Peter acknowledges his love for Ellie, his incompleteness without her. More significant still is his recognition that Ellie is a woman he cannot completely control. . . . The old know-it-all Peter cannot smoothly incorporate this woman into the life he has imagined for himself. . . . This is a real change from the position of masculine superiority that he had previously occupied.[24]

Moreover, Peter's description of himself as a "little screwy myself" represents a 180-degree reversal from his sense of himself as a commonsense, working-class man of the people. The journey has not only freed Ellie from her gilded cage; it has liberated Peter from his class prejudices, his insistence on his superiority, and—the enemy of all comedy—the need to be normal.

As a chronicle of Peter and Ellie's love story, *It Happened One Night* exemplifies Lent's portrayal of the function of games and playfulness in the romantic relationships in screwball comedy (which she considers this film to be). She observes that such films, especially in the 1930s, "illustrate the value of play as a means of establishing the companionship so essential to contemporary love. . . . Play itself became the language by which the authentic lovers discovered their affinity."[25] The "fun" often takes the form of role-playing. Ellie and Peter take on various roles, sometimes quite deliberately, and occasionally unconsciously. On the bus, Peter pretends to be Ellie's husband to free her from the clutches of the obnoxious Mr. Shapeley. He also, of course, pretends to be her husband when he rents a room for the night at the auto-camp. They continue this charade when they hitch a ride with the jovial Mr. Danker (Alan Hayes). They let Danker think that they are on their honeymoon, and when he stops at a hamburger stand, rather than tell him that they have no money, they say that they are not hungry, prompting Danker to observe that "young people in love are never hungry."

Fast-talking Peter is a natural at playing roles. At one point on the bus trip, Shapeley, having read about Ellie in the papers, tries to extort hush money from Peter. Peter reacts by offering a very believable imitation of a gangster (and a bit of a parody of earlier Gable roles) with such remarks as "I got a notion to plug you. . . . You know too much" and a threat to "go after" Shapeley's children as he did with a certain Bugs Dooley, who "got a little too talkative." The role-playing works, as Shapeley leaves the bus and runs for his life. Later, in their first night together, Peter plays a rather seductive role as he pretends to reveal to Ellie the way that a man undresses for bed, stripping down to his trousers. He then fancifully creates the "walls of Jericho" when he hangs the blanket over a clothesline between their separate beds. Even such practical activities and arrangements are played out by Peter as very much like a game.

Ellie, on the other hand, is a bit of a novice in this department. She reveals hidden talent, however, when their breakfast in the auto-camp is interrupted by Mr. Dyke, the owner of the auto-camp, announcing the arrival of the detectives sent by Ellie's father to track her down. Wartenberg describes the scene vividly, saying the following:

> Aware of their approach, Peter has seated Ellie on the bed, and as he combs her hair down over her face, he loudly recounts his conversation with Aunt Bellah from Wilkes-Barre. At first, Ellie has no idea what he is doing, but she quickly catches on and plays along with him. . . . When Peter feigns anger at one of the detectives to distract him from his quarry, Ellie jumps in to "calm" Peter. She even introduces her own variations on the story he has been fabricating. After Peter protests to Dyke, "They can't come in here and start shooting questions at my wife!" Ellie turns on him—"Don't get excited, Peter. They just asked a civil question"—capturing the bickering tone of old marrieds so well that it throws Dyke and the detectives off the scent.[26]

As Wartenberg observes, Ellie "clearly gets a kick out of pretending to be Peter's wife," not only because it prevented her from getting caught and returned to captivity, but because she enjoyed "how they played off one another" and how she had been "forced to use her wits" and discovered a "capacity that her sheltered existence had kept hidden and unused." It also causes Peter to realize that "there is more to Ellie than the spoiled brat he has so far disdained—she has reserves of character undeveloped by her privileged way of life."[27] Peter is so impressed, in fact, that he playfully suggests that they could go on the road as a two-person acting troupe. Wartenberg sees this as Peter's first suggestion that their relationship could develop, if not into a romantic bond, at least into a "joint undertaking that transcends short-term mutual convenience." When Ellie suggests that their troupe could do "Cinderella," she "reveals that her imagination is already headed that way."[28]

Later, Ellie is introduced to the joys of piggybacking as Peter carries her across a stream, and they argue about the nature of an authentic piggyback ride.

The lesson in doughnut dunking is a bit of a game as well, with Peter claiming to be a master of the "art." The hitchhiking lesson turns into a competition, with Ellie the clear winner. A great deal of their conversation, when they are not arguing or bickering, is comprised of the sort of play that combines gender and class competition but also mild explorations of the possibilities of a deeper romantic relationship.

The play gets sexualized at times as well. Lent maintains that such physical antics "function as a substitute for expressions of overt sexuality" that had been banned by the Motion Picture Production Code, which, coincidentally, came into effect the very year that *It Happened One Night* was released. "Allusions to sexuality replace the overt, explicit physical sexuality depicted in earlier films, and double entendre, allusion, humor, symbol and metaphor abound."[29] Ellie and Peter experience physical contact almost immediately when she falls into his lap when the bus abruptly starts moving out of the Miami station. At the first stop on the route, Ellie, having fallen asleep, wakes up to find that she has been resting her head on Peter's shoulder. They enjoy more physical contact during the piggyback ride. Then, when they spend the night out in a field, Ellie thinks that Peter has wandered off. When he returns and her fears are relieved, she instinctively embraces him. When the embrace lingers a bit, romantic sparks seem to fly between them, even more so when he bends over her as she settles into her bed of hay and they almost kiss. They both deal with the awkwardness of the situation with some hostile remarks, but, as she falls asleep, Peter steps away and lights a cigarette to calm his emotional stirrings. As Lent remarks, the "extreme physicality allows the characters to touch intimately, but humorously, offering alternative outlets for repressed sexuality."[30]

Sexuality is expressed verbally as well. As McDonald remarks, "There are a number of elements in the film that are suggestive of sexual desire as well as of romantic intimacy between the pair."[31] When Peter sets up the blanket on the clothesline between their beds, he proclaims assuringly, "Behold the walls of Jericho. Maybe not as thick as the ones that Joshua blew down with his trumpet, but a lot safer. You see, I have no trumpet." Later, when Peter offers Ellie a raw carrot, she says that she doesn't like "those stiff things." Peter's attention to his "thumb" as something a man uses for hitchhiking is matched, of course, by Ellie's "limb." When, at the film's conclusion, Peter and Ellie end up back in a motel room, the audience hears the sound of a trumpet blowing at last. Such allusions are consistent with Glitre's observation that the Motion Picture Production Code had actually allowed for a "system of representation that allowed 'sophisticated' viewers to draw conclusions that were unavailable to 'innocent' viewers."[32]

Finally, *It Happened One Night* reaches into archetypal levels of comedy in its evocation of the life force of springtime. Francis MacDonald Cornford's classic study of early Greek comedy traces its origins to various spring fertility rituals and the "fight of summer and winter" that celebrates the new life of nature at the time of the spring equinox in ancient Greece and many other cultures.[33] Frye describes comedy as the "mythos of spring" and explores Shakespeare's romantic comedies as the "drama of the green world" with affinities to the medieval tradition of seasonal ritual play of Maypoles and Morris dances. Shakespeare sends his lovers into forests, seacoasts, and distant islands with the "same rhythmic movement from normal world to green world and back again."[34] If one considers Ellie's wealthy lifestyle as the "normal world," which she escapes and then returns to, then her life on the road and in the woods is the "green world," which brings an end to her dead-end existence and raises her to a new life of adventure, romance, and sexual fulfillment. *It Happens One Night* becomes a celebration of the very mysteries that have been celebrated since earliest times. One can also point to a bit of springtime symbolism in the warm-weather rain that they encounter on their first night and a hint of Easter in the one egg Ellie is allotted for her breakfast.

Glitre's study of romantic comedy hearkens back to Frye's treatment of Shakespeare. Although at this point in her analysis, she is primarily considering screwball comedy, Glitre's interpretation of the Shakespearean comic formula nicely describes the two worlds of *It Happened One Night*:

> The normal world is characterized as a world of irrational law and parental tyranny, while the green world functions as a festive "holiday" space in which social conventions can be flouted . . . and magical things can happen. . . . The normal world's tyranny stems from its rigidity, which has resulted in social (and economic) stagnation; this is counteracted by a resurgence of playful irrationality, often empowered by the move into the green world. The contrast between artifice and nature remains, therefore, but is recast as a contrast between dehumanizing, urban existence and liberating, pastoral play.[35]

She admits, however, to one flaw in her application of the Shakespearean pattern to screwball comedy, which is significant for this study. Glitre concedes the following:

> The green world as screwball comedy shares some of these traits but not all. . . . The green world does not represent an alternative society; it is usually occupied by the couple alone. Consequently, no matter how beneficial the time spent in the green world is for the screwball couple, there is little sense of *social* renewal, and the couple tends to remain unreconciled with their original society.[36]

This point might well be the final proof that *It Happened One Night* is indeed better understood as a romantic rather than a screwball comedy. Unlike the screwball comedy interludes, the "green world" that Ellie enters on her journey offers a genuine alternative to the only world she has known throughout her wealthy upbringing. It is a society composed of bus drivers, auto-camp managers, traveling salesmen, sailors, farmers, an out-of-work mother and her son, an assortment of singing bus passengers, and a wisecracking newspaper reporter. It is a world of communal bathrooms, flooded-out bridges, and bus schedules that wait for no one. These represent, in Capra's vision, the real American society, much more alive than the world of Ellie's father's yachts and mansions and King Westley's hydroplanes.

And as she returns from her trip into that "green world," there is a great deal of traditional comic reconciliation, between Ellie and Peter, of course, but also between Peter and his editor, who hires him back; between Ellie's father and Westley, who happily agrees to an annulment in exchange for a $100,000 check; and, most significantly, between Ellie and her father. After all, the entire story began with a quarrel between them, stemming from their long-standing battle over control of her life. In a touching scene just before she marches out to the wedding that will not happen, Ellie's father embraces her warmly as she confesses, "I wouldn't hurt you for anything in the world." More broadly, the marriage of Peter and Ellie brings together the working class and the wealthy in a romantic honeymoon night back on the road when the "walls of Jericho," and so many other walls, come tumbling down.

Romantic comedies continue to emerge from Hollywood's dream factories, with the same undeniable appeal and constantly renewable energy of "chemistry" created by each year's hot new couples. While variations on the formula abound, it is hard to match the original magic of *It Happened One Night.*

A Sampling of Romantic Comedies

The Philadelphia Story (1940)
The Shop around the Corner (1940)
Adam's Rib (1949)
Roman Holiday (1953)
Pillow Talk (1959)
Manhattan (1979)
Moonstruck (1987)
When Harry Met Sally (1989)
Pretty Woman (1990)
As Good as It Gets (1997)

Notes

1. For the record, the ten comedies—or mixtures of comedy and drama—that have received an Academy Award for Best Picture include *You Can't Take It with You* (1938), *The Apartment* (1960), *Tom Jones* (1963), *The Sting* (1973), *One Flew over the Cuckoo's Nest* (1975), *Annie Hall* (1977), *Driving Miss Daisy* (1989), *Forrest Gump* (1994), *Shakespeare in Love* (1998), and *The Artist* (2011).

2. Mason Wiley and Damien Bona, *Inside Oscar: The Unofficial History of the Academy Awards* (New York: Ballantine Books, 1996), 58.

3. Accounts of this meeting vary considerably, of course. One version of the story can be found in Warren G. Harris, *Clark Gable* (New York: Harmony Books, 2002), 111–12.

4. Tina Olsin Lent, "Romantic Love and Friendship: The Redefinition of Gender Relations in Screwball Comedy." In *Classical Hollywood Comedy*, Kristine Brunovska Karnick and Henry Jenkins, eds. (New York and London: Routledge, 1995), 327.

5. Thomas E. Wartenberg, *Unlikely Couples: Movie Romance as Social Criticism* (Boulder, Colo.: Westview Press, 1999), 49.

6. Lent, "Romantic Love and Friendship," 314.

7. Kathrina Glitre, *Hollywood Romantic Comedy: States of the Union, 1934–1965* (Manchester, UK, and New York: Manchester University Press, 2006), 22.

8. Elizabeth Kendall, *The Runaway Bride: Hollywood Romantic Comedy of the 1930s* (New York: Doubleday, 1991), 54.

9. Wes D. Gehring, *Romantic vs. Screwball Comedy: Charting the Difference* (Lanham, Md.: Scarecrow Press, 2002), 5–6.

10. Tamar Jeffers McDonald, *Romantic Comedy: Boy Meets Girl Meets Genre* (London and New York: Wallflower Press, 2007), 22, 24.

11. Lent, "Romantic Love and Friendship," 314.

12. The following five points with the accompanying quotations are taken from Gehring, *Romantic vs. Screwball Comedy*, 1–4.

13. Ted Sennett, *Lunatics and Lovers* (New Rochelle, N.Y.: Arlington House, 1973), 90–91.

14. Sennett, *Lunatics and Lovers*, 94.

15. Gehring, *Romantic vs. Screwball Comedy*, 11–12.

16. Jim Leach, "The Screwball Comedy." In *Film Genre: Theory and Criticism*, Barry K. Grant, ed. (Metuchen, N.J.: Scarecrow Press, 1977), 82–83.

17. Northrop Frye, *Anatomy of Criticism: Four Essays* (Princeton, N.J.: Princeton University Press, 1957), 163–86.

18. McDonald, *Romantic Comedy*, 21, 24.

19. Wartenberg, *Unlikely Couples*, 53.

20. Maria di Battista, *Fast-Talking Dames* (New Haven, Conn.: Yale University Press, 2001), 163.

21. Wartenberg, *Unlikely Couples*, 47, 54.

22. Wartenberg, *Unlikely Couples*, 9.
23. Wartenberg, *Unlikely Couples*, 50.
24. Wartenberg, *Unlikely Couples*, 65.
25. Lent, "Romantic Love and Friendship," 322.
26. Wartenberg, *Unlikely Couples*, 59.
27. Wartenberg, *Unlikely Couples*, 59.
28. Wartenberg, *Unlikely Couples*, 60.
29. Lent, "Romantic Love and Friendship," 328.
30. Lent, "Romantic Love and Friendship," 328.
31. McDonald, *Romantic Comedy*, 23.
32. Glitre, *Hollywood Romantic Comedy*, 21.
33. Francis MacDonald Cornford, *The Origin of Attic Comedy* (Ann Arbor: University of Michigan Press, 1993), 12–19.
34. Frye, *Anatomy of Criticism*, 182.
35. Glitre, *Hollywood Romantic Comedy*, 74.
36. Glitre, *Hollywood Romantic Comedy*, 74.

CHAPTER 3

Screwball Comedy

BRINGING UP BABY (1938) AND
WHAT'S UP, DOC? (1972)

The comic genre known as "screwball" has several distinctive elements. It involves a complicated plot; the action moves at a frantic pace; the screenplay provides witty, rapid-fire dialogue; the scenario involves destruction of property and even physical damage to its characters; and, typically, a romantic relationship develops between the main characters, often despite their class differences and some gender issues. Two features, however, define the category more precisely: All or almost all of the characters are eccentric or downright crazy in one way or another, and the main characters seem to have little moral compunction or concern for the needs of others as they pursue their personal goals.

When the conversation turns to the subject of screwball comedy, Howard Hawks's 1938 film *Bringing Up Baby* is often considered the premier example. Starring Katharine Hepburn as madcap heiress Susan Vance and Cary Grant as the befuddled paleontologist Dr. David Huxley, the film develops its plot around David's pursuit of a million-dollar gift to his museum of natural science and, later in the film, the search for an intercostal clavicle, the prehistoric bone that he needs to complete his reconstruction of a brontosaurus skeleton, while Susan attempts to lure him away from his impending marriage to his scientific colleague, Alice Swallow (Virginia Walker). Susan's main device for keeping David's attention is her request that he accompany her as she takes a tame leopard named Baby up to her aunt's home in Connecticut. A series of mishaps occur involving a search for Baby, who escapes into the woods; an encounter with a far more dangerous leopard who has escaped from a traveling circus; and a hunt for David's bone, which Susan's aunt's dog, George, has stolen and buried.

It becomes clear to the audience that marriage to Miss Swallow would be an unromantic existence. Miss Swallow even opposes David's plans for a honeymoon, saying, "I see our marriage as completely dedicated to your work," she tells David. She insists that there be "no domestic entanglements of any kind."

Madcap heiress Susan Vance (Katharine Hepburn) gets her man, Dr. David Huxley (Cary Grant), as they search for Baby, her lost leopard, in *Bringing Up Baby* (1938).

David mildly protests, pathetically suggesting that they might have some sort of physical "entanglement" once they are married, but the domineering fiancée will have none of that.

Five minutes into the film, Susan appears, and the screwball antics begin. David encounters Susan at the country club where he is playing golf with a certain Mr. Peabody (George Irving), a lawyer arranging the potential million-dollar gift. In the course of a few minutes, Susan manages to steal David's golf ball and then damage his automobile, which she seems to mistake for her own car. She drives away from the country club with David on the running board, taking him away from Peabody. That evening, as David attempts another meeting with Peabody for dinner, he again encounters Susan. Sitting at the restaurant bar and attempting to learn a trick that involves popping olives from her hand to her mouth, she drops one olive. David, of course, slips on the olive and falls flat on his back. As she follows David away from the bar area, Susan manages to take another woman's purse; she rips David's suit jacket, saying, "Oh, you've torn your coat," and then, when he accidentally steps on the train of her evening gown, exposing the backside of her undergarments, they exit the restaurant with Peter walking closely behind her to hide the problem and again losing the opportunity to meet with Peabody.

In these two scenes, Susan is revealed as the "modern woman," playing golf, driving a sports car, drinking cocktails, and engaging in party tricks. She displays no respect for other people's ownership of property and never admits to being the cause of any mix-up, whether it be with a golf ball, an automobile, a purse, or an item of clothing. She also has the habit of not allowing others to finish their sentences, managing to inject her own opinion and interpretation into every conversation to everyone's befuddlement. During the course of the film, Susan continues her oblivious behavior, crashing her car into the back of a truck full of chickens, parking her car next to a fire hydrant, driving off in another person's car, tossing a rock through Mr. Peabody's window and knocking him unconscious, breaking David's eyeglasses, getting David and herself soaked by trying to cross a creek that she claims is shallow, and finally, causing major disruption at David's museum. Kathleen Rowe sees such disregard for property as a "function of her own class privilege, but . . . also a marker of her unruliness. . . . She brings to both property and language a sense of play hostile to the spirit of capitalism . . . outside the middle class and free from its conventionality."[1]

Susan is an expert at lying and scheming to get her way. In the first of her fairly transparent ploys, on the morning after their encounters at the golf course and the restaurant, Susan calls David, "because you are the only zoologist I know," (he's actually a paleontologist) to ask for his help in transporting Baby, a tame leopard that her brother has sent from Brazil to be delivered to their aunt's home in Connecticut. When David refuses, she starts screaming and pretending that the leopard is attacking her, thus obliging the gentlemanly David to rush to her assistance. When he arrives to discover that she was lying, he angrily leaves her apartment. Susan prompts Baby to follow David into the street, where she drives up to them and packs them into her car, bound for Connecticut. Once there, she is confronted by the town constable (Walter Catlett) for parking by the fire hydrant. When she sees Baby moving over to an adjoining automobile, she says that the other car is hers and, when David returns, they drive off together in the stolen vehicle. Upon arriving at her aunt's house and convincing David to take a shower, she steals his clothes so that he cannot return to the city for his appointment to marry Miss Swallow. At the dinner table that evening, she hides David's identity by claiming that he is Mr. Bone, a wild game hunter. Finally, when she and David end up in the county jail, she pretends to be a gangster's moll, "Swinging Door Suzy."

The majority of the film is spent in a hunt for David's brontosaurus bone, which her aunt's dog, George, has stolen and buried, and a parallel hunt for Baby, who has escaped into the Connecticut woods. The confusion is resolved when Baby returns, the bone is found, and Susan gets her man, managing in the meantime to acquire the million-dollar grant for his museum. Susan is the ultimate "madcap heiress" of screwball comedy, focused throughout all the antics on her one goal of marrying the hero; she remains oblivious to other people's concerns, especially the hero's, and capable of illogical arguments, physical escapades, and outlandish lies to triumph over it all.

Hepburn's performance is all the more impressive when one realizes that she had never appeared in a film comedy before. Her Hollywood career had begun only five years earlier, with her very successful debut as John Barrymore's daughter in *A Bill of Divorcement* (1933). Within a year, she won her first Academy Award for her role as an ambitious actress in *Morning Glory* (1934). She continued to star in a dozen more films which, while quite different in their locales and narratives, always portrayed her as a strong, independent woman, ranging from Meg, the outspoken New England adolescent in *Little Women* (1933), to the regal Mary Stuart in *Mary of Scotland* (1934), to a mountain girl faith healer in *Spitfire* (1934), to a young woman disguised as a man in *Sylvia Scarlett* (1935), to one of the many struggling actresses in *Stage Door* (1937). All of these roles tended toward the melodramatic, and not all of the films were well-received at the box office. These middling successes, along with her brash off-screen personality and unconventional behavior, earned Hepburn the famous title of "box-office poison" by the Theater Owners of America.

While *Bringing Up Baby*, which, like most films, was not a box-office success at the time, it marked a major turning point in Hepburn's career. She had finally found a role that drew upon her own upper-class Connecticut background as a "self-absorbed, uppity East Coast young woman of privilege."[2] It also made use of her previously untapped ability at fast-paced dialogue and physical comedy. She is described by Maria di Battista as an agile performer who "skips, ambles, strolls, lopes, ducks, crouches, squats, and in general reproduces the entire repertoire of human postures and gaits."[3]

Hepburn's next film, *Holiday* (1938), a milder screwball comedy, again paired her with Cary Grant; however, this film also faltered at the box office. Reconsidering her future in films, Hepburn bought out her contract from RKO studios and went back to New York City to star in *The Philadelphia Story*, a play written by Philip Barry with her in mind. The venture turned out to be a huge critical and commercial success. After buying the movie rights, she returned to Hollywood and, once again with Cary Grant as her leading man, finally experienced box-office success with the 1940 film version of *The Philadelphia Story*. Hepburn was at last a genuine movie star, and she continued as such, winning three more Academy Awards, until her death in 2003.

Her next film would be a definitive experience, both professionally and personally. *Woman of the Year* (1942), in which she plays a witty, independent career woman, paired her with Spencer Tracy. The film created the screen persona that would characterize almost all of the many roles she would play for the rest of her career and also began her romantic partnership with Tracy, which continued until his death in 1967.

Cary Grant, however, was no stranger to light comedy and even some screwball films. Born Archibald Leach in Bristol, England, in 1904, he began his stage career at the age of fourteen and moved to America in 1920. Arriving in Hollywood in 1932, he proceeded to appear (and, most often, star) in more than thirty films by the time he made *Bringing Up Baby*. While his remarkable good looks earned him many romantic roles, he had also appeared in action films, light comedies, and bedroom farces, costarring with the likes of Carole Lombard, Tallulah Bankhead, Loretta Young, Myrna Loy, Jean Harlow, and even with Katharine Hepburn in the 1935 melodrama *Sylvia Scarlett*. His most memorable roles in the period, however, were as the target of Mae West's seductive wiles in *She Done Him Wrong* (1933) and *I'm No Angel* (1935). Just the year before *Bringing Up Baby*, he had starred in the sophisticated farce *Topper* and one of Leo McCarey's best screwball comedies, *The Awful Truth*, with Irene Dunne.

Despite his experience and popularity, Grant was reluctant to step back from his usual persona as the handsome debonair sophisticate to play an absent-minded and sexually inexperienced professor. Fredric March, Ronald Colman, and other Hollywood leading men at the time, protective of their own romantic personae, had already turned down the role; however, Hawks convinced Grant that he could play the role by imitating Harold Lloyd's nerdy bespectacled roles.[4] A great admirer of Lloyd, Charlie Chaplin, and other stars of silent film comedy, Grant took on the challenge. With black-rimmed eyeglasses, a crumpled top hat, an oversized homburg, and a short-stepping pace, he transformed himself into an egghead. He would also bring to the role his history of slapstick comedy from his teenage years of acrobatic comedy as one of the "knockabout boys" in Robert Pender's music hall shows. (It was one of the popular act's tours of America that brought the young Archibald Leach to the United States, where he stayed to become Cary Grant.[5])

Throughout *Bringing Up Baby*, Grant's character combines a physical awkwardness—constantly bumping into objects and people, slipping on an olive or a muddy creek bank, tripping over animals, being forced to wear a woman's dressing gown, at one point getting snagged by a butterfly net, and even fainting after Susan and he have caged the wild leopard in a jail cell—with an unavoidable touch of class. Pauline Kael comments that the "assurance he gained in slapstick turned him into the smoothie he had aspired to be. He brought elegance to low comedy."[6] And as Kathleen Rowe observes, Grant also manages to portray the professor as the rigid character of Bergsonian analysis whom the "unruly woman" will rescue and bring back to life:

> A fossil, the bone represents all that the film opposes: David's avoidance of the chaos of life—of live animals rather than dead ones, and of lively women rather than women like Miss Swallow. David prefers

the morgue-like quiet of a museum of natural history, where he pursues his work as a paleontologist, studying the remains of extinct reptiles. . . . The fossil's rigidity corresponds to the sense that David himself is not fully awake or alive.[7]

Rowe also delights in analyzing the two major symbols in the film, David's "bone" and Susan's leopard. The bone is a "manifestation of the phallus, or symbol of social power. . . . It has meanings related not only to sexuality but to gender and to the organization of property and language, all of which undergo a massive assault at the hands of Susan."[8] Meanwhile, the leopards—both the tame one and the wild one—associate Susan with live animals, not dead animals' skeletons:

> The leopard is as unsubtle a symbol as the bone, but effectively establishes what Susan represents—the "live animal" repressed within the ossifying David. While Baby is tame and gentle, there's also the other leopard, the dangerous double. The film acknowledges the latent danger in the sexuality that David has repressed and through Susan links it with women. Women, it suggests, can be gentle like Baby or dangerous like Baby's double, and their appearances are deceiving. Yet the alternative is worse, and life without the danger Susan brings to it resembles something like death.[9]

This victory of life over death is graphically exemplified in the film's famous final sequence at the museum. The previous scene brings all the film's major characters (played by some of the finest comic actors of the 1930s) into the county jailhouse. David and Susan have been arrested for acting as "peeping Toms" lurking about the premises of the psychiatrist Dr. Fritz Lehman (Fritz Field), and Constable Slocum (Walter Catlett) and his police crew suspect that they may be the thieves who have been terrorizing the county. Susan's aunt, Elizabeth Random (May Robson); her lawyer, Mr. Peabody (George Irving); Aunt Elizabeth's guest, the wild-game hunter Major Horace Applegate (Charles Ruggles); and Aunt Elizabeth's handyman (Barry Fitzgerald) have all assembled to serve as victims, character witnesses, and the like. Eventually, even Miss Swallow and Mr. Peabody show up. Confusion reigns as the bewildered constable tries to sort things out. He is particularly mystified when Susan goes into an impersonation of a gun moll named "Swinging Door Suzy," spinning a stunning tale of criminal activity that distracts the police enough to enable her to steal the key to her jail cell. By the end of the scene, both leopards return, as does the dog, George, with the missing brontosaurus bone. Presumably, all problems are solved.

Finally, back at work, David is found busily inserting the intercostal clavicle in the brontosaurus skeleton. Susan arrives to tell David that she has convinced her Aunt Elizabeth to contribute the million dollars to the museum and, more to the point, to make a final attempt to capture David's heart. Miss Swallow has just broken off their engagement. When David admits that his experience with Susan "was the best day of my life" and confesses that he loves Susan, who has climbed up onto the skeleton, they reach out to kiss each other and, in what Gehring calls "probably the biggest pratfall in slapstick history," the entire skeleton collapses into smithereens.[10]

And so *Bringing Up Baby* entered the annals of Hollywood comedy, but it did not receive its proper critical due at the time. It "was apparently more than audiences could take in 1938. It was a box-office disappointment, deemed too silly and crazy by the critics."[11] According to Kathryn Bernheimer, the film began to receive proper recognition in the 1960s, and "its reputation was further enhanced by Peter Bogdanovich's 1972 homage *What's Up, Doc?*, which created renewed interest in the revered classic."[12]

Bogdanovich, a young film critic and historian who had turned to film directing, had catapulted to A-list status in 1971 with his multiaward-winning drama *The Last Picture Show*. As a follow-up to this achievement, Bogdanovich decided to display his familiarity with and affection for classic Hollywood fare by writing and directing a remake of—or at least an homage to—*Bringing Up Baby*, titling it *What's Up, Doc?*

In the opinion of most critics, *Bringing Up Baby* still remains the superior work. Bernheimer's description of the film as the "fastest, funniest, wildest, most demented screwball farce in movie history" is typical of the critical praise this classic film has received.[13] When the American Film Institute composed its various lists of the top 100 films in each genre, *Bringing Up Baby* ranked number fourteen, while *What's Up, Doc?* trailed far behind at number sixty-one. Yet upon closer investigation, Bogdanovich's remake can be more properly appreciated not just as a tribute to Hawks but as a return to screwball comedy for a new generation, making use of a clever screenplay, a talented cast, and much more developed cinematic techniques.

The first challenge Bogdanovich faced was to update a film genre that was closely associated with the 1930s and 1940s and the social tensions of the period. Tina Olsin Lent summarizes the challenge, saying the following:

> Many critics and historians have offered interpretations of which audience interests, needs, and desires screwball comedies addressed. Some writers have asserted that the characters' eccentric behavior and "lunacy" provided models for sanity and survival in a crazy and overly conventional world. Other writers have maintained that screwball comedy constructed a model for reconciling the socioeconomic disparities that threatened national unity.[14]

Dr. Howard Bannister (Ryan O'Neal) attempts to explain to his host, Mr. Larrabee (Austin Pendleton), and his rival, Hugh Simon (Kenneth Mars), the uninvited presence of the troublesome Judy Maxwell (Barbra Streisand) at the Larrabee Foundation banquet in *What's Up, Doc?* (1972).

Gehring identifies a similar pattern in screwball comedies' presentation of social class for Depression-era audiences, writing the following:

> While the comedy of the pre–MGM Marx Brothers and W. C. Fields is truly iconoclastic toward high society, screwball comedy merely pokes survivable—status quo—fun at the eccentricities of the rich. While satire can and does exist, the screwball comedy viewer is allowed to grow fond of these wealthy wackos, in a superior sort of way, while also enjoying the escapism of beautiful people in beautiful settings. Most screwball comedies minimize any socioeconomic differences of the leading duo and key on the initial conflicts concerning eccentric behavior.[15]

Bogdanovich's 1970s version followed the formula, first, by creating a setting where the hero, a befuddled academic occupying a relatively elitist position in society, ventures into the even more elite world of philanthropy in pursuit of a $20,000 grant to fund his research. The heroine is a free-spirited college dropout, a familiar figure in the culture of the early 1970s, suggesting the iconoclasm of campus protests and Timothy Leary "tune in, turn on, and drop out" attitude. Bogdanovich cast the Hollywood heartthrob Ryan O'Neal to assume the Cary Grant role as a handsome but clueless professor of musicology, Dr. Howard Bannister, and Barbra Streisand, an Oscar-winning actress better known for her musical career, as the kooky flower child and serial college student Judy Maxwell. The much-expanded "Miss Swallow" role of the uptight fiancée, Eunice Burns, was played by newcomer Madeline Kahn. While Bogdanovich came up with the story, he wisely enlisted Buck Henry, David Newman, and Robert Benton to craft the screenplay. Henry had only recently collected numerous screenwriting awards for *The Graduate* (1967) and an Emmy for writing the popular television spy spoof *Get Smart* (1965–1970). Newman and Benton were best known in Hollywood at the time for the numerous screenwriting awards they had received for the 1967 darkly comic gangster drama *Bonnie and Clyde*. With such talent at his command, Bogdanovich had everything he needed to create a delightful screwball comedy.

Bogdanovich's decision to honor Hawks's screwball legacy led him to recreate that director's attitude toward his main characters, well described by Gerald Mast:

> Like his noncomic films, Hawks's comedies refuse to sentimentalize or moralize. They show bizarre, lunatic people doing "screwball" things without ever explicitly telling us why they do them and without ever saying (or even implying) that underneath the surface lunacy they are just plain folks. Hawks never apologizes for his comic characters and never strips away the veneer to let them bare their souls. They remain unswervingly true to their bizarre schemes, hopes, and interests. . . . If his characters seem loony, it is simply because they are wrapped up in their own heads. They can't see beyond their own intentions—and they don't want to.[16]

The screwball comedies of the 1930s and early 1940s account for some of the finest work of the era's best directors. Besides *Bringing Up Baby*, Hawks turned out several classics of the genre, including *Twentieth Century* (1934), *His Girl Friday* (1940), and *Ball of Fire* (1942). Preston Sturges directed *The Lady Eve* (1941) and *The Palm Beach Story* (1942). Leo McCarey's *The Awful Truth* (1937) and George Cukor's *Holiday* (1938) and *The Philadelphia Story* (1940) continued the popular pattern. Frank Capra's two screwballish gems, the romantic comedy *It Happened One Night* (1934) and the farcical *Arsenic and Old Lace* (1944), served as bookends for the period. Other notable screwball films by respected directors include *My Man Godfrey* (1936), *Theodora Goes Wild* (1936), and *Nothing Sacred* (1937). It is not surprising that Bogdanovich, with his critical appreciation of these directors' achievements, would be tempted to try his hand at this revered genre.

Like these classic comedies, the plot of *What's Up, Doc?* is certainly complicated, perhaps too much so, involving numerous obsessive characters all staying in the same hotel. Howard Bannister and his fiancée, Eunice Burns, have come to San Francisco in hopes of winning a $20,000 grant from the Larrabee Foundation for his musicology research. While the Bristol Hotel is playing host to the Larrabee Foundation banquet that evening, it is also welcoming several other visitors who all own suitcases with the same red scotch plaid design. Howard's suitcase holds his precious igneous rocks, which are central elements in his research. The suitcase belonging to wealthy dowager Mrs. Van Hoskins (Mabel Albertson) contains a considerable amount of expensive jewelry. The suitcase of a third visitor, Mr. Smith (Michael Murphy), holds highly classified government documents that he has stolen, intending to expose government scandals, à la the Pentagon Papers. The fourth suitcase is simply filled with Judy's clothes. The confusion of the bags and various parties' pursuit of those bags—with special concern for and occasional risqué references to Howard's "rocks"—supply the skeleton for the frantic plot. Meanwhile, Judy's persistent schemes—like Susan Vance's in *Bringing Up Baby*—to win the professor's affection provide the rest of the film's comic adventures.

The three major players turned out to be excellent choices. Although Barbra Streisand eventually moved on to more serious roles (*The Way We Were* [1973], *A Star Is Born* [1976], *Yentl* [1983], and *Nuts* [1987]), her earliest films prior to *What's Up, Doc?* displayed a kooky, offbeat persona: the Jewish ugly-duckling turned Ziegfeld Follies star Fanny Brice in *Funny Girl* (1968), her New York ethnic interpretation of Dolly Levi in *Hello, Dolly* (1969), a feisty Manhattan call girl in *The Owl and the Pussycat* (1970), and a time-traveling psychic seeking therapy in *On a Clear Day You Can See Forever* (1970). Even earlier, in her Greenwich Village nightclub performances and her Emmy-award winning television musical specials *My Name Is Barbra* (1965) and *Color Me Barbra* (1966), she delivered offbeat interpretations of classic Tin Pan Alley and Broadway standards. She had already been awarded a Best Actress Oscar for her 1968 film debut in *Funny Girl* (an award which, coincidentally, she won in a tie vote with Katharine Hepburn). In this array of attention-grabbing performances, Streisand played off her Brooklyn and Greenwich Village roots, the shape of her eyes and nose, and her idiosyncratic wardrobe choices to present herself as a determined and talented young woman to be reckoned with, even if she sometimes appeared wildly off-base—in other words, the perfect screwball heroine.

Her performance as Judy Maxwell also includes elements of Groucho Marx and, of course, Bugs Bunny, both of them fast-talking con men. Her first words to Howard, as she munches on a carrot stick (stolen off of a passing waiter's tray), are "What's up, Doc?" (he does, after all, have a Ph.D.). Also, her comments to Howard and others often resemble the side-of-the-mouth derogatory comments of Groucho. She thus enhances the traditional screwball-heroine formula with the addition of a Looney Tunes smart-aleck element, as well as the hostility and anarchy of the Marx Brothers classics of the 1930s.

Ryan O'Neal only needed to be good looking and clueless, putty in the hands of his domineering fiancée and bewildered by the antics of Judy, the newly arrived trickster. In fact, the more handsome he is, the better. Gehring finds this a significant element in screwball comedy, noting the incongruity of a "handsome leading man like Cary Grant being so often flustered by women."[17] Mast, however, considers the casting of O'Neal to be one of the many defects of a film that he considers to be far inferior to its prototype:

> Although it is possible to accept the premise of Barbra's blatant sexual attraction to Ryan, it is not possible to accept the premise that Ryan O'Neal (a) is an intellectual; (b) if he were an intellectual, could acquire Eunice for a fiancée; and (c) knows anything at all about igneous rocks except how to pronounce the word. Cary Grant may not be very credible as a zoologist, but the sheer speed of his performance diverts us from considering potential incredibility.[18]

O'Neal's career began in the mid-1960s with his role as the rich and hunky teenage love interest Rodney Harrington on the popular nighttime soap opera *Peyton Place*; however, he graduated to Hollywood stardom by playing the Harvard law student Oliver Barrett IV, who watched his college sweetheart succumb to cancer in the blockbuster 1970 weepie *Love Story*. In this sense, he was firmly in the tradition of the young Cary Grant, who began his career in films as the handsome love interest of so many leading ladies of the early 1930s to emerge by the end of the decade as the personification of the screwball hero. O'Neal faced a bigger challenge than Grant, however. There was the very real possibility that he would always be associated in the public mind with the image of *Love Story's* doomed young lover. To his credit, by donning horn-rimmed glasses and a bow tie (much as Grant had done to play the wimpy professor in *Bringing Up Baby*), O'Neal managed to make the transformation from the romantic Harvard frat boy to befuddled professor-researcher credibly enough.

In writing and casting the third major role in the film, Bogdanovich and his writers created some major comic alchemy. They transformed what could have been a thankless role of the uptight female rival into an amalgam of maniacal control, ruthless ambition, and complete hysteria called Eunice Burns. It was a brilliant film debut for Madeline Kahn. Kahn would later receive an Oscar nomination for the role of Trixie Delight in Bogdanovich's next film, *Paper Moon* (1973), and then join the company of Mel Brooks's zanies in such classics as *Blazing Saddles* (1974), *Young Frankenstein* (1974), and *Silent Movie* (1976). She raised the stakes of the film's madcap lunacy whenever she appeared on the scene in a role that was much more prominent than her counterpart in *Bringing Up Baby*. In *Bringing Up Baby*, Miss Swallow appears only three times, and then rather briefly. Mast maintains that "Eunice becomes a major figure in *What's Up, Doc?*—simply because she is funnier and more interesting than anything else in the film." She is a major instance in what Mast sees as Bogdanovich's shift of focus "from the stars to the supporting players and to impersonal cinematic gimmicks" like the elaborate chase near the end of the film.[19]

The film's narrative can be broken down into eight sequences: 1) the arrival of Howard, Eunice, and several other characters at the San Francisco airport and then on to the Hotel Bristol for Judy and Howard's first meeting in the hotel drugstore; 2) the preparation for and attendance at the banquet thrown in the hotel ballroom by the Larrabee Foundation; 3) the late-night chaos created in Howard's hotel room when he finds Judy taking a bubble bath, then sends her out on a window ledge so that he can deal with a frantic Eunice, and finally sets the room on fire; 4) a romantic interlude the next morning when Howard, thrown out of his hotel room, discovers Judy in the hotel's rooftop ballroom, having spent the night sleeping on a piano; 5) a return to mayhem at the awards ceremony held at Mr. Larrabee's Russian Hill residence; 6) an elaborate and frantic chase up and down the hills of San Francisco, ending with several automobiles landing in the bay; 7) the reunion of all parties when they are hauled into night court, where, in the tradition of classical comedy, a secret is revealed that settles most of the issues; and 8) in a coda that ends the story where it began, the departure of various parties from the San Francisco Airport.

The primary force driving the screwball machine is Streisand's portrayal of the central character, Judy Maxwell, in relentless pursuit of the object of her affection. Gehring remarks that "screwball comedy turns the American courtship system on its ear; the female leads the charge, while the male holds back in the manner of the stereotyped weaker sex."[20] In her romantic pursuit, like all the classic screwball heroines, Judy is carefree, irresponsible, obsessed, verbally adroit, surprisingly intelligent, and—through it all—lots of fun. Most of her zany 1930s predecessors developed their frivolous attitudes because they were spoiled heiresses who never had to concern themselves with the consequences of their obsessions and irresponsibility. Judy, however, arrives on the scene with no apparent source of income and no apparent reason to be in San Francisco, yet she is equally oblivious to the people or objects in her environment. Without money and hungry, she follows a pizza delivery man across a busy street, avoiding and ignoring the collision of two motorcycles in her wake, as well as two cars halting in front of her and crashing into one another. More importantly, her insouciant jaywalking causes Howard and Eunice's taxi to come to a sudden halt as well, giving Howard the headache that will occasion their meeting in the hotel drugstore.

Judy's hunger continues to motivate her throughout the first half of the film, as she follows the pizza man into the hotel where Howard and Eunice are staying, steals the aforementioned carrot, orders food delivered to a hotel room that she knows is unoccupied, sneaks her way into the foundation banquet, and, still hungry after the banquet, finishes the night by ordering a roast beef sandwich from room service.

Judy's hunger is only the tip of the iceberg in terms of her devotion to her own needs regardless of other people's concerns. Careless of Howard's desires throughout the film, she rips his suit jacket and pajama bottoms, reads his mail, makes herself at home in his hotel room, takes a bubble bath in his bathroom, and generally ignores his pleas for her to leave him alone. She is even more cruelly dismissive of Eunice's feelings, constantly luring Howard away from her, stealing Eunice's identity to join Howard at the Larrabee Foundation banquet, and even misdirecting Eunice away from the final foundation awards ceremony to a dangerous mob hideout where her life is threatened.

Judy displays the obsessive nature typical of the screwball heroine in her wooing of Howard by any means necessary. Judy is not alone in her obsessions, however. Almost every other character in the film is driven toward a goal and will stop at nothing to achieve it. Howard's devotion to his research, Eunice's determination to win the grant money, Mr. Smith's determination to expose the U.S. government with his documents, and the hotel house detective's pursuit of Mrs. Van Hoskins's jewelry all drive them to lunatic extremes.

Judy's chief weapon in pursuing her goals is not physical violence or firearms, but, like Hepburn's Susan Vance and Groucho's character in all his films, it is language, coming fast and illogically, employed either to confuse her listeners or impress them with an elaborate lie. Howard is almost too easy a victim. When Judy meets him in the drugstore and he describes his interest in igneous rocks, she responds with a list of other rock formations. She continues to stalk him throughout the store, accusing him of rejecting her like a "piece of ripe fruit you can squeeze the juice out of and cast aside . . . a mistake, a clerical error you can just erase." As they leave the drugstore, Judy attempts to purchase a radio, telling the clerk to charge it to her husband, Howard, whom she has renamed Steve. She follows Howard out of the store, where, encountering Eunice, she accuses "Steve" of alternately cheating on her and Eunice, bewildering both of them.

Judy's finest verbal performance, however, comes when she lies her way into the foundation banquet where, pretending to be Eunice Burns (but preferring to be called "Burnsie"), she proceeds to flirt shamelessly with Mr. Larrabee (Austin Pendleton) and astound him with elaborately fabricated tales of Howard's achievements, while interrupting every attempt by Howard to explain that she is not, in fact, his fiancée. When his competitor, Hugh Simon (Kenneth Mars), dismisses Howard's attempts to connect igneous rocks and prehistoric music, she informs him that Howard had already been in conversation with Leonard Bernstein about "conducting an avalanche in E-flat." She then spins a tale about their "incredible adventure" onboard their plane trip to San Francisco when the pilot fainted from an "overdose of fear," sending the plane into a dive, until Howard entered the cockpit and, connecting two of his igneous rocks to airline instruments "with a particularly high magnetic content, set up an electronically induced field-pattern on the gyrocom . . . just possibly saving 112 passengers from a tragic, fiery death!" Larrabee, charmed by Judy's flirtatiousness and her stories, informs Howard that, should he be awarded the grant, the achievement will be due as much to her charms as to Howard's work. Forced to realize Judy's importance to his quest, when the real Eunice tries to join them at the banquet table, Howard denies that he even knows the woman, another victory for Judy, the charming liar. Still later, when discovered in the bathtub of Howard's hotel room, Judy once again reduces Howard to helplessness with a barrage of double-talk as he tries to eject her, resist her romantic advances, and ultimately explain all the commotion when Eunice bursts into the room.

During the course of her verbal displays, it also becomes obvious that Judy is quite an educated and intelligent—albeit unorthodox—young woman, whose remarks combine accurate information with more dubious statements. Mast remarks that in Hawks's screwball comedies, the "human moral center is the brain. . . . The Hawks characters love each other precisely because of their strong-willed, independent minds. . . . One strong mind feels attraction to the strength and integrity of another."[21] In her drugstore conversation with Howard, Judy responds to his references to igneous rocks by confessing that she is more interested in the "metamorphic or sedimentary rock categories. I mean, I can take your igneous rocks or leave 'em. I relate principally to mica, quartz, feldspar." A few minutes later, when a shocked Eunice asks her, "Don't you know the meaning of propriety?" Judy immediately answers, "Propriety (noun): conformity to established standards of behavior or manners; suitability, rightness, or justice. See etiquette." At the banquet, in her tall tale of Howard's airplane adventure, Judy engages in a highly technical description of aeronautical instruments. She later explains some odd behavior as an attempt to study "verbal reverberations under spinal pressure." She charms Mr. Larrabee by recognizing a remark of his as a quotation from Ralph Waldo Emerson. At one point, she describes to Howard her eclectic education at numerous institutions: political science at Colorado State, advanced geology at Wellesley, musical appreciation at Bennington, comparative literature at Northwestern University, archeology at the Tuskegee Institute, general semantics at the University of Chicago, and veterinary medicine at Texas A&M, among others. Finally, she exposes the plagiarism of Howard's competitor for the grant, Dr. Hugh Simon, by identifying his "research" as the little-known "Findlemeyer Proposition" and citing its publication in the 1925 Harvard Press Musicological Review.

At the same time, Judy is more connected to the physical world and her bodily desires than Howard, the reserved professor. Her hunger motivates her earliest activity in the film. She deals with physical danger rather adroitly, managing to climb back onto the hotel ledge from which she was hanging and avoiding any number of threats to life and limb as she and Howard run, drive, and bicycle their way up and down the hilly streets of San Francisco in the film's colossal chase sequence. Such precarious activity is part and parcel of the screwball tradition. Lent documents the pattern of a screwball couples' outlandish physical antics and fights, quoting a 1930s critic's observation: "Today a star scarcely qualifies for the higher spheres unless she has been slugged by her leading man, rolled on the floor, kicked downstairs, cracked over her head with a frying pan, dumped into a pond, or butted by a goat."[22] Lent attributes this physical activity in the classic screwball comedies to the restrictions imposed by the 1930 Motion Picture Production Code:

> The screwball antics . . . functioned as a substitute for expressions of overt sexuality. . . . Aside from obvious sexual innuendo, screwball antics drew attention to both the sexual and companionable aspects of the developing romantic relationship. . . . The extreme physicality allowed the characters to touch intimately, but humorously, offering alternative outlets for repressed sexual energy.[23]

As a creature of the 1970s, however, Judy can express her sexuality much more openly. She shamelessly encourages Mr. Larrabee to place his hand on her breast to "feel [her] heart pounding" when she first meets him, which he is happy to do. She is even more blatantly erotic in her encounters with Howard. At one point, she leans into him quite closely when he is attempting to explain to her the importance of his research. She is not shy when Howard discovers her in the bubble bath and, when he orders her out, she offers to step out of the tub naked. Then, as Howard panics at that prospect and falls back on the floor, Judy, wrapped only in a towel, climbs on top of his seminude body to attend to his needs, particularly concerned that he might have injured his "coccyx." She turns quite seductive when, meeting Howard on the hotel rooftop, she serenades him with "As Time Goes By," rendered in romantic Streisand style. While still on the roof, she hands him the letter announcing that he is being given the grant. Howard impulsively kisses her. She responds with a much more serious kiss. As they continue, the camera moves away from them to show a house painter arriving on the scene. From his startled reaction and the cigar that drops out of his mouth and into his paint can, viewers can presume that the kissing has led to more intimate sexual activity.

Judy's physical appearance and behavior, however, also involve a certain degree of gender reversal in both erotic and aggressive manifestations. This too fits the screwball formula. Gehring's observations, published in 1986, may be a bit dated, but they can be fairly applied to the cultural milieu of *What's Up, Doc?*:

> There has always been a sexual double standard as to how society responds to the reversal of stereotype gender activity. A girl with certain masculine overtones is perfectly acceptable; the notion of a tomboy is actually celebrated in our society. But any male attempts to reciprocate such a gender crossover are still strongly verboten in American society, Boy George notwithstanding. This allows the screwball heroine to be more aggressive in her male hunt without leaving the accepted normal range of female activity. At the same time, she often is able to break down the male's rigidity, an antisocial state not allowing for his interaction with society.[24]

At the beginning of the film, Judy's newsboy cap and trousers give her a tomboy look. She is definitely the aggressor in the romance, observing Howard with a lusty gaze as he first enters her view, stalking him in the drugstore, initiating their first conversation, refusing to let go of his hand, and otherwise pursuing him mercilessly throughout the rest of the film. In the bubble bath sequence, she clearly enjoys staring at him dressed only in his boxer shorts and bow tie, Chippendales-style. At the banquet, she even threatens Dr. Simon with a wise-guy bit of macho aggression, whispering, "How would you like a sandwich-de-knuckles?"

And through it all, she is a lot of fun. With her quick repartee, her facility at tale-spinning, and her brushes with disaster, Judy slowly brings the repressed Howard to life. The first change in Howard occurs at the banquet when, realizing that to get the grant money he must deny that he knows Eunice, he and Judy look at one another in naughty complicity. In the hotel rooftop scene, the viewer discovers that Howard actually plays the piano and, in the brief romantic interlude, the smile he wears reveals that he might be beginning to enjoy the company of this madcap woman. In the departure scene at the airport, after all the mayhem, Judy quietly asks Howard, "It wasn't all so bad, was it? . . . See, sometimes it's kind of fun." Judy's one admission of a dark element in her life comes when she lists the number of colleges she has attended. She admits that she has been trying to please her father, who was "very upset when I was asked to leave the first college I ever went to." And now that she has once again been dismissed from the umpteenth college because of an explosion she caused in a chemistry class, she confesses, "I'm really scared to go home."

Howard comes from a long line of screwball comedy professors who need to be rescued from their fates by the life force of the film's heroine. Gehring refers to a statement of Henri Bergson that "any individual is comic who automatically goes his own way without troubling himself about getting into touch with the rest of his fellow human beings."[25] The Bergsonian "mechanical inelasticity" is vividly displayed by Howard as the "comically rigid professor type" with the "overly rational, overly detached academic mind [that] has allowed other goals and/or values to get in the way of romance."[26] The film's first shot of Howard waiting for a taxi at the airport shows him staring blankly into space, awaiting his next set of orders from his overbearing fiancée. In the taxi ride to the hotel, he obsesses over his igneous rocks, testing their tonal quality, so attentive to his rocks that he is unaware that he is in San Francisco. Registering at the hotel, he notices that the desk clerk's bell is flat. In the drugstore to get aspirin, he pauses to test the tonal quality of a souvenir rock from Alcatraz. At this point, however, Judy appears, the one who will release him from his intellectual prison and impending marriage to Eunice.

Howard's physical awkwardness constantly contrasts with Judy's bodily ease and energy. Leaving the drugstore and desperately trying to escape from her persistent chatter, Howard clumsily climbs up the down escalator. He cannot tie his own bow tie for the banquet. Once at the banquet, he pins his identification badge on upside down, after which he is often informed, "You are upside down." Meeting Mr. Larrabee, Howard is unable to shake his hand because he is holding two drinks in his own hands; he instead manages to bump into Larrabee and spill one of the drinks on Larabee's tuxedo. Upon seeing Judy in his bathtub, he drops his pajama bottoms and, when she offers to get out of the tub, he trips over his fallen pajama bottoms and ends up on the floor, fearing that he has broken something. "I can't breathe," he announces. "Is it possible to break a lung?" In the ensuing chaos in his hotel room, he pulls the knob out of the television set and then, trying to turn off the set by pulling out the cable cord, he sends sparks flying and starts a fire in the room. The next morning, when he is asked to leave the hotel, he cannot even manage the elevator. He pushes the down button, but the elevator takes him to the roof. In the climactic chase scene, he is constantly at loose ends, unable often to see where he is driving. Yet, aware that he is being chased by men with guns and inspired by Judy's fearlessness, he manages to run, ride a bicycle, and eventually drive a car through the city's hilly terrain, avoiding numerous collisions and demonstrating a remarkable physical agility that he did not seem to possess earlier in the film.

Howard is absentminded and socially awkward as well. Early in the film, Eunice needs to remind him of several facts: that they are in San Francisco; that his trip to the drugstore is to get aspirin; that he is holding his bow tie in his hand; that he needs to pull the door to exit her hotel room; and, often, that he needs to keep on a tight time schedule. Socially inept, he needs to be coached by Eunice for his words of introduction to Mr. Larrabee. Throughout the film,

Howard is constantly interrupted and rendered incapable of arguing against his rival, Dr. Simon, the fast-talking Judy, the domineering Eunice, and the enthusiastic Larrabee; however, in the courtroom scene near the end of the film, when he volunteers to be the one in the crowd to explain the whole situation to the judge, his absentmindedness is replaced by a precise awareness of each incident and a new social poise and confidence. Although the story's complications and judge's questions challenge him, Howard persists in recapitulating the entire story. His transformation is impressive. From his adventures with the free-spirited Judy, he has acquired amazing physical, social, emotional, and verbal skills.

And, of course, Howard is sexually repressed. As Eunice is fixing his bow tie and expressing her suspicion that he is attracted to Judy, it becomes obvious that his plans to marry Eunice are rather unromantic. He confesses, "I don't think of you as a woman, Eunice. I think of you as . . . as . . . Eunice." The fact that her name is uncomfortably close to "eunuch" reinforces the prospect of a loveless marriage, which, apparently, is fine with Eunice. When Howard admits that "I know that I don't seem to be a very romantic person," Eunice assures him, as Miss Swallow assured David in *Bringing Up Baby*, "I'm not looking for romance."

Romance, of course, will come in his several physical encounters with Judy, culminating in the rooftop-ballroom sequence. When Howard discovers Judy sleeping on top of a grand piano that he has sat down to play, she is no longer the tomboy. With her hair loosened for the first time in the film and falling down onto her shoulders, Lauren Bacall style, Judy quotes Humphrey Bogart's famous line from *Casablanca*, saying, "Of all the gin joints in all the towns in all the world, [he] had to walk into mine. Play it, Sam." She then begins a lush rendition of *Casablanca*'s love song, "As Time Goes By," and then moves in for a kiss. Howard, once again trying to resist, falls backward and lands both of them on the ballroom floor, where they eventually engage in heavy romantic activity, adding his sexual liberation to his other newfound freedoms.

The third member of the triangle, Eunice, undergoes her own transformation. Her frantic need to control her life and Howard's, another example of the obsessive quality of all of the film's characters, is expressed not only in her nasal whining and shrill and frequent screaming, but in her starched, perfectly arranged but staid outfits and the equally stiff 1970s flip of her rust brown wig. Her encounters are all exercises in frustration, leading to her inevitable loss of Howard's affections and the end of their engagement. Gehring describes Eunice's role as typical of the screwball formula, commenting that "most screwball comedies 'telegraph' the hero's, or heroine's, choice long before the conclusion—generally because there is such a marked difference between the competition."[27] Eunice's asexual control of Howard is defeated by Judy's free-spirited love. Eunice, the domineering mother figure, is cast off as part of Howard's psychosexual maturity. Constantly attentive to their schedule and the competition for the Larrabee grant, Eunice infantilizes the absentminded Howard. Yet, she herself is hardly a model of mature behavior. In her finest comic scene, she is refused entrance into the foundation's banquet because Judy has swiped her identification badge to sneak into the event. Told by the banquet host that they do not have "a Eunice Burns," she screams, "I am not *a* Eunice Burns; I am *the* Eunice Burns," and she proceeds to barge her way into the banquet hall, with the host clinging to her leg. When Howard denies that he knows her, she is dragged screaming out of the hall, humiliated and physically damaged. Later, when she hears suspicious noises coming from Howard's room, she adds to the chaos by loudly insisting that he let her in, which forces Howard to shove Judy out onto the window ledge, and then demanding that Howard turn off the blaring television set, thus causing the fire in the room and setting her off on another screaming jag.

Eunice endures more than humiliation, eventually encountering threats on her life. When she attempts to join Howard at the awards ceremony at the Larrabee mansion, she follows the deceptive directions Judy has given her and ends up in a deserted warehouse, where she is threatened by the thugs who have mistakenly gotten hold of Howard's suitcase instead of the one containing Mrs. Van Hoskins's jewels. From then onward and throughout the chase scene, she—along with Mr. Larrabee and Dr. Simon—is held at gunpoint by the thugs.

Eunice suffers her final humiliation when, in the courtroom scene, she claims that the gangsters tried to molest her, to which the judge replies, "That's unbelievable." She survives the ordeal, however, and, in the process seems to reveal what may have been her true motives all along. Having shared the terrifying chase in the close physical company of Mr. Larrabee and being told that the grant will not be given to Howard, she stays on in San Francisco with the philanthropist, whom she immediately proceeds to order around as they leave the airport.

Two sequences late in the film reward closer observation. The chase scene, which lasts a full ten minutes, is reported to have taken a month to film and to have cost one million dollars to produce, a quarter of the film's entire budget. It would be difficult to match it for the amount of near misses, actual collisions, and damage to property. It begins at the awards ceremony at the Larrabee mansion on Russian Hill, when Judy, realizing that all four of the plaid suitcases are present in the room, convinces Howard to help her grab them and run away from the gangsters, the government detective, the hotel detective, and everyone else who wants one of the bags. While Judy and Howard confiscate a grocery delivery bicycle for their escape, the others follow in three different cars: Mr. Larrabee's limousine, a taxi, and a convertible. Eventually, having crashed the bicycle into a costume shop, Judy and Howard pass by a church and steal the Volkswagen Bug waiting there with a "Just Married" sign on its door. The four automobiles continue a frantic chase up and down the steep hills of the city, finally heading toward the dock of the Sausalito ferry. Attempting to drive their car onto the ferry, they miss the boat and end up in the harbor, followed by all three of the other automobiles and almost by several police cars that have joined in the chase.

Several outlandish events occur in the process. Early on in the chase, Howard and Judy, encountering a Chinese dragon parade as they speed down a hill, drive the bicycle directly inside the long dragon puppet and then find themselves attached to it until they crash into the costume shop. At one point, ignoring all traffic lights, the various cars cause a seven-car pileup at one intersection, but they all escape unharmed. One car manages to knock over a line of garbage cans, which then roll down the steep hill, causing a pedestrian to jump out of their way over a wall and onto the table of diners at an outdoor restaurant. Another scene shows the cars maneuvering the curves of the famous Lombard Street. Later, Judy and Howard lead all of the automobiles down the numerous concrete steps of Alta Plaza Park. The most dramatic and suspenseful moment comes early in the chase when all of the cars encounter a man on a tall ladder hanging a banner over a street while two other workers attempt to cross the street carrying a large pane of glass. Each of the four vehicles succeeds in missing the ladder and the glass in their first run through the intersection, but, with the mercilessness of comedy, their chase brings them back to the street corner. The bicycle and two of the vehicles avoiding hitting the ladder and the glass one more time, but the fourth vehicle finally bumps against the ladder, knocking it down and sending the banner-hanging workman swinging like Tarzan on the banner's rope, crashing into the glass pane and shattering it into a million pieces. Did Mack Sennett or Buster Keaton produce any chase quite so elaborate?

The sequence pits the playfulness and irresponsibility of the screwball characters against the work ethic and bourgeois respectability of several of the victims of the collateral damage incurred during the chase. They steal the bicycle of a young grocery delivery man; they hamper the efforts of the banner hanger, the workers carrying the pane of glass, a man who is attempting to lay concrete in one of the side streets through which they run, and another work crew delivering sand to a construction spot; and they confiscate the "Just Married" car parked in front of a church just as the newlyweds emerge from the ceremony. Even the mild revelry of a Chinese dragon parade is ruined. The massive amount of havoc reminds viewers that comedy seldom places much value on physical property and, indeed, often delights in its destruction as the price of the hero's escape from threat. The end of the chase captures the eternal optimism of comedy. As they race down the hill toward the dock and the ferry to Sausalito, Judy shouts, "We can make it . . . we can make it!" As the ferry slips away from the dock before they can board it and the automobile flies into the drink, viewers hear Judy wistfully admit, "I don't think we can make it." Yet, of course, they do "make it," since, in compliance with an urban myth of the 1970s, their Volkswagen remains afloat in the water while all the other vehicles sink.

Also, in a nod to comedy's ancient roots, at one frantic point Howard complains that he cannot see anything. Judy cleans his glasses. When he puts them back on, he cries out, "Oh God, I can see!" Preferring otherwise, he throws his eyeglasses out of the window and proceeds relatively blindly, perhaps a comic allusion to the blinded but wiser Oedipus. Apparently, Howard abandons his glasses for good. As a sign of his release from his uptight professorial life, he wears no eyeglasses for the rest of the film. This also parallels the scene in *Bringing Up Baby* when Susan knocks David over during their hunt for the brontosaurus bone and causes him to break his glasses, whereupon she remarks that he looks "much nicer" without them.

The next scene follows logically as all parties are hauled into night court for their numerous offenses. This sequence, also lasting ten minutes, is a triumph of comic screenwriting meant to echo the climactic jailhouse-interrogation sequence in *Bringing Up Baby*. It features some brilliant work by a latecomer to film comedy, Liam Dunn, who, like Kahn, went on to contribute hilarious performances in Mel Brooks's *Young Frankenstein, Blazing Saddles,* and *Silent Movie.* His night court magistrate is a wicked combination of pessimism, misanthropy, hypochondria, acute nervousness, and—when he starts rolling steel balls in his palm—Captain Queeg-like paranoia. While the judge insists on "peace, calm, and order" in his courtroom, he is instead presented with pandemonium. Throughout the proceedings, he gulps down a variety of pills, administers some nasal spray, and takes spoonfuls of medicinal fluids. In side-of-the-mouth comments to his long-suffering bailiff, he refers to the session as "tonight's horror show," another example of the "endless parade of human debris" he is forced to witness night after night. The judge confesses that were it not for his deep "compassion," he would love to "send every one of them to an island somewhere, wrapped in heavy chains," inviting comparisons to the judges in *Les Misérables* or *The Count of Monte Cristo*—all of this before the rambunctious cast of characters comes rushing into the courtroom.

And rush in they do—about twenty of the people involved in the chase along with a couple of police officers. After pounding his gavel for order several times and then listening to the charges against the defendants, he announces that "in this case—and I think the Supreme Court'll back me up on this—I am seriously considering setting up a torture chamber," with visions of whips and red-hot irons. As several of the perpetrators try to explain what led them to his courtroom, the judge insists on hearing "this whole ridiculous story told by one person." Howard steps up and takes a stab at it, only to be interrupted several times by the judge's questions attempting to clarify Howard's accurate but confusing recapitulation of the film's chaotic plot.

The entire comic construction comes tumbling down when the judge notices that one person in the crowd, covering herself with a blanket, has said nothing. The judge barks, "Well, what do you have to say for yourself, young lady?" Peeking out from under the blanket, Judy whispers, "Hello, Daddy." Judge Maxwell—the father whom Judy had earlier said she was afraid to face—throws up his hands and drops his head to the desk, and the desk collapses into pieces. Order in the court, indeed!

The revelation of the judge's relationship to Judy exemplifies another frequent feature in screwball comedy, a supporting character whom Gehring identifies as a "fatherly but antiheroic type" to whom few people within the story pay any attention but who has a "fatherly interest in the well-being of the genre's heroine."[28] Judge Maxwell, as it turns out, is the man whom Judy had earlier described as "very upset" about her failures at various colleges and who was the reason she was "really scared to go home." Her reason for showing up in San Francisco at the film's beginning is finally revealed in the closing moments: The prodigal daughter was coming home.

True to the long literary tradition, the justice that should prevail in a court of law gives way to mercy and forgiveness and the incredible good luck bestowed by the gods of comedy. In the airport coda that immediately follows, viewers find that each suitcase has been returned to its rightful owner (including the government documents in a suitcase that is handcuffed to the federal detective). Then, thanks to the timely deus ex machina of Judy's recalling the journal article about the Findlemeyer Proposition and thus revealing Dr. Simon's plagiarism, Mr. Larrabee promises to write another check to Howard and walks off with Eunice. Howard boards the plane, finds Judy sitting in the row behind him, and confesses that he loves her, ending the film with the Hollywood kiss. In the only allusion to Ryan O'Neal's public image, when Howard says that he is sorry for the way he treated Judy, she bats her eyelashes several times and says, "Love means never having to say you're sorry" (the infamous line from *Love Story*). After a long pause, Howard responds, "That's the dumbest thing I ever heard." Then, as the airline's onboard Bugs Bunny movie ends with Bugs and Elmer Fudd singing "What's up, Doc?," Porky Pig concludes the Looney Tunes cartoon—and Bogdanovich's screwball gem—announcing, of course, "That's all, folks!"

A Sampling of Screwball Comedies

Twentieth Century (1934)
Theodora Goes Wild (1936)
The Awful Truth (1937)
His Girl Friday (1940)
Ball of Fire (1941)

The Lady Eve (1941)
The Palm Beach Story (1942)
Arsenic and Old Lace (1944)
Arthur (1981)
Victor/Victoria (1982)

Notes

1. Kathleen Rowe, *The Unruly Woman: Gender and the Genres of Laughter* (Austin: University of Texas Press, 1995), 150.

2. Wes D. Gehring, *Romantic vs. Screwball Comedy: Charting the Difference* (Lanham, Md.: Scarecrow Press, 2002), 119.

3. Maria di Battista, *Fast-Talking Dames* (New Haven, Conn.: Yale University Press, 2001), 19.

4. Kathryn Bernheimer, *The 50 Funniest Movies of All Time: A Critic's Ranking* (Secaucus, N.J.: Carol Publishing Group, 1999), 20.

5. Gehring, *Romantic vs. Screwball Comedy*, 57.

6. Pauline Kael, "The Man from Dream City." *New Yorker*, July 14, 1975, p. 54.

7. Rowe, *The Unruly Woman*, 140.

8. Rowe, *The Unruly Woman*, 150.

9. Rowe, *The Unruly Woman*, 150.

10. Wes D. Gehring, *Screwball Comedy: A Genre of Madcap Romance* (New York: Greenwood Press, 1986), 78.

11. Bernheimer, *The 50 Funniest Movies of All Time*, 21.

12. Bernheimer, *The 50 Funniest Movies of All Time*, 21.

13. Bernheimer, *The 50 Funniest Movies of All Time*, 20.

14. Tina Olsin Lent, "Romantic Love and Friendship: The Redefinition of Gender Relations in Screwball Comedy." In *Classical Hollywood Comedy*, Kristine Brunovska Karnick and Henry Jenkins, eds. (New York and London: Routledge, 1995), 315.

15. Gehring, *Screwball Comedy*, 154.

16. Gerald Mast, *The Comic Mind: Comedy and the Movies*, 2nd ed. (Chicago: University of Chicago Press, 1979), 250.

17. Gehring, *Screwball Comedy*, 153.

18. Mast, *The Comic Mind*, 255–56.

19. Mast, *The Comic Mind*, 256.

20. Gehring, *Screwball Comedy*, 163.

21. Mast, *The Comic Mind*, 250–51.

22. Lent, "Romantic Love and Friendship," 327–28.

23. Lent, "Romantic Love and Friendship," 328.

24. Gehring, *Screwball Comedy*, 165.

25. Gehring, *Screwball Comedy*, 160.

26. Gehring, *Screwball Comedy*, 161.

27. Gehring, *Screwball Comedy*, 169.

28. Gehring, *Screwball Comedy*, 166.

CHAPTER 4

Musical Comedy

SINGIN' IN THE RAIN (1952)

Since the advent of sound with *The Jazz Singer* (1927), Hollywood has been producing movie musicals of every kind. Over the years, many of the musicals achieved blockbuster commercial success, critical raves, and even the Oscar for Best Picture (*An American in Paris* [1951], *Gigi* [1958], *My Fair Lady* [1964], and *Chicago* [2002], among others). Some of the most successful of them can rightfully be dubbed "musical comedies" for their attempts to combine comic characters and plots with musical numbers (*The Wizard of Oz* [1939]). But only a handful of films have managed to make most of their musical numbers comical in themselves: the early Marx Brothers films; some of Eddie Cantor's and Mae West's comedies; the film versions of such Broadway musical comedies as *A Funny Thing Happened on the Way to the Forum* (1966), *Funny Girl* (1968), *Grease* (1978), or the 2005 version of Mel Brooks's *The Producers* (1968).

However, the 1952 MGM masterpiece *Singin' in the Rain*, which Pauline Kael, along with many other critics, called the "best Hollywood musical of all time," infuses almost every musical number with comic attitude and, in the process, pays tribute to the great comedians of the silver screen. Such an accomplishment supports John Mariani's claim that "only a very few musicals are as well integrated . . . and none is funnier or more literate" than *Singin' in the Rain*.[1]

In the early 1950s, Arthur Freed was the head of what had come to be known as the Freed Unit of MGM, which had been responsible for producing *Babes in Arms* (1939), *The Wizard of Oz* (1939), *Cabin in the Sky* (1943), *Meet Me in Saint Louis* (1944), *An American in Paris* (1951), the 1951 version of *Show Boat*, and *The Band Wagon* (1953); and it would eventually produce more than thirty other popular and award-winning MGM musicals. Freed had just been given the Irving G. Thalberg Memorial Award at the 1951 Academy Awards ceremony. He invited the playwriting and songwriting team of Betty Comden and Adolph Green out to Hollywood with only the slimmest idea for a film. In

Don Lockwood (Gene Kelly) blissfully celebrates his revived film career and newfound love by singing and dancing in a downpour in *Singin' in the Rain* (1952).

1949, Freed and his songwriting partner, Herb Nacio Brown, sold MGM their entire catalog of songs that they had turned out over a period twenty years for the studio, beginning with the 1929 Academy Award winner *Broadway Melody*. Shortly after the sale, Freed announced that he intended to make a musical titled *Singin' in the Rain,* to be constructed around the Freed-Brown song catalog.

By the following year, plans for the film had gotten more specific. It was to be codirected by Stanley Donen and Gene Kelly.

Kelly, who would also be starring in the film, was at the top of his career. Only a year earlier, *An American in Paris*, for which he was both star and choreographer, had won five Academy Awards, including Best Picture. Kelly himself received an Honorary Academy Award that year "in appreciation of his versatility as an actor, singer, director, and dancer, and specifically for his brilliant achievements in the art of choreography on film." Comden and Green had gotten to know Kelly when they worked together in summer stock theater in 1939, and they had written the screenplay for Freed's 1949 film version of their Broadway hit *On the Town*, with Kelly as one of its stars.

After listening to numerous songs from the Freed-Brown catalog, Comden and Green came up with a story built around the changeover of Hollywood from silent films to sound. It took them only three months to write the screenplay, along with one original song, "Moses Supposes." The end result was a movie about the movies, a witty spoof that Christopher Ames describes as "what happens when the self-referential genre of the movie about Hollywood meets the self-referential genre of the musical."[2] It was a while, however, before audiences and critics alike got the joke. Peter Wollen points out that it took more than twenty years for *Singin' in the Rain* to enter the ranks of the most esteemed Hollywood films. It finally made it onto the list because, according to Wollen, the cinema of the 1960s and 1970s, with films like Federico Fellini's *8½* (1963) and François Truffaut's *Day for Night* (1973), created an "increased interest in self-reflective cinema, in films [that] themselves dealt with the process of filmmaking . . . [and] the fascination with the foregrounding of conventionally concealed technology."[3]

The special blend of music and comedy in *Singin' in the Rain* owes much to the nature of the story, which takes an affectionate look back at both the directors' experimentation with sound techniques and the fragile egos of actors whose futures depended on the quality of their speaking voices. The comic plot of *Singin' in the Rain* is built on the desperation of the studio bosses, the hysteria of the directors and sound engineers, and the deceitfulness and tyranny of one silent film diva, Lina Lamont. While spoofing this particular era in Hollywood history, Comden and Green play with the very essence of the film medium itself.

The comic conflicts revolve around the idea of film itself as an illusion. The motion picture experience, created by the projection of light onto a screen in synchronization with a track of electrical sound signals, lures the movie audience into believing that what they are watching is actually occurring before their very eyes and ears. This suspension of disbelief allows the audience to laugh, cry, or become otherwise excited by what is actually only a combination of light and sound signals. When the signals fall out of synchronization, however, the illusory nature of the experience becomes clear.[4] This self-reflexive experience becomes the running joke throughout the film, and most of the musical numbers contribute to the humor.

Michael Dunne describes this as a process of "demystification." He perhaps gives the film's audience more credit than they deserve when he proposes that the film's depiction of a Hollywood studio's first bumbling attempts to record dialogue for their first "all-talking" film by the use of hidden microphones and recording booths, as well as the disastrous moment at the film's premiere when the sounds and the film get out of synch "can only make the viewers of *Singin' in the Rain* more conscious that they are themselves recipients of sounds delivered through a similar system."[5]

Singin' in the Rain's proposition that that the entire Hollywood enterprise is based on illusion shapes the film's opening sequence. At the premiere of *The Royal Rascal*, the latest silent film historical romance starring Don Lockwood (Gene Kelly) and Lina Lamont (Jean Hagen), at Grauman's Chinese Theater, the crowd of fans outside the theater were driven to near hysteria in expectation of the arrival of Don and Lina, who are not only beloved costars but are reported to be real-life sweethearts as well. Their romance is a publicity department's lie; however, the dim-witted and egotistical Lina actually believes it, despite Don's frequent private denials. Don cooperates with the studio's publicity department, however, as he coyly avoids answering the enthusiastic radio interviewer's question about their rumored wedding plans.

Don indulges in a much more complicated fiction when he is asked by the interviewer to recount his rise to Hollywood stardom, since, as the interviewer proclaims, the story is an "inspiration to young people all over the world." The presentation of Don's life story is the film's first use of the opposition of picture and sound. As the voice-over provides a highly fictionalized version of Don's story, the visual information portrays the truth. He speaks of having been educated in the finest schools and performing for his parents' society friends. Meanwhile, the camera shows Don and his childhood friend, Cosmo Brown (Donald O'Connor), dancing in pool halls. He claims to have accompanied his parents to the theater to see the works of "Shaw, Moliere, and the finest of the classics." The screen image reveals the young scamps sneaking into a movie theater to watch a horror film. The "rigorous musical training at the Conservatory of Fine Arts" is, in actuality, shown to be performances on piano and fiddle in a smoky saloon. While Don states that the two friends "rounded out our apprenticeship at the most exclusive dramatics academy," they are seen performing the corniest baggy-pants and seltzer-bottle routines in a rinky-dink vaudeville setting. Don describes one phase of their career as a "dance concert tour" at the "finest symphonic halls in the country," as the on-screen montage includes towns named Dead Man's Fang, Arizona; Oatmeal, Nebraska; and Coyoteville, New Mexico.

Their dance routine in the rowdy music halls of the Wild West offers the first example of the film's combination of music and comedy, as Kelly and O'Connor perform a rapid-fire slapstick number, "Fit as a Fiddle" (for which Freed wrote the lyrics). Their green and white checkered baggy suits, floppy hats, and relentless smiles endow them with clownish personas, and their nonchalance in handling their fiddles is delightful to watch. The song's lyrics express the comic affirmations of their joy in being physically "fit as a fiddle," as well as their romantic optimism, because they are "ready for love"; however, as their tap dancing speeds up and as they continue playing the fiddle while kneeling and squatting and performing other amazing physical stunts, their extraordinary athleticism and intricate tap-dancing skills become high physical comedy in this almost throwaway minute-and-a-half number.

Don continues his fabricated life story by describing the offers that "came pouring in" from Hollywood. On-screen, the truth unfolds, as we see Cosmo Brown working as a mood music pianist for silent film production (a job, incidentally, that Freed had held in his early Hollywood days) and Don as a stuntman who unsuccessfully attempts to flirt with the star, Lina. In the voice-over, Don describes his movie roles as "urbane, suave, sophisticated," as the visuals show him as a wordless human object risking his life in daredevil stunts. This sequence offers the first example of *Singin' in the Rain*'s multilayered interplay of reality and illusion. The on-screen sequence shows Don substituting for the silent film's stars by getting knocked out in a Western saloon fight, crashing a plane into a building, driving a motorcycle off of a cliff, and running into a building that explodes; however, those very stunts are actually being performed in the film by one of Hollywood's most successful stuntmen, Russell Saunters, who served in that capacity in several of Kelly's films, including *An American in Paris*.

Don ends his elaborate lie by repeating the motto that he claims has guided him throughout his performing career: "Dignity. Always dignity." The viewers have seen, however, the variety of indignities that Don and Cosmo have endured on Don's path to stardom. The reality-illusion motif is thus solidly introduced in the first few minutes of the film. Ames points out the following:

> *Singin' in the Rain* announces early that it will focus on the border regions . . . to frame the contrast between illusion and reality along the lines suggested in the opening scene: the conflict between celebrity publicity and genuine personality, the struggle between "dignity" and folk art, the gap between sound and image, and the contrast between duped audience and privileged audience.[6]

In her conversation after the showing of *The Royal Rascal*, it becomes obvious that Lina's voice, a highly nasalized, standard New Yorkese dumb-blonde screech, does not fit her glamorous silent screen image, leaving the studio desperate to keep her from ever speaking in public. The inside joke is that the actress Jean Hagen is imitating the voice of Judy Holliday, who had only recently garnered an Academy Award for her brilliant portrayal of just such a dumb blonde in the acclaimed comedy *Born Yesterday* (1950). Holliday was a close friend of Comden and Green, who had teamed up with them several years earlier in their night club comedy troupe the Revuers.

On his way to the premiere party, Don is mobbed by fans and, in his escape, ends up jumping into the car of Kathy Selden (Debbie Reynolds), a struggling dancer-actress. When she realizes that she is in the presence of a major film star, she claims to be unimpressed by his accomplishments. She says that she saw one of his films and remarks, "If you've seen one, you've seen them all." She then gives an imitation of Don's typical performing style of exaggerated facial expressions and other acting clichés, which, from the excerpt shown during the premiere, seems fairly accurate. Kathy contrasts Don's film work with "real acting" on stage, calling him "just a shadow on film . . . a shadow, not real flesh and blood," which is, in fact, an accurate description of the illusion created by the film medium. Ames points out that Kathy's critique pointedly "invokes the terms of Don's self-presentation at the premiere," in which he claimed to have been trained in classical theater and repeatedly emphasized his devotion to "Dignity. Always dignity."[7] According to Kathy, film acting not only lacks the dignity of stage performances, but, compared to the "real acting" of live theater, it is illusory. Her criticism clearly bothers Don, who, when he finally makes it to the premiere party, immediately takes his friend Cosmo aside and asks him if he thinks that he is a good actor.

Meanwhile, it is soon revealed at the premiere party that Kathy is merely a chorus girl, and, as Ames points out, the "gap between her speech to Don and her real entertainment self-duplicates the gap between Don's words and the visual images that reveal his vaudeville background."[8] She pops out of a cake and joins other chorines in a cheesy version of the Freed-Brown standard "All I Do Is Dream of You." When Don recognizes Kathy, he gleefully teases her about her "acting career." Her angry response is to toss a cake at Don, only to see it land in full force in Lina's face in another one of the film's many tributes to the silent film comedy tradition.

At the party, studio producer R. F. Simpson treats the crowd to a demonstration of a "talking picture" with synchronized sound and images. R. F. tells everyone about Warner Brothers' upcoming sound film, *The Jazz Singer*, which he predicts will be a flop. Film history will make the prediction comically ironic.

The next major musical number in *Singin' in the Rain* presents what is surely O'Connor's greatest film performance. Cosmo attempts to cheer up his lovelorn pal, Don, with the musical advice, "Make 'Em Laugh." The song itself is another example of the interplay of reality and illusion. Freed is listed as the composer of the song; however, he uses the melody of another song, "Be a Clown," composed by Cole Porter and featured in an earlier Freed-Kelly collaboration, *The Pirate* (1948), originally sung by Kelly himself and Judy Garland as music hall comedians. But Porter's authorship is not acknowledged in the film's credits or elsewhere. Rudy Behlmer's study of the making of the film testifies that "no one has ever discovered whether this was an amazing coincidence, a private joke between songwriters, or an innocent and amusing pastiche. Everyone in the unit preferred, apparently, not to bring up the subject to Freed."[9] Another commentator has remarked that "only a man of Cole Porter's tact and distinction would have chosen to ignore" the obvious theft of his melody.[10]

In any case, the number makes brilliant use of O'Connor's talent in a stunning display of acrobatic dance. Wollen's analysis of the film explains that O'Connor came from a circus family. His father had been an acrobat for Ringling Brothers, and his mother had been a tightrope walker and bareback rider. By the time O'Connor was born, his family had developed a vaudeville act that incorporated their circus stunts with more traditional singing and tap dancing. Wollen relies on O'Connor's own description of his and Kelly's development of the number, writing the following:

> The two of them went to the rehearsal room and brainstormed and tried things out before finally coming up with what was basically a compendium of gags and shtick I'd done for years—in fact, going right back to my vaudeville days. Every time I got a new idea or remembered something that had worked well for me in the past, Gene wrote it down and, bit by bit, the entire number was constructed.[11]

The number is prefaced by a sequence in which Cosmo and Don walk past several sets for productions in progress: a jungle adventure, a circus performance, and a train robbery using the scenery roller background—all reminders of the artificiality of movie sets. The number itself is performed on various sections of the soundstage filled with fake backdrops, prop furniture, costumes, and workers carrying lumber and equipment around the sets. O'Connor interacts with many of these items and people while employing grotesque facial expressions, dangerous pratfalls, collisions with real and fake walls and pieces of lumber, and bodily contortions and leaps that display his admirable gymnastic skills—in many ways a tribute to the physical wizardry of Buster Keaton.

The number can be divided into five parts. In the first part, Cosmo's song urges his pal to remember that, while he is a serious actor, he could be much more popular if he could do comedy and "make 'em laugh." He urges Don to "*ridi, pagliacco*" ("laugh, clown") and describes various bits of comic shtick while he himself gets hit by pieces of lumber and other props. In the brief second part of the number, after Cosmo has slammed his face into a wall that was hidden behind a fake doorway, he attempts to sing a second verse of the song while manipulating his nose, eyes, and cheeks as if his face were made of silly putty. In the third part, he evokes Charlie Chaplin as he flirts with a headless dummy seated on a couch. Then, falling behind the couch with the dummy, he engages in a fight that is dramatized by throwing the dummy up in the air to appear above the couch, followed by Cosmo himself (or is it also a dummy?) likewise flying into the air. Then, pulling the dummy in front of the sofa, Cosmo fails to do a gymnastic handstand using the limp dummy for support. In the fourth section of the number, Cosmo attempts numerous gymnastic body twists and turns but is hampered by his uncooperative legs. He concludes his performance by running up two walls of the set to do high-altitude somersaults. When he attempts the same trick on a third wall, the wall proves to be made of cardboard, and he crashes through it, only to bounce back through the hole his crash has created to sing the final words of the song "Make 'Em Laugh."

The entire number is a major tribute to the slapstick comedy of the great silent film comedians. It also furthers *Singin' in the Rain*'s motif of reality versus illusion. Ames observes the following:

> Behind the backstage area in which he dances, there stands a photographed set that gives the illusion of an outstretching colonnade. Cosmo's dance takes him right up the set decoration, which thus destroys the illusion of depth it offers. The dance ends with him crashing through a wall. . . . He is creating illusion while unmasking it. . . . He creates the illusion of a spontaneous joyful dance while breaking the illusions of sets and props around him.[12]

The next scene continues the theme of synchronization of sight and sound in the film medium. As they prepare to shoot a romantic scene for their next film, *The Dueling Cavalier*, Lina tells Don that she got Kathy fired from her chorus girl job. As they act out their silent movie love scene together, Don tells Lina how deeply he hates her for having Kathy fired, while Lina makes even more threats against Kathy; however, as the director enthusiastically remarks, it all looks perfectly romantic on camera. But before they can do another take, the boss of Monumental Pictures, R. F. Simpson, announces that they are shutting down production until the studio is equipped to produce sound pictures.

The next musical number illustrates the immediate popularity of sound pictures with a montage of musical numbers, all using songs from the Freed-Brown catalog, concluding with a full-length performance of the song "Beautiful Girl," which turns into a mild spoof of the Hollywood versions of Ziegfeld girls posing in the latest 1920s fashions. It chronicles the historical reality that most of the early talking pictures were musicals. As Rick Altman remarks, "When film first learned to speak, it sang instead."[13]

The frantic montage is followed by the least comic musical performance in the film. Yet, in its own way, this number is the clearest manifestation of the theme of cinematic artificiality. Don had been searching unsuccessfully for Kathy for several weeks after his first encounter with her in her automobile and at the premiere party. She comes back into his life when he sees her performing as one of the chorus girls in the filming of the "Beautiful Girl" number. Thanks to Don's pleading with R. F., Kathy gets a job in an upcoming film. As Don and Kathy walk around the studio lot, Don attempts to tell her that he loves her, but he claims that, as a "ham" actor, he cannot express his feelings without the proper setting.

He takes her into a large, bare soundstage. Then he flips on the appropriate lighting, turns on wind and smoke machines, and projects a pink and blue backdrop. As Don describes it to Kathy, he is creating a "beautiful sunset, mist from the distant mountains, colored light in a garden. . . . Then we add 500,000 kilowatts of star dust, a soft summer breeze." He places Kathy on a ladder to serve as her balcony and proceeds to serenade her with the lovely ballad "You Were Meant for Me." Throughout most of the number, which includes a gentle soft-shoe duet by Kelly and Reynolds, many of the shots include the klieg lights, the wind and mist machines, and the ladder. But even with such clear presentation of the artifice of the medium, by the director's use of zooms and pans and the benefit of a lush orchestral accompaniment, not to mention Kelly's gently romantic tenor vocals, viewers are swept into the romanticism of the song. With this artful combination of visual images and sound, the filmmakers have once again "made magic" and seduced viewers into an emotional response to what is, in actuality, a projection of light and sound signals on a screen. As Dunne remarks,

> The demystification is extreme—even down to Don's use of techni-
> cal terms like *kilowatts* and *rose-colored spot*—but the remystification
> is extreme also—so that viewers end up seeing that Don is in love
> with Kathy instead of realizing that Gene Kelly has just performed a
> very clever musical number.[14]

Jane Feuer concurs in her appreciation of the scene, commenting on the following:

> Once again the technology seems to become the show. Yet *Singin' in
> the Rain* ultimately denies that technology is responsible for pleasure.
> "You Were Meant for Me," the romantic number on the deserted
> sound stage . . . demystifies only in order to restore illusion. Although
> Kelly gives us a look at the hardware behind movie magic (the wind
> machine, the soft lights) in an introduction to the song, the camera
> arcs around and comes in for a tighter shot of the couple during the

central portion of the number, reframing to exclude the previous exposed equipment. We regress from an exposé of romantic duets to an example of a romantic duet, which, along with all the others, lies about its past. The early talkie musical may be a product of a show of technology, but *Singin' in the Rain* remains, rhetorically at least, the product of magic.[15]

The following comic sequence chronicles the challenge facing the studio's newly hired diction coach, Phoebe Dinsmore, to cure Lina of her painfully nasal voice. The diction coach hired for Don has a much easier task, but his pompous affectations become the targets of Don's and Cosmo's mockery. Singing the only song composed for the film by Comden and Green, "Moses Supposes," Kelly and O'Connor, dressed in casual slacks and sweaters that make them look almost like collegiates of the Rudy Vallee era, come across as "regular guys" who find the diction coach pretentious. Professing enormous admiration for the coach's expertise, they break into song, using lyrics inspired by the diction exercises: "Moses supposes his toeses are roses/But Moses supposes erroneously/But Moses he knowses his toeses aren't roses/As Moses supposes his toeses to be." They then go into an elaborate tap duet, dancing on the professor's desk and chairs and playing with the window curtains. The professor suspects that he is being put on but watches helplessly until his two students seat him on his desk, pile furniture on top of him, scatter the contents of the wastebasket in something of a Marx Brothers moment of anarchy, and sing out their final note, a jubilant letter A. Their boyish song-and-dance number serves as a talented expression of undergraduate rebellion against academic pomposity. In doing so, it offers an exhibition of pure joy.

Having reached its midpoint, the film offers its most outrageous spoof of filmmaking as it chronicles several attempts of the high-strung director to film and record the same romantic scene from *The Dueling Cavalier* that had worked so beautifully when Don and Lina performed in the silent film format. Hilarious mishaps occur as Lina cannot speak directly into the microphone, whether it is placed in a bush located in front of her, sewn in the bodice of her dress (where it picks up the sound of her heartbeat), or hidden in a flower on her shoulder.

When the film premieres, they discover, to their horror, that the sound track includes several unintended noises, since the microphone has picked up on the rattling sound of Lina playing with her pearl necklace, the crashing noise of Don's elegant walking stick as he tosses its aside to rush into Lina's arms, the uneven volume of Lina's dialogue as she moves toward and away from the microphone hidden in the bush, the exaggerated volume of the sound created when Lina taps Don's shoulder (bearing a hidden microphone) with her elegant fan, and other inappropriate sounds that threaten to drown out the lovers' dialogue. The most outrageous moments occur when an accident in the film projection causes the picture and sound to go out of synchronization so that Don appears to be speaking Lina's lines and vice versa. The audience attending the premiere screams with laughter, mocking the dialogue and shouting its derision at the screen. The studio has a major disaster on its hands, and Don and Lina's film career may well be over.

Don, Kathy, and Cosmo retire to Don's mansion, contemplating their fate and staring at the rain coming down outside their window. Don even begins to see himself as the sort of "dumb show" performer that Kathy described the first time they met. In their attempts to lift Don's spirits, Cosmo suggests that Don fall back on his vaudeville song-and-dance career. The mention of singing and dancing inspires Kathy to propose remaking *The Dueling Cavalier* as a musical. They become excited at the possibility of this opportunity to save Don's career, and, as they realize that they have been talking through the night until 1:30 a.m., they greet the new day—and the new future for Don—with an ebullient song and dance number, "Good Morning." The number is a lively moment of pure comedy, an exercise in playfulness, optimism, and sheer joie de vivre.

The sequence, however, must have been particularly challenging for Reynolds. She was only eighteen years old at the time, and not a very accomplished singer, with practically no training or experience as a dancer. Reynolds herself has confessed, "I was totally untrained. . . . All I knew was time step and soft show. No ballet, no jazz, no real tap."[16] "Good Morning" required a great deal from her, especially in terms of some very rapid tap dancing. In an interview years later, Reynolds recalls that Kelly kept shouting, "Dance harder! More energy." When they finished filming the number, Reynolds fainted and was carried to her dressing room. Her family doctor arrived and saw that the blood vessels in her feet had burst.[17]

The number begins with the three of them singing and dancing in the kitchen. They move into the dining room for the second verse. Reynolds expresses the mood of celebration as she sings, "When we left the movie show, the future wasn't bright/But came the dawn, the show goes on. I don't want to say goodnight." They then proceed to the mansion's foyer and staircase, singing "Good morning" in various languages. Reynolds finally joins in the tap dancing up and down the staircase. Grabbing their bright yellow raincoats and hats off of the coatrack, they play peek-a-boo with them and perform a variety of dances using the raincoats as props. The dances include an Irish jig, the cancan, a hula dance, the flamenco, and the Charleston, finishing with a jump onto the mansion's bar and, turning it into a barre, they execute ballet steps. They continue their feverish tap dancing trio into the living room, where, somersaulting over one couch, they kick over another couch and tumble into it exhausted but laughing uproariously.

Their laughter subsides when it dawns on them that the one obstacle to achieving their dream of a musical is the awful quality of Lina's voice. As they playfully recall the moment at the premiere when the sound and picture fell out of synchronization, Cosmo comes up with the concept of voice dubbing. He proposes that they record Kathy's voice to be dubbed for Lina in the production of the film. As he mouths the lyrics of "Good Morning" with Kathy singing behind him, Cosmo demonstrates the dubbing process for viewers, once again reminding them of the artifice involved in film production.

This scene is immediately followed by arguably the most famous number in the history of Hollywood musicals, Kelly's iconic performance of the film's title song. The sequence expresses Don's carefree attitude as he realizes how good his life is. Not only does he still have an acting career thanks to his friends' ideas, but he has also fallen in love. "What a glorious feeling," he sings. "I'm happy again." To express this profound joy, Kelly's choreography and song-and-dance performance employ an array of comic movement and gesture.

Wollen offers an excellent shot-by-shot analysis of this unforgettable five-minute sequence (which is composed of only ten shots), suggesting but not fully exploring how each shot includes some type of comic performance. In the first shot, as Don and Kathy kiss good night at her front door, Kathy jokingly refers to the rain that is falling as "California dew." Don claims not to notice it. "From where I stand," he says with comic irony, "the sun is shining all over the place." In the second shot, Don, in an exaggerated gesture of graciousness, waves away the taxi he and Kathy had taken to her house and then "saunters cheerily down the sidewalk to an introductory vamp, singing a kind of half-hummed doo-de-doo-de-do-doo-de-do," eventually deciding to lower his umbrella and let the rain fall on him regardless of its effect on his clothes. In the third shot, Kelly actually begins "singin' in the rain." His pace picks up a bit, and he leaps onto a lamppost in what Wollen calls Kelly's "acrobatic, Douglas Fairbanks mode." When he jumps down from the lamppost, he then hugs it, and, "with a huge Kelly grin," sings, "I'm ready for love." Thus a simple lamppost becomes a device for comic exuberance and a bit of playacting, with the lamppost as the object of his affection.

In the fourth shot, Don passes by a couple who are moving as quickly as possible, using a newspaper to shield themselves from the rain. They pause briefly to turn around and stare at this fool who is not making use of his umbrella in the downpour, but Don defies the gods of the weather, singing out, "Come on with that rain; I've a smile on my face." His joy is his means of coping with natural disasters like rain. The fifth shot is more extended than the earlier ones, as Don continues to stroll down the street. In this section, Kelly evokes the spirit of Chaplin in his interplay with the umbrella. He swings it around like Chaplin's cane, juggles it a bit, uses it as his partner as he begins dancing, and finally strums it like a ukulele. (Wollen points out that the original song was first introduced in *The Hollywood Revue of 1929* by a ukulele player.)

In the sixth shot, having stopped in front of a pharmacy with a display window that features a bathing beauty enjoying the sunshine on a beach, Kelly stops singing and moves into pure dance mode. While the beach depicted in the window would seem to be a more desirable location, Don seems perfectly content in the opposite environment, a dark and rainy sidewalk. This comic inversion of values furthers the number's reference to Chaplin's tramp character. The display window becomes a backdrop as Kelly turns the sidewalk into a stage for a tap-dancing routine featuring more Chaplinesque play with the umbrella. In the seventh shot, Kelly continues dancing with his umbrella, while a gushing waterfall from a rainspout looms dangerously behind him. He finally ends up directly under the spout and, in joyful surrender, lowers the umbrella and blissfully allows the water to pour over his smiling face. Kelly then takes a giant leap into the street for the eighth shot, where, continuing to partner with his umbrella, which he has fully opened by now, he dances in a wide celebratory circle in the street, heedless of any possible traffic, completely absorbed in the moment.

In the last two shots of the sequence, Don becomes positively childish. He jumps back onto the sidewalk to engage in all sorts of play, described by Wollen as the following:

> This begins with a hopping one-foot-up, one-foot-down movement along the curb, then a pantomimed tightrope walk along the edge, followed by heavy splashing on the sidewalk, with Kelly kicking and stomping in the prepared puddles, and then jumping into the shallow, water-filled pit in the road, with exuberant sounds as he stomps and splashes water around wildly, but still rhythmically, in an uninhibited frenzy of childishness.[18]

Unbeknownst to Don, a police officer arrives—a representative of adult authority and civic responsibility. During one of his turns with his umbrella, Don catches sight of the officer, and, with the classic pose of a *commedia* character—Arlechinno caught in the midst of some mischief—Don stops in his tracks and slowly tries to assume a calmer, more adult stance. In the sequence's final shot, Don turns to face the officer and, flashing his most charming grin, simply sings to the officer, "I'm singin'. . . and dancin'. . . in the rain." He can offer no defense for his childish disturbance of the peace. Sensing that the humorless policeman is not appreciative of his actions, however, he moves away as smoothly as possible, offering a hopeful wave of his hand at the officer as he departs. Moving down the rain-soaked street, Don generously gives away his umbrella to a passerby. What need does this blissfully happy man have for an umbrella or anything else?

Director Stanley Donen has remarked that this famous dance number "works because of its utter simplicity, and there's no better idea for a movie than to dance for joy."[19] Ames points out that it is also the most famous example in Hollywood films of a "reflexive" song in "which a performer sings and dances as he sings about singing and dancing. . . . In doing so it captures in miniature the self-referential theme of the movie: a song about singing in a musical about musicals in a Hollywood movie about Hollywood."[20]

The comic plot darkens, however, as the studio agrees to rework *The Dueling Cavalier* into *The Dancing Cavalier*. R. F. insists that the process of dubbing Lina's voice with Kathy's must be kept a secret from Lina, who sees Kathy as serious competition for Don's affections; however, *Singin' in the Rain*'s filmmakers use this opportunity to engage in the most complicated self-reflexive joke of the movie. According to Gary Marmorstein, the newcomer Reynolds's voice still carried a bit too much of her native Texas accent to convey the sophisticated tones of the romantic noblewoman played by Lina, so in the "famous scenes in which Reynolds appears to be dubbing for Jean Hagen as the aluminum voice silent screen actress . . . it is actually Hagen, speaking normally, dubbing herself."[21] Then, in a further step in the process of illusion, Kathy is shown dubbing for Lina's singing voice in the recording of the love song, "Would You?"; however, attentive viewers may notice that the singing voice is not the same as the one that sang "All I Do Is Dream of You" or "Good Morning" earlier in the film. The song is actually being sung by an uncredited performer, Betty Noyes (listed elsewhere as Royce). When the final sound transfer of the "Would You?" number is shown, the audience of *Singin' in the Rain* sees Hagen, as Lina, supposedly lip-synching the voice of Reynolds as Kathy, while in actuality Reynolds is lip-synching Noyes. Carol Clover finds this double lip-synching somewhat ironic given the film's theme of giving credit where credit is due:

> Maybe the split between a movie's story and its production practices is so complete that it didn't occur to anyone that there was something funny about not crediting Noyes's/Royce's voice in a film that is precisely about the crediting of voices in film.[22]

The sequence concludes with a further reminder of film artifice, as the Technicolor picture of Lina singing morphs into a black-and-white presentation of the final filmed version shown in the studio screening room.

After Don, Cosmo, and R. F. have watched the "Would You?" footage, Don tells R. F. that there is only one more musical number to be filmed for *The Dancing Cavalier*. Cosmo had earlier suggested that to have modern dance numbers in a film set during the French Revolution, the entire *The Dancing Cavalier* story could be presented as a dream experienced by a Broadway hoofer who has been hit on the head by a sandbag while reading *A Tale of Two Cities*.

By means of this elaborate shoehorn, Kelly is able to include a long and lavish production number, "Broadway Melody," as an opportunity for the same mix of ballet, modern dance, and tap dancing in his triumphant dance performance to Gershwin's music in *An American in Paris* a year earlier. In the film's self-reflexive stance, it is also something of a salute to Arthur Freed, recalling the Academy Award-winning film that was Freed's first taste of Hollywood success.

The opening lines of the main song offer a comic message, as Kelly, spotlighted in a tuxedo and a rakishly tipped straw hat, sings, "Don't bring a frown to old Broadway. You gotta clown on Broadway . . . for Broadway always wears a smile." Then, as the number's narrative begins, Kelly appears as the naive bumpkin pounding on theater agents' doors, singing "Gotta Dance." His character resembles Harold Lloyd with Lloyd's trademark floppy porkpie hat, snappy-vested suit, and black-rimmed eyeglasses. Later in the number, when he encounters the strikingly beautiful Cyd Charisse (in her first major dancing role in film) as a speakeasy femme fatale, Kelly offers only a mild version of Lloyd's innocence, as she seductively insists on removing his eyeglasses and kicking them out of his reach. Kelly's and Charisse's dance duet, however, is much too sexy to continue the Lloyd persona, as Kelly's character evolves into a smooth Times Square denizen.

After Charisse rejects Kelly in favor of her gangster boyfriend, Kelly starts his climb to stardom, first appearing in a baggy-pants burlesque routine, then in a George M. Cohan red-white-and-blue number, and, finally, as a star in the Ziegfeld Follies; however, although he eventually achieves fame and the attention of gorgeous ladies, he finds that the woman of his dreams still prefers her gangster boyfriend. As Kelly stands alone and rejected, he spots a younger Lloydish arrival to the big city singing "Gotta Dance." The sight of the hopeful newcomer reminds the star of his original enthusiasm, and he vigorously joins in the singing. The number ends, and, in another moment of self-reflexive humor, Don asks R. F. what he thinks of it. R. F. replies in a remark that Freed himself was known to say often, stating, "I can't quite visualize it. I'll have to see it on film first." Of course, *Singin' in the Rain*'s audience has just done that.

Meanwhile, part of the plan for Kathy is that, after *The Dancing Cavalier* is released, the studio is prepared to promote her as a star in her own right; however, Lina catches Don and Kathy kissing, is told of the plan, and initiates her own publicity campaign hailing her musical performance in the film. Having talked to her lawyers, she discovers how much control and legal power she enjoys. She threatens to sue the studio unless they remove Kathy's name from the film's credits and require Kathy to continue to dub her voice for Lina's future films.

Her downfall occurs at the premiere of *The Dancing Cavalier*. With delightful comic logic, Lina's powermongering goes too far. As they listen to the thunderous applause at the end of the showing, Lina informs everyone of the arrangement she has forced upon R. F. and the studio. Buoyed by the enthusiastic reception of the audience and her newfound awareness of her legal rights, she begins threatening everyone. Even R. F. seems powerless against her. At that point, someone reports that the audience is demanding that Lina come onstage and speak to them. Reminding everyone that the studio has always kept her silent, she now insists on "doing my own talking." The subsequent address is hilarious. Lina's nasal screech and grammatical ignorance shock the audience, as she tells them, "If we bring a little joy into your humdrum lives, it makes us feel as though our hard work ain't been in vain for nothin'. Bless you all!" The confused audience requests that she sing for them with that beautiful voice she displayed in the film. Lina panics.

But Don comes up with a plan that will bring down the tyrant. Ames properly recognizes this scene as "crucial in revealing the problematics of truth and illusion" of the film. Lina is the "classic blocking character, standing in the way of the happy ending by virtue of her faith in the studio publicity that says Don loves her."[23] Her inability to see what went wrong at the premiere of *The Dancing Cavalier*, her lack of awareness of her vocal limitations, her belief in praise lavished on her as a "glittering star in the firmament" written by her publicist, and her willingness to use her star power to tyrannize the studio all point to a moral and esthetic ignorance that must be exposed and disempowered.

R. F. tells Lina to go onstage and orders Kathy to stand behind the curtain near a microphone so that she can sing while Lina lip-synchs the words in front of the curtain. Kathy, not informed of the plan, feels betrayed by Don, but, knowing that she is under contract to R. F., she agrees to sing. Lina proceeds to "perform" "Singin' in the Rain." As she heads into the second verse, however, R. F., Don, and Cosmo pull open the curtain behind Lina, revealing Kathy as the actual singer. The audience explodes in laughter, especially after Cosmo replaces Kathy and sings a line or two of the song himself. Don runs onstage and announces to everyone that it was Kathy's voice that everyone enjoyed so much and that "she is the real star of the picture." He underlines her new status by crooning the song "You Are My Lucky Star" to her. Although she was running out of the theater in anger and humiliation, Kathy turns back toward the stage and joins Don in the singing.

The final moments of the film play even more explicitly with the film's motif of reality versus illusion. The camera moves in for a close-up of Don's face in profile (reality) as he kisses Kathy. The shot fades into a poster of the same profile on a billboard (illusion). The camera backs up to reveal the entire poster, which is an advertisement for Monumental Pictures' new release, *Singin' in the Rain*, starring Don Lockwood and Kathy Selden, whose picture also graces the poster. The camera widens to show Don and Kathy admiring the billboard on a California hillside (reality). The camera then moves in again to a close-up of Don and Kathy engaging in a major Hollywood kiss. "The End" then appears written on a blank screen, reminding the viewers that they have been watching a film (illusion). The movie theater lights come up, and viewers rise from their seats to return to their own lives (reality).

Of course, the film advertised on the poster, *Singin' in the Rain*, does not star Don Lockwood and Kathy Selden. It stars Gene Kelly and Debbie Reynolds, and it has just ended. And, as Ames points out, the ending shows the righting of several of the tensions we identified at the film's outset:

> Unabashed musical comedy replaces the pretensions to dignity in silent melodrama, the raising of the curtain behind the lip-synching Lina unites visual image and soundtrack, and perhaps the billboard even looks forward to uniting privileged audiences with the "mob" audience within the film (who can now see *Singin' in the Rain*).[24]

Singin' in the Rain offers film aficionados a feast of in-jokes built around the film's references to the silent movie era. Comden and Green are said to have come up with the idea of the transfer from silent to sound films because they had bought the house they lived in while working on the film from a former silent film star whose career was killed by the advent of sound. The film's costume designer, Walter Plunkett, had worked in films since 1929, and many of his anecdotes about those transitional years also inspired many of the bits, like the loud tapping of Lina's fan on Don's shoulder, where a microphone had been placed. Many of the characters who show up for the movie premiere in the beginning of the film are caricatures of such silent film stars as Pola Negri, Clara Bow, Gloria Swanson, and the gossip columnist Louella Parsons.

The screenplay is also peppered with many references to MGM itself. The producer, R. F. Simpson, is said to be a parody of Louis B. Mayer, and his initials are a reference to Arthur Freed himself. The frantic director, Roscoe Dexter, might be recalling the highly emotional director Erich von Stroheim. Many of the costumes and sets are drawn from several of Gene Kelly's earlier MGM star vehicles, including *The Pirate* (1948), *The Three Musketeers* (1948), *Words and Music* (1948), *Summer Stock* (1950), and even his most recent film prior to *Singin' in the Rain*, *An American in Paris*. The car that Kathy is driving early in the film was originally Andy Hardy's jalopy in the MGM Andy Hardy series in the 1930s. The dressing room Don steps out of to film *The Dueling Cavalier* had been that of Norma Shearer, the MGM star and wife of the powerful studio chief Irving Thalberg. The incredibly high wig that Lina wears in the same scene was worn by Shearer in the 1938 MGM epic *Marie Antoinette*, provoking considerable in-group humor when Lina whines, "What dope would wear a thing like this?"

MGM and its Freed Unit provided ample material for both musical numbers and comic spoofs, but no other film has managed to combine music and comedy in the same scenes as well as *Singin' in the Rain*. As John Kenneth Muir observes, the musical numbers are "staged in a manner that exhibits a joie de vivre uncommon in film story. Bursting with energy, the *Singin' in the Rain* numbers have become iconic."[25] The musical numbers do little to advance the film's plot. Rather, they serve as musical and comedy spectacles that force the story to pause while they celebrate, in joyous fashion, the film's narrative. Whether it be the rise of someone to Hollywood stardom, the value of clownish buffoonery, the romantic spell surrounding newly discovered love, the dawn of a new day, or the sheer joy of singing in the pouring rain and feeling completely alive, *Singin' in the Rain* is a truly comic musical, maybe the best one yet.

A Sampling of Musical Comedies

Annie Get Your Gun (1950)
Gentlemen Prefer Blondes (1953)
Seven Brides for Seven Brothers (1954)
Guys and Dolls (1955)
The Court Jester (1956)
Funny Girl (1968)
Hello, Dolly! (1969)
Grease (1978)
Chicago (2002)
Hairspray (2007)

Notes

1. John Mariani, "Come on with the Rain." *Journal of Popular Film and Television*, vol. 14, no. 3 (May–June 1978), 7.
2. Christopher Ames, *Movies about the Movies* (Lexington: University Press of Kentucky, 1997), 60.
3. Peter Wollen, *Singin' in the Rain* (London: British Film Institute, 1992), 53.
4. Henri Bergson, *Laughter: An Essay on the Meaning of the Comic*, trans. Cloudesley Brereton and Fred Rothwell (New York: Macmillan, 1924), offers many examples of the effect of separating sound from action to comic effect.
5. Michael Dunne, *American Film Musical Themes and Forms* (Jefferson, N.C., and London: McFarland & Co, 2004), 167.
6. Ames, *Movies about the Movies*, 56.
7. Ames, *Movies about the Movies*, 56.

8. Ames, *Movies about the Movies*, 61.

9. Rudy Behlmer, *America's Favorite Movies: Behind the Scenes* (London: Samuel French, 1990), 262.

10. Hugh Fordin, *M-G-M's Greatest Musicals: The Arthur Freed Unit* (New York: DaCapo Press, 1996), 359.

11. Wollen, *Singin' in the Rain*, 34.

12. Ames, *Movies about the Movies*, 61–62.

13. Rick Altman, *The American Film Musical* (Bloomington: Indiana University Press, 1987), 131.

14. Dunne, *American Film Musical Themes and Forms*, 168.

15. Jane Feuer, *The Hollywood Musical* (Bloomington: Indiana University Press, 1982), 46–47.

16. Mariani, "Come on with the Rain," 11.

17. Mariani, "Come on with the Rain," 11.

18. Wollen, *Singin' in the Rain*, 27.

19. Mariani, "Come on with the Rain," 12.

20. Ames, *Movies about the Movies*, 66, 67.

21. Gary Marmorstein, *Hollywood Rhapsody: Movie Music and Its Makers, 1900–1975* (New York: Schirmer Books, 1997), 257.

22. Steve Cohan, *Hollywood Musicals: The Film Reader* (New York: Routledge, 2002), 158.

23. Ames, *Movies about the Movies*, 69.

24. Ames, *Movies about the Movies*, 70.

25. John Kenneth Muir, *Singing a New Tune: The Rebirth of the American Musical from* Evita *to* De-Lovely *and Beyond* (New York: Applause Books, 2005), 36.

CHAPTER 5

Sex Farce

SOME LIKE IT HOT (1959)

When the American Film Institute placed Billy Wilder's *Some Like It Hot* at the top of its list of the 100 greatest comedies ever made, Anthony Lane reported the achievement in *The New Yorker*, commenting how amusing it was that the "most entertaining cultural spectacle of the last 100 years has been, by common consent, a pair of full-grown American males wearing falsies." "Falsehood," he observes, "is the fuel of this famous movie. It is rabid with deception."[1] Indeed, it seems that every other line that comes out of the mouths of these "full-grown American males"—and others as well—is a lie, and various disguises are assumed with similar frequency. The film, in fact, displays all the standard devices of the sex farce genre: rapid-fire dialogue, role reversals, tightly overcrowded spaces, frantic escapes, chases, near misses, and coincidental run-ins with dangerous characters. And all of it occurs in desperate pursuit of sex, money, or survival. And then there is the frenzied pace of the film. As Gerd Gemunden describes it, "From the film's opening chase scene, through the ribaldry on the overnight train, shots of elevators endlessly going up and down, and the pivotal use of a bicycle, to the final getaway in a motor boat, there is constant movement and action."[2] All of this is sustained by comedy's archetypal struggle of life versus death, introduced in the earliest sequence of the film set in a funeral parlor and maintained in the several attempts on our heroes' lives throughout the rest of the narrative.

The story is relatively simple by the standards of farce. Two down-on-their-luck musicians, Joe (Tony Curtis) and Jerry (Jack Lemmon), having witnessed the St. Valentine's Day Massacre in Chicago, escape from the killers by disguising themselves as "Josephine" and "Daphne" and joining an all-girls' orchestra on their way to an engagement in Florida. On the band's train ride to Miami, they meet Sugar Kane Kowalczyk (Marilyn Monroe), the

Sugar Kane Kowalczyk (Marilyn Monroe) sings "Runnin' Wild," accompanied by Joe/Josephine (Tony Curtis) on the saxophone and Jerry/Daphne (Jack Lemmon) playing the bass, along with other members of Sweet Sue's "all-girl" band in *Some Like It Hot* (1959).

ukulele player and lead singer with her own hard-luck story in the romance department: her penchant for always falling for the wrong guy. Arriving in Florida, Joe and Jerry continue to masquerade as members of the all-girls' orchestra. Joe, however, soon assumes another disguise in his pursuit of Sugar. Donning a sporty yachtsman's outfit (which he stole from the band director's assistant's suitcase), he pretends to be "Junior," a dashing young oil mogul. Jerry, meanwhile, totally melting into his new identity as "Daphne," attracts the attention of a millionaire senior citizen, Osgood Fielding III (Joe E. Brown), who pursues Jerry/Daphne relentlessly and eventually proposes marriage. Meanwhile, the Chicago mob boss who supervised the St. Valentine's Day shootings, Spats Colombo (George Raft), and his thugs show up for a gangland convention at the very hotel in Florida where the girls are performing, and, recognizing Joe and Jerry as witnesses to the shooting, they proceed to pursue them once again with murderous intent. Chaos ensues, and (almost) everything is resolved by the final frame.

The enormous success of *Some Like It Hot* upon its release should have surprised no one. The film's appeal was fairly guaranteed by the popular perception of its three stars. Marilyn Monroe was the reigning sex goddess at the time, having captivated both audiences and critics with her performances in some of the most popular comedies of the period, including *Gentlemen Prefer Blondes* (1953), *How to Marry a Millionaire* (1953), *There's No Business Like Show Business* (1954), *The Seven Year Itch* (1955), and *Bus Stop* (1956).

Tony Curtis was one of Hollywood's hottest romantic leading men who had already appeared in thirty-five films in the previous decade. His good looks had served him well in a variety of genres, including romantic comedies, tough-guy melodramas, war movies, and costume spectacles. He eventually landed leading roles in many highly respected films, in portrayals that combined his physical appeal with macho dramatics. He played the lead in *Houdini* (1953), he appeared opposite Burt Lancaster in the circus melodrama-spectacle *Trapeze* (1956) and the dark satire *The Sweet Smell of Success* (1957), and he joined up with Kirk Douglas in *The Vikings* (1958). He had recently earned an Oscar nomination for his role as an escaped convict chained to fellow escapee Sidney Poitier in *The Defiant Ones*, a controversial 1958 drama about racism.

Jack Lemmon had already earned his Academy Award in 1956 as the nervous Ensign Pulver in the hit comedy *Mister Roberts*, and he solidified his reputation in several more successful comedies of the 1950s, usually playing the nervous or sexually inept Everyman. *Some Like It Hot* was the first of many successful collaborations between Lemmon and Billy Wilder.

Wilder, one of the most respected and award-winning screenwriters and directors in Hollywood, seems to have mastered every film genre. Many of his films are now considered classics of their type, including *Double Indemnity* (1944), *The Lost Weekend* (1945), *Sunset Boulevard* (1950), *Stalag 17* (1953), *Sabrina* (1954), *The Seven Year Itch* (1955), *The Spirit of St. Louis* (1957), *Witness for the Prosecution* (1957), and, after *Some Like It Hot*, several starring vehicles for Jack Lemmon, namely *The Apartment* (1960), *Irma la Douce* (1963), *The Fortune Cookie* (1966), and *The Odd Couple* (1968). By 1958, Wilder had already won two Oscars for Best Director, and he went on to win two more during his career.

Wilder and his coscreenwriter, I. A. L. Diamond, employed some of the most time-honored techniques in developing the film's award-winning screenplay. Joe and Jerry represent the classic comic pair, stretching back at least as far as Don Quixote and Sancho Panza, all the way up to their twentieth-century incarnations in Laurel and Hardy and, in the 1950s, Dean Martin and Jerry Lewis. Joe, the handsome smooth-talker, is the braggart-schemer of the two, while Jerry is the nervous, cowardly complainer, at least in the first fifteen minutes of the film. Sugar, meanwhile, embodies the ultimate distillation of the Marilyn Monroe persona: the luscious blonde cupcake who, while she oozes sexuality, is either too dim-witted or, for some reason, too innocent to realize the spellbinding effect she has on men. Yet, she is also a variation on the classic comic ingénue in the long tradition of farce: the lovely young lady with limited mental capacities but abundant physical attributes and ardent appetites. Many other classic comic devices propel the film's plot and dialogue.

Besides the tweaking of the established images of the film's stars, the script and the casting also made self-referential use of a variety of Hollywood clichés dating back to the glory days of the 1930s. George Raft resurrects his wisecracking mobster persona as the Chicago gangster Spats Colombo. Pat O'Brien reassumes his standard role as an equally hard-boiled detective, Officer Mulligan. Joe E. Brown, one of Hollywood's top moneymakers in the 1930s, revives his flagging film career, employing his cavernous mouth, broad grin, and wide eyes to depict a mischievous old millionaire with only one thing on his dirty mind. And when Tony Curtis assumes his identity as "Junior," the dashing young millionaire, halfway through the film, he offers a fairly good imitation of Cary Grant's performances in the comic hits *The Philadelphia Story* (1940) and *Bringing Up Baby* (1938).

Some Like It Hot, however, is not simply a pastiche of farcical devices, brilliant one-liners, and tributes to earlier Hollywood product. The genius of this comic masterpiece is the careful structure of the narrative, which is divided into four "acts," each approximately half an hour long, with half of the action taking place in Chicago and on a train and the other half in Miami. Each act includes elements of both sexual adventure and physical danger, and each sequence is built around deception and desperation. Wilder and Diamond's brilliant display of transgression and frenzy is a triumph of controlled design. As Neil Sinyard and Adrian Tucker observe,

> *Some Like It Hot* is one of the most brilliantly constructed of Wilder's films. The film is tightly organized around a consistent range of polarities—a tension between two constantly shifting worlds of male and female, gangster and musician, Chicago and Miami, romance and death, reality and unreality, dream and nightmare. It is the contrast, conflict, and confrontation between these complementary worlds that provides the film with its energy, tension, and coherence.[3]

Act 1: Life versus Death

In *Some Like It Hot*, the comic action literally becomes a death-defying strategy. The narrative begins with the on-screen information "Chicago 1929." The historical context of the Eighteenth Amendment's prohibition of the "manufacture, sale, or transportation of intoxicating liquors" sets up the eternal conflicts inherent in comedy: authority versus individuality, upright sobriety versus intoxicated folly, and responsibility versus revelry. The classical basis for farce is clearly established by placing the action in the Prohibition era, which "made transgression routine and channeled ordinary citizens toward illicit avenues of gratification. Prohibition in the film evokes all manner of efforts to prohibit universal behaviors and desires."[4] Like the decrees of tyrannical parents or rulers in the classical comedy tradition, the Volstead Act is seen as the government's ultimately futile attempt to keep people from enjoying themselves. In the comic universe, all such efforts are doomed to failure.

The criminal violence that the Prohibition era created, however, also provokes the ultimate comic conflict between life and death. The first sequence announces this contest as directly as possible. The film opens with a tracking shot of a hearse driving through the dark streets of a city, the standard mise-en-scène of the gangster films of the 1930s. Inside the hearse viewers can see the pallbearers, the coffin, and an impressive flower arrangement. Suddenly, shots are fired from a police car chasing the hearse. The pallbearers, pulling back the curtained ceiling of the hearse to reveal a fully supplied gun rack, respond with their own barrage of gunfire. A high-speed chase ensues, with both the hearse and police car getting riddled with bullets, until the police car crashes and gives up the chase. The hearse, likewise crashing into other cars, finally comes to a stop. The screen then shows liquid spewing out of the bullet holes in the coffin. The coffin lid is raised, displaying its contents, dozens of bottles of bootleg liquor. The words "Chicago 1929" flash across the screen. As Gemunden remarks, this opening sequence also "efficiently establishes the central metaphor of counterfeit and camouflage and the binary opposition of being and appearance . . . that provides the central structuring device of the film."[5]

References to death continue in the sequence that follows. The hearse arrives at Mozzarella's Funeral Parlor, which is actually a speakeasy. Shortly afterward, Officer Mulligan arrives with several other police cars to raid the joint. He is told by his informant, Toothpick Charlie (George E. Stone), that he should tell the funeral director that he has come to attend the "old lady's funeral." He is further instructed that if he wants an inside table, he should tell them that he is "one of the pallbearers," and he is given a black armband as his ticket into the "funeral service." Mournful organ music is playing in the foyer of the funeral home until the organist pulls out one of the organ stops and opens the "chapel" doors. In an instant, uproarious jazz music replaces the melancholy organ melody. As Mulligan surveys the room filled to overflowing with raucous partygoers and long-legged chorines dancing the Charleston to "Sweet Georgia Brown," he comments appreciatively, "Well, if you gotta go, that's the way to do it." When he requests to sit at the table that belongs to Spats Colombo, the waiter informs him that the table is "reserved for members of the immediate family." Mulligan suggests that the place could be raided. The waiter asks, "Who's gonna raid a funeral parlor?" Mulligan replies, "Some people got no respect for the dead."

The mayhem in this early section of the film also establishes a pattern of "multiple images of spillage and overflow" throughout the narrative, according to Daniel Lieberfeld and Judith Sanders, illustrating the film's "preoccupation with the transgressive":

> In the very first scene, bootleg liquor leaks from a coffin. Next, a speakeasy customer spills his drink on mob boss Spats Colombo. Gasoline overflows the tank of Joe's and Jerry's car as they inadvertently witness gangsters spilling each other's blood during the St. Valentine's Day Massacre. Aboard the bumpy train to Florida, Sugar's hidden whiskey flask shakes loose as she sings, "Running wild/lost control." "We might spill something," Sugar frets later, as she and Jerry, disguised as Daphne, share an illicit drink. "So spill it," exults Daphne, "Spills, thrills, laughs, and games!"[6]

They also observe that each of these spills is followed by some threat of retribution, emphasizing the danger of such trangressive behavior.

The next several sequences show Joe and Jerry playing out the schemer-worrier dynamic. As members of the speakeasy's jazz orchestra, Joe on saxophone and Jerry on bass fiddle, they argue about what to do with the money they will be paid for the gig that night. While Jerry hopes to spend the money on getting a filling in his tooth, Joe proposes that they spend the money betting on a "sure thing" at the dog races. When Jerry suggests that the dog Joe picks might lose the race, Joe asks him, "Why must you paint everything so black?" Their conversation is interrupted by the police raid on the joint. Joe and Jerry manage to escape, but, in the meantime, they don't get paid for the night's work. Joe, still devoted to his "sure thing" gamble, suggests that they pawn their overcoats to cover their bets at the dog races. Jerry once again complains that it's the middle of winter; Joe replies that, when their gamble pays off, "tomorrow, we'll have twenty overcoats!" In a quick cut, the next shot shows them on the morrow—coatless—in a Chicago snowstorm, with Jerry complaining that he is hungry with a hole in his shoe, while the incorrigible Joe tries to convince Jerry to hock their instruments for another gambling scheme.

Their roles, however, change for a couple of minutes when they visit their agent's office and find out that there is a job available for a saxophonist and a bass player, only with an all-girl orchestra, Sweet Sue and her Society Syncopaters. This time it's Jerry who imagines how they could disguise themselves as women and join the band for the three-week engagement in Miami, while it is Joe who refuses to go along with the scheme. Instead, sweet-talking the secretary, Joe manages to borrow her car to drive to a one-night stand at a Valentine's Day dance at the University of Illinois.

The death motif returns for the following sequence at the garage where Joe and Jerry go to pick up the secretary's automobile. As they are filling her car with gasoline, Spats Colombo arrives at the location and proceeds to pay back the informer, Toothpick Charlie, and his buddies in a round of gunplay that becomes the St. Valentine's Day Massacre. Once the shooting stops, Joe and Jerry are discovered hiding behind their borrowed automobile. Just as Colombo's gang aims their guns at the two witnesses, the thugs are distracted, and, in the ensuing chaos, Joe and Jerry once again manage to escape disaster. Joe immediately realizes that the job in Florida provides a more secure removal from the threat of death. Affecting a female voice, he telephones the agency and takes the job for the both of them. In a quick cut to the next scene, Joe and Jerry, in perfect drag, are shown joining the all-girl orchestra boarding the train to Florida.

The sexual element was inserted into the plot with Joe's leering appreciation of the dancing chorus girls at Mozzarella's Funeral Parlor and his outrageous, but effective, flirtation with the agency secretary. The coincidence of a murder occurring on a holiday for lovers, St. Valentine's Day, maintains the interplay of violence and sexuality that pervades the narrative. Sexuality enters the story definitively, however, with the arrival of Monroe as Sugar Kane Kowalczyk. Her entrance into the film is iconic. It is set up by the on-screen appearance of Lemmon and Curtis looking like proper young ladies of 1929 for all the world to see, perhaps a bit heavy on the makeup but otherwise perfectly groomed. Jauntily and sometimes awkwardly prancing in their high heels, they rush to board the train on time. Jerry continues to complain about his situation: the discomfort of the high heels, the draft he feels from wearing a skirt, and the feeling that everyone is staring at him.

Still adjusting to their new female identity, they suddenly get a look at "The Real Thing" in the form of Sugar. As Sugar gingerly bounces by them and skips to avoid a burst of steam from the train, Jerry expresses his astonishment at the way she moves: "like Jell-O on springs . . . with some sort of built-in motor." Marilyn arrives on the scene to illuminate the rest of the film. Meanwhile, Joe/Josephine and Jerry/Daphne manage to do a fair impersonation of the fair sex, enough to inspire Beinstock (Dave Barry), the band's manager, to comment that the band finally has a couple of "real ladies." He is, in fact, smitten enough by Daphne's charms that he pats her posterior as she bends over to pick up her luggage.

Even amid the thrill of this new scheme and the sexual excitement generated by Sugar's appearance, the boys cannot forget the death threat looming over them. Before boarding the train, Jerry, the coward-complainer, continues to express his reservations about this latest scheme; however, as a newsboy walks by shouting the headlines about the massacre and the "bloody aftermath" that is expected, Jerry finally comprehends the level of the threat on their lives and buys into the plan. When they introduce themselves, Beinstock tells them, "You girls saved our lives." Jerry/Daphne replies, "Likewise, I'm sure." The cliché response, in this case, is truer than their rescuers know. Sex and death—Sigmund Freud's two great forces—have met in this moment, which brings an end to the Chicago segment of the story.

Curtis's and Lemmon's transformation at the end of what one might call act 1 of the film was extraordinary for its time. As Gemunden comments, "There is general agreement that Wilder's transvestites go further in becoming actual women than anyone before them in the long Hollywood . . . tradition of cross-dressing," and she mentions two of the most popular examples, Bob Hope's drag act in *Road to Zanzibar* (1941) and Cary Grant's in *I Was a Male War Bride* (1949).[7] She refers to the analysis of Patrice Petro, who writes the following:

> Although not entirely or exactly feminist, the film nonetheless forces its audience (and its central male characters) to experience the world differently, as women do—subject to unwanted sexual overtures, male voyeurism, and the constraints and pleasures of feminine culture. This is the source of much of its humor—for both women and men.[8]

Act 2: Riding for Their Lives

Act 2 exploits the crowded conditions of the train ride to Florida for comic effect. If the Chicago environment was a predominantly male environment, with its dark streets and illegal venues populated by violent criminals, bootleggers, and law-breaking revelers, the overnight train is a woman's world, a sorority house on wheels where the girls party clandestinely, tell ribald jokes about one-legged jockeys, and sing about "running wild."

Once they board the train, Joe's and Jerry's new identities reverse their previous roles. Joe, the playboy, presents his alter ego Josephine as the "refined type," announcing that they are both graduates of the Sheboygan Conservatory of Music, while Jerry, the nervous complainer, turns into Daphne, a giddy, fun-loving flapper who enjoys being one of the girls, gabbing with them about "this divine seamstress" he/she has found to do his/her outfits. Joe becomes the worrier, afraid that Jerry's playfulness with the other band members will lead to sexual indiscretion which, in turn, will result in the uncovering of their masquerade. In his hesitancy and concern, Joe does not adapt to their new situation as easily as Jerry; he even gets reprimanded by the bandleader, Sweet Sue (Joan Shawlee), for not "picking up the beat" with his saxophone playing during Sugar's performance of "Running Wild." Jerry, however, moves right into the swing of things, getting to know all the girls on a first-name basis and otherwise fitting nicely into his new role and environment. According to Lieberfeld and Sanders, this should come as no surprise, since "Joe and Jerry are polarized as gender examplars throughout the film":

> Joe plays the phallic tenor sax, Jerry the womanly double bass. And if holes connote femaleness, Jerry is full of them: Besides the hole in his tooth, there is one in his shoe; his blood type is O; and his instrument is shot full of holes. Jerry embraces his new identity by discarding his Geraldine alias and adopting the more flamboyant Daphne. Joe sticks with Josephine, a conservative choice that indicates the transience of his transgression.[9]

This sequence also provides a great deal of exposition of Sugar's situation. While breaking up a block of ice in the train's bathroom sink, Sugar provides Joe with information he will later find quite invaluable: her incurable attraction to saxophone players; her bad experiences with men (whom she describes as treating her exactly as the viewers have seen Joe treating the secretaries at the talent agency); and her plans to find a millionaire in Florida to marry, preferably one with a yacht and wearing glasses because his eyesight has deteriorated from "reading all the tiny print in those columns in the *Wall Street Journal.*"

Monroe's sexual persona is emphasized by the camera shots of her throughout this sequence. The focus on her curvaceous figure as she moves to board the train, the opening shot of her leg with the whiskey flask in her garter during her first conversation with Joe and Jerry, and the framing and lighting for the energetic bodily movements during her rendition of "Running Wild" depict Monroe "in terms of her fractionated body. . . . In each instance the male characters' gaze, accompanied by a soundtrack of lasciviously growling horns, cues viewers to regard Sugar in terms of fetishized body parts."[10] Sugar's singing performance is bookended by the sight and sounds of the train's wheels roaring down the tracks and setting the pace for the almost frantic delivery of her song. Like Joe and Jerry in their flight from their murderous pursuers, Sugar is also "running away" from the men in the bands with whom she has sung, especially the saxophone players who were always seducing and abandoning her.

As they settle into their sleeping berths for the overnight train ride to Florida, the boys find their role-playing severely compromised by the proximity of the playful young ladies in the orchestra. First, Sugar visits Jerry's berth in the middle of the night. Her innocent cuddling with Jerry, as she describes the nights she would climb under the covers with her sister when they were young, drives Jerry to the heights of sexual frustration, neatly foreshadowing Sugar's "seduction" of Joe on the yacht later in the film, when Joe will likewise have to engage in sexual pretense. Then, in a scene that Wilder has called "my homage to the stateroom scene in *Night at the Opera*," several other band members join them in Jerry's sleeping berth for a slumber party with crackers and cocktails, crowding into the narrow space until the screen is filled with the faces of a half dozen blondes (including Jerry/Daphne).[11] Their rambunctious mood, fueled by the alcohol, threatens to reveal Jerry's disguise as they reach under his nightgown to slip ice cubes down his back. In a desperate attempt to preserve the masquerade, Jerry puts a stop to the female bonding by pulling the train's emergency brake, abruptly flinging the partygoers out of his berth and onto the floor of the train and effectively ending the train sequence of the film with a bang.

Act 3: Double Sexual Pursuits

With another quick cut, the screen is filled with the blinding sunlight of Miami Beach, as the band arrives for their engagement at the resort hotel. Thus begins act 3 of the comedy, the longest section of the film, at about forty minutes, which is filled with frantic action that seriously raises the ante of deception and disguise, as well as the level of sexual display by both Monroe and Curtis. Jerry/ Daphne barely makes it up the steps of the hotel veranda before he/she is greeted by Osgood Fielding III, the most aggressive of the many elderly millionaires awaiting the arrival of the band ladies. Meanwhile, upon entering his hotel room, Joe is forced to deal with the sleazy comments of an aggressive bellboy. With this new awareness of "how the other half lives," Jerry wants to abandon their disguises now that they are far away from Spats Colombo, but Joe insists that they must maintain the masquerade because Colombo is still searching for them in every male band in the country. In the film's continuous interchange of sex and death, Jerry, however, knows that Joe really wants to stay with the band to pursue Sugar.

Joe begins his pursuit by assuming yet another disguise. Donning a pair of eyeglasses and dressing in some gentlemanly beach attire that he has stolen from Beinstock's luggage, Joe becomes "Junior," a handsome young oil tycoon, and heads out to the beach. Encountering Sugar on the beach, Joe lies his way into her heart by using all the information she had given him earlier: stealing a beach chair from a little boy named Junior and adopting his name; reading the *Wall Street Journal* with his horn-rimmed glasses; pointing out his yacht in the harbor; and, prompted by the sight of the shells the little boy had been collecting, informing Sugar that his family is so devoted to shells that they gave the name to their oil company. What is surprising is Sugar's similar capacity to instantly create her own false identity, describing herself as a Bryn Mawr debutante playing in a band with other college girls as a "lark," having studied at the Sheboygan Conservatory of Music, and finding all the coming-out parties, opera openings, and so forth in her debutant existence such a bore. When Jerry/Daphne joins the conversation, Sugar even encourages Daphne to play along as another Vassar or Bryn Mawr girl.

The elaborate deception then spins into overdrive. When Sugar insists that they run back to the hotel to tell Josephine all about her newfound millionaire, Jerry readily agrees, certain that Joe's disguise will be revealed. Instead, Joe, having moved quickly, is found soaking in the tub, as Josephine had said she would be doing, the bath bubbles concealing the fact that he is still wearing his beach attire. When Sugar assures them that Junior will attend the band's performance that night, Jerry once again hopes that Joe will not be able to be both Junior and Josephine at the same time and in the same place.

But that too will be managed by Joe. While Joe and Jerry are playing in the band that evening, Sugar receives a note from Junior (in a flower arrangement that had actually been sent to Daphne by Osgood) saying that he cannot attend the performance but will meet Sugar at the dock after the show to take her out to his yacht (which, of course, actually belongs to Osgood).

In the midst of this elaborate con game, Monroe presents one of her finest on-screen musical performances, a daring version of "I Wanna Be Loved by You." Monroe's dress (designed by Orry-Kelly, who won the film's only Academy Award for this achievement) features a low-slung décolletage and sheer bodice that, under certain lighting, practically disappears. The outfit is skillfully designed to emphasize Monroe's breasts. She sings her seductive number directly to the camera (and, hence, the viewer), even pointing a delicate finger at the camera when she sings the words, "by you."

The sequence on the yacht is a triumph of Joe's talent at deception. Having lured Sugar into the main cabin of the yacht for what she expects to be a romantic rendezvous, Joe informs her that, traumatized by his role in the accidental death of his former sweetheart, he has lost all sexual interest in women. He announces that if any woman could ever revive his libido, he would marry her. Sugar eagerly takes up the challenge and engages in passionate kissing and significant bodily contact with the supposedly sexually disabled Junior. Soft lighting and lush romantic music enhance the mood.

However, working with two of the most glamorous stars in Hollywood at the time, Wilder needed to keep the audience's focus on the comedy rather than voyeuristic thrills. He manages this trick brilliantly by interrupting the erotic sequence with crosscuts to scenes of Daphne and Osgood dancing the night away in what, in different circumstances, would be a passionate tango. Jack Lemmon's female impersonation reaches new heights in this scene, which, in its absurdity, manages to distract the film audience from the sexual excitement of watching Monroe seduce Curtis.

As a coda to all the sexual confusion, Joe returns to his hotel room to find Jerry celebrating because he has just received a wedding proposal—along with a diamond bracelet—from Osgood. He intends to take Osgood up on his offer and marry him "for security." Jerry's sexual masquerade has reached its logical conclusion. It is one example of a pattern that Gemunden points out in all of Jack Lemmon's roles in Wilder's films: "He has the greatest problems distinguishing where the self ends and its performance begins . . . because he falls in love with his masks."[12] On the other hand, Curtis's on-screen persona is too definitively masculine to ever convey any sense of sexual confusion in Joe. He remains committed to his heterosexuality and his realization of the genuine love he feels for Sugar. Confused or not, however, both men need to resolve their romantic situations.

Act 4: Deliverance, Revelation, and the "Perfect" Ending

Romantic resolution for Joe, and in some sense for Jerry, however, will coincide with the greatest threat on their lives. In the pattern of horrible coincidences that propel every farcical narrative, Spats Colombo and his entourage, followed closely by Officer Mulligan and his crew, arrive at the hotel in Miami for a mob convention. With the return of the mobsters and Mulligan, the pattern of violence and deception that dominated the first act of the film returns in this fourth act. The gangsters are once again gathering under false pretenses. Instead of the funeral service at Mozzarella's Funeral Parlor, they are attending a banquet for the "Friends of Italian Opera." In the midst of the speeches of the rival mob bosses, a gunman pops out of the elaborate cake on the table, and, in a barrage of automatic gunfire like the one that was used to kill Toothpick Charlie and the others in the Chicago garage, Colombo and his cohorts are assassinated. Joe and Jerry, who happen to be hiding under the banquet tables, have once again witnessed a gangland massacre and must run for their lives from another group of thugs and their syndicate boss, Little Bonaparte (Nehemiah Persoff). In a nice touch, at one point they manage to elude the killers by riding on the bottom shelf of a gurney, hidden by a long sheet that simultaneously covers them and Colombo's corpse.

In this convergence of death and desire, Joe discovers that his genuine love for Sugar has transformed him from a smooth-talking heel into a man with a conscience. When, still dressed in their Daphne and Josephine disguises, they encounter the mobsters in the hotel lobby and the elevator, Joe and Jerry decide to leave the hotel as quickly as possible. As they are frantically packing their suitcases, Joe feels the need to telephone Sugar to bid her good-bye. In an elaborate bit of double role-playing, Curtis (still dressed as Josephine but speaking on the telephone in the voice of Junior) spins another elaborate tale, telling Sugar that he must leave immediately to marry a Venezuelan oil mogul's daughter in a "corporate merger." Sugar, for her part, maintains her debutante identity as she replies that she will call her broker and instruct him to invest in Venezuelan oil.

However, Joe the fast-talker has clearly undergone a transformation far deeper than his previous incarnations. This time, unlike his previous use of lies to seduce women, he is fabricating a story to spare the feelings of a woman whom he actually has come to love. Discreetly slipping it under her hotel room door, he gives Sugar Jerry's diamond bracelet that was going to buy his and Jerry's financial freedom. Still wearing their female disguises, Joe and Jerry run out of the hotel. In the midst of their escape attempt, however, Joe overhears Sugar singing a melancholy ballad in the hotel ballroom. Risking his life, he runs up on stage to wipe away her tears, saying, "None of that, Sugar. No guy's worth it." He then kisses her, revealing to Little Bonaparte and the other mobsters in the audience that he's "no dame." Thus, two of the primary goals of farce-chases—pursuit of financial gain and escape from danger—have been sacrificed in this public profession of love. The kiss, meanwhile, signals to Sugar that "Josephine" is also "Junior." She races to join him and Jerry as they head to Osgood's yacht to live happily ever after.

The film's final section also rounds out Monroe's musical performances, which have been carefully designed within the four-act structure as a showpiece for the range of her talents. Absent from act 1, she makes her stunning entrance into the film at the beginning of act 2, the train ride section. While on the train escaping from her disappointing love affairs, she offers a bouncy little jazz number about "running wild," declaring that she, "don't need nobody." In act 3, after she meets her dream millionaire on the beach, she performs her seductive baby doll number, "I Wanna Be Loved by You." In act 4, feeling abandoned once again, she sings the soulful torch song, "I'm Through with Love." Each number exhibits a different facet of her iconic personality, moving from her character as a carefree adventurer in the sexual marketplace to a well-endowed and available temptress to, finally, a wounded victim of men's sexual irresponsibility.

The film's concluding moments are too famous to need much description; however, they should be recognized for their allusions to the film's earliest sequences. As Joe, Jerry, Osgood, and Sugar all jump into the speedboat that will take them to the yacht for their escape, viewers get to enjoy two final arguments conducted by the schemer-worrier pair. Oddly enough, both Joe and Jerry are, for once, speaking the truth and making sense, but common sense does not win the day. Joe, whom the audience first saw as the master of verbal persuasion, now attempts to prevent Sugar from following him, accurately describing himself as a "liar and a phony, a saxophone player, one of those no-goodniks you keep running away from." Sugar responds, almost mocking his glibness, saying, "That's right. Pour it on. Talk me out of it," and she effectively ends the discussion with her best rhetorical device, a passionate kiss. In this crucial moment, Joe the fast-talker loses the argument. Jerry, who had begun the film nervously arguing against all of Joe's unlikely schemes, once again offers a list of objections to Osgood's far more absurd proposal of marriage. When, in desperation, Jerry finally reveals the information that should logically settle the matter—the fact that he is a man—Osgood's absurdist response ends the conversation as effectively as Sugar's kiss. Grinning and hopelessly in love, Osgood replies with the ultimate rationale for all comedy, saying "Nobody's perfect."

The film's conclusion completes the farcical action quite satisfactorily. Joe and Jerry escape death. Joe and Sugar find true love. Also, thanks to the diamond bracelet that Sugar is conveniently wearing as she boards the boat, combined with Jerry's continued relationship (however unusual) with Osgood, they have all achieved some financial security. Little Bonaparte may still want to chase Joe and Jerry down, but for now the boys seem to be out of harm's way. Maybe nothing or "nobody" is perfect, but this comic masterpiece, in its carefully constructed design of all its farcical action, comes awfully close.

A Sampling of Sex Farces

The Seven Year Itch (1955)
The World of Henry Orient (1964)
Kiss Me, Stupid (1964)
Bob & Carol & Ted & Alice (1969)
Shampoo (1975)
10 (1979)
Porky's (1982)
There's Something about Mary (1998)
American Pie (1999)
What Happens in Vegas (2008)

Notes

1. Anthony Lane, "Boys Will Be Girls," *New Yorker*, October 22, 2001, p. 72.

2. Gerd Gemunden, *A Foreign Affair: Billy Wilder's American Films* (New York: Berghan Books, 2008), 103.

3. Neil Sinyard and Adrian Tucker, *Journey Down Sunset Boulevard: The Films of Billy Wilder* (Ryed, Isle of Wight: BCW Publishing, 1979), 215.

4. Daniel Lieberfeld and Judith Sanders, "Comedy and Identity in *Some Like It Hot.*" *Journal of Popular Film and Television*, vol. 26, no. 3 (Fall 1998): 130.

5. Gemunden, *A Foreign Affair*, 102.

6. Lieberfeld and Sanders, "Comedy and Identity in *Some Like It Hot*," 130.

7. Gemunden, *A Foreign Affair*, 118.

8. Patrice Petro, "Legacies of Weimar Cinema." In *Cinema and Modernity*, Murray Pomerance, ed. (Piscataway, N.J.: Rutgers University Press, 2006), 251.

9. Lieberfeld and Sanders, "Comedy and Identity in *Some Like It Hot*," 132.

10. Lieberfeld and Sanders, "Comedy and Identity in *Some Like It Hot*," 132.

11. Quoted in Charlotte Chandler, *Nobody's Perfect: Billy Wilder, a Personal Biography* (New York: Simon & Schuster, 2002), 208.

12. Gemunden, *A Foreign Affair*, 108.

CHAPTER 6

Satire

DR. STRANGELOVE OR: HOW I LEARNED TO STOP WORRYING AND LOVE THE BOMB (1964)

Satire employs humor, often quite sophisticated, to attack what its author considers stupid or immoral. Fortunately, every generation in human history has provided enough stupidity and immorality for such attacks, presented in literary or dramatic modes. Athens had the plays of Aristophanes; Roman culture produced the poets Horace and Juvenal. Over the centuries, satirical comedy has been produced by some of Europe's most renowned authors of their day: One thinks of Geoffrey Chaucer, Giovanni Boccaccio, François Rabelais, Desiderius Erasmus, and even the saintly Thomas More. The Enlightenment's rediscovery of the devastating power of the pen produced some of the best literature of the seventeenth and eighteenth centuries with the plays of Moliere, Oliver Goldsmith, and Richard Sheridan; the novels of Miguel de Cervantes and Daniel Defoe; and the caustic essays and verse of John Dryden, Alexander Pope, Jonathan Swift, Samuel Johnson, and other wits inhabiting the coffeehouses of London. America brought forth the likes of Mark Twain, Ambrose Bierce, H. L. Mencken, Sinclair Lewis, Dorothy Parker, Joseph Heller, Kurt Vonnegut, and others.

Until the twentieth century, the locus of satire was limited to print and theater. The arrival of motion pictures added new weapons. The wit and bile of language and the portrayal of bizarre characters in the theater could be enhanced with the advantages of close-ups, camera angles, lighting, framing, editing, and other cinematic techniques. Stanley Kubrick's 1964 hit movie *Dr. Strangelove or: How I Learned to Stop Worrying and Love the Bomb* brilliantly demonstrates the potential of film to use language, characters, settings, and camera work to create a classic work of modern satire.

The traditional analysis of satire has usually divided the genre into two types. One approach is labeled Horatian, in tribute to the first-century Roman poet Horace, whose satires were gentle, lighthearted reminders to his countrymen of their failure to exhibit the virtuousness of the Roman Republic's ideals.

Dr. Strangelove (Peter Sellers) explains to the president and his advisers the intricacies of worldwide nuclear destruction in *Dr. Strangelove or: How I Learned to Stop Worrying and Love the Bomb* (1964).

He ridicules the social climbers, fortune hunters, bad poets, and sycophants in his upper-class circle, as well as the constant instances of envy, lust, avarice, gluttony, drunkenness, and other luxurious behavior; however, his attacks are "never on famous individuals, but instead on types, sometimes named, sometimes not," and, with his frequent retreats into self-deprecating humor, the "poet uses this stance to create a disarming position from which to launch his criticisms of Roman morals and Roman society."[1] As a result, the slings and arrows of such mild criticism were easily avoided, causing a bit of guilt and embarrassment but no real change.

The more aggressive satire composed approximately 100 years later by the poet Juvenal employed scorn, ridicule, and a sense of outrage in a serious attempt to improve the behavior of his fellow Roman citizens and put an end to their stupidity or immorality. Juvenalian satire mainly railed against the vices of the upper classes of Roman society for their marital infidelity and other sexual misconduct, greed, social climbing, political plots, hypocrisy, and the generally lascivious and luxurious behavior that Horace had also attacked, but it also named names.[2] Some historians claim that Juvenal was, in fact, so critical of the mores of the time that at one point he was exiled from Rome. This style of angry satire is eloquently memorialized by the inscription on Jonathan Swift's tomb in St. Patrick's Cathedral in Dublin, which describes it as a place "where fierce indignation can no longer lacerate the heart."

More current examples of both of these types can be found in the rich supply of late-night television show material. Horatian satire can be found in the stand-up routines of most late-night hosts. *Saturday Night Live* typically pokes fun at the White House and various political figures or newsmakers in its opening sketch and "Weekend Update" segments, usually mocking personal flaws (Gerald Ford's clumsiness, Ronald Reagan's pompadour, Bill Clinton's fondness for junk food, Barack Obama's ears) rather than challenging any of their controversial foreign or domestic policies. The jokes and sketches are not usually intended to drive these people out of office; in fact, the writers relish these flaws as comic inspiration. *The Daily Show with Jon Stewart* and its spin-off, *The Colbert Report*, however, actually do express disapproval of the objects of their humor, expressing anger or frustration, and in Colbert's case, in his persona as a right-wing pundit, with a satirical irony matching Jonathan Swift's "A Modest Proposal" (1729) or Mark Twain's "The War Prayer" (1916). Colbert's performance at the 2006 White House Correspondents' Dinner illustrates the difference between the two types of satire. When Colbert was invited, it was expected that he would follow in the tradition of speakers over the years who have gently spoofed or poked fun at the president. Instead, Colbert, employing his on-air Republican identity, defended President George W. Bush; however, with his ironic compliments, he offered a harsh critique of the man who was sitting only a few feet away from him. At one point, he explained his devotion to "my hero" George W. Bush because he is "steady. . . . He believes the same thing Wednesday that he believed on Monday, no matter what happened Tuesday." He offered his words of mock consolation to the president, urging him to "pay no attention" to his current approval rating of 32 percent. While one could say that 68 percent of the country disapproved of the job President Bush was doing, Colbert noted that the polls also showed that "68 percent approve of the job he is *not* doing." Needless to say, Colbert received a major amount of criticism for not playing by the rules.

Kubrick's *Dr. Strangelove* falls definitively into the Juvenalian camp, angrily attacking America's Cold War paranoia, its politicians' secrecy and impotent diplomacy, and its military leaders' fascination with weaponry and technology as machismo run amuck. It also hopes to expose everyone's "listless acquiescence to the possibility—in fact, the increased probability—of nuclear war."[3]

The screenplay, credited to Kubrick, Terry Southern, and Peter George, began as a serious adaptation of a suspense novel written by George, a former RAF navigator, published in the United Kingdom with the title *Two Hours to Doom* in 1958 (under the pseudonym Peter Bryant), and the next year in the United States with a new title, *Red Dawn*. The novel told the story of an "insane U.S. Air Force general who, learning that he is suffering from a fatal disease, orders an unprovoked attack against Russia, urging Washington to follow his lead and wipe out the Soviet Union."[4] In the novel, with B-52 bombers in the air, the governments of the United States and Soviet Union end up working together to ensure that the planes do not reach their destination. But no such happy ending occurs in Kubrick's film. Instead, as Kubrick worked on the adaptation, he gradually came to realize that a "more truthful" story could be told in a comic mode:

> I started work on the screenplay with every intention of making the film a serious treatment of the problems of accidental nuclear war. As I kept trying to imagine the way in which things would really happen, ideas kept coming to me [that] I would discard because they were so ludicrous. I kept saying to myself, "I can't do that—people will laugh." But after a month or so I began to realize that all the things I was throwing out were the things [that] were most truthful. After all, what could be more absurd than the very idea of two mega powers willing to wipe out all human life because of an accident?[5]

Thus a darkly comic narrative emerged, which, in its comic portrayal of America's fear of the Soviet threat and the possibility of nuclear disaster, also satirizes Hollywood's serious treatment of these topics. It begins with the same premise as its novelistic source: The insanely paranoid General Jack D. Ripper (Sterling Hayden), convinced that the communists are attempting to contaminate America's water supply, orders the B-52 bombers flying out of Burpleson Air Force Base to drop nuclear bombs inside the Soviet Union. Once the planes are airborne, the mission can be aborted only with the use of recall codes known only to Ripper. Captain Lionel Mandrake (Peter Sellers), an RAF officer on loan to the U.S. Air Force as part of an "officers' exchange program," pleads with Ripper to recall the aircraft, but Ripper refuses.

When President Merkin Muffley (Sellers again) hears of this development, he convenes his military cabinet for an emergency meeting in the Pentagon War Room, where the hawkish General "Buck" Turgidson (George C. Scott) fervently argues in favor of the attack. Instead, President Muffley orders the army to attack Burpleson Air Force Base, uses the War Room's emergency hotline to warn the Soviet premier of the impending attack, and agrees to a plan to have the B-52s shot down before they can drop their nuclear payload. This becomes all the more urgent when the Russian ambassador, Alexi de Sadesky (Peter Bull), who has been invited to the meeting despite Turgidson's objections, informs them of the Soviets' "doomsday machine," a device designed to trigger automatically in the event of a nuclear attack and set off a chain reaction that will wipe out all life on the planet.

Mandrake finally figures out the recall code and relays it to President Muffley, who manages to recall all but one of the bombers. The lone aircraft, named "The Leper Colony" and piloted by the Texan major T. J. "King" Kong (Slim Pickens), continues toward its target. Back in the War Room, the president's scientific adviser, a wheelchair-bound ex-Nazi named Dr. Strangelove (Sellers yet again) proposes a plan to save a remnant of U.S. citizens (including, of course, the members of the War Room cabinet) by placing them in underground mineshafts. Before this matter can be acted upon, however, the lone aircraft reaches its target and drops a fifty-megaton nuclear bomb, triggering the doomsday machine and destroying the world. So much for the happy ending.

While little of this synopsis suggests much humor, other than pure lunacy and absurdity, Kubrick infuses the narrative with the interaction of several comic motifs, creating what Norman Kagan describes a "nightmare comedy using the lethal paradoxes of accidental war" and portraying almost everyone as "grotesques" or "people trying to behave normally in the middle of a nightmare."[6] Robert Brustein dubs the film a "nightmare farce" designed to express "outrage against the malevolence of officialdom."[7] David Hughes observes, "From the opening shot to the explosive climax, *Dr. Strangelove* is a relentlessly inventive combination of satirical didacticism, political polemic, and hysterical humor," quoting Pauline Kael's opinion that *Dr. Strangelove* "ushered in a new era of satire."[8] Randy Rasmussen's extensive critique of the film begins by describing it as a "satiric odyssey through the labyrinth of one of modern civilization's most elaborate creations: military deterrence in the nuclear age."[9]

Kubrick, clearly protesting the U.S. military's standard policies, had been concerned with the nuclear arms race for quite a while before making the film. Kagan reports that Kubrick had read more than seventy books on the subject of nuclear combat and control, while also subscribing to *Aviation Week* and the *Bulletin of the Atomic Sciences*.[10] Thomas Allen Nelson comments that *Dr. Strangelove* "merely exaggerates and externalizes the satiric irony" of Kubrick's 1957 antiwar drama *Paths of Glory*.[11] U.S. foreign policy and Cold War military strategy were both built on the possibility of nuclear war and the Soviet Union's threats. Hughes offers a concise description of the period's crises and policies, writing the following:

> The Cuban missile crisis, in which Kennedy and Khrushchev played a dangerous game of nuclear brinksmanship until the Russian premier agreed to withdraw Soviet missiles from bases in Cuba, had occurred just two years earlier. As part of America's defense strategy, fully laden nuclear bombers were flown daily toward Russian targets, instructed to continue their missions until the recall code at their "fail safe" points.[12]

The anti-Soviet Union posture of Washington had been amply demonstrated in the 1960 Kennedy–Nixon campaign debates and in President John F. Kennedy's 1960 inaugural address. The fact that Kennedy's assassin, Lee Harvey Oswald, had spent some time in the Soviet Union and was married to a Russian woman enhanced American distrust of the Soviet Union. The House Un-American Activities Committee, although its influence was fading, was still active in the 1960s, serving subpoenas to Jerry Rubin, Abbie Hoffman, and other political activists in the mid-1960s as possible communist agents.

Even Hollywood highlighted the Soviet threat and possibilities of nuclear annihilation. The 1959 film *On the Beach*, a major studio release directed by the distinguished Stanley Kramer and featuring film stars Gregory Peck and Ava Gardner, presented a picture of life on earth in the aftermath of a nuclear war, presumably between the United States and the Soviet Union. The film's apocalyptic narrative shows the cities of San Diego and San Francisco deserted after the nuclear disaster. Coincidentally, the story was set in 1964. In *Dr. No* (1962), the first of the hugely popular series of James Bond movies, the villain planned to destroy a U.S. moon rocket with a nuclear weapon. The second film, *From Russia with Love* (1963), revolves around Bond's search for a decoding machine that can access Russian state secrets. With such steady Hollywood messages, the Soviet threat and the dangers of nuclear weapons figured prominently in the public mind of 1964 America.

Meanwhile, the Sidney Lumet film *Fail-Safe* (1964) had finished production and was ready for release at the same time as *Dr. Strangelove*, with a plot uncannily similar to Kubrick's film. In Lumet's version, a technical malfunction in the Pentagon's strategic control system causes an erroneous order to be sent to a B-58 bomber squadron on a routine training mission. The pilots are ordered to fly beyond their fail-safe distances to attack targets in the Soviet Union. To convince the Soviets that this was a mistake, the president, played by all-American Henry Fonda, orders the Strategic Air Command to help the enemy shoot down the U.S. planes. Kubrick had, in fact, initiated a plagiarism suit against *Fail-Safe's* producers and others in 1963, claiming that both had copied George's book. Columbia Pictures, which was distributing both films, agreed to hold the release of *Fail-Safe* until December, ten months after *Dr. Strangelove. Dr. Strangelove* turned out to be Columbia Pictures' biggest box-office success for 1964.[13] *Fail-Safe*, its serious theme undermined by Kubrick's successful satire, did not do as well.

Clearly, the time was ripe for another take on the nuclear conflict between the two superpowers. A comic critique of the entire military system and its nuclear strategy could focus on several points of its target. As Brustein observes, "*Dr. Strangelove* is a satire not only on nuclear war and warriors, but also on scientists, militarists, military intellectuals, diplomats, statesmen—all those, in short, whose profession is to think about the unthinkable."[14] The largest amount of scorn is directed toward the military leadership as irresponsibly and obsessively aggressive, with generals Ripper and Turgidson as prime examples. Ripper first appears as a paranoid liar and authority figure turned control freak. He is usually shown in a low-angle shot with strong lighting on his face from the fluorescent fixture above his desk and a totally black background, almost always munching on his phallic cigar. The angle gets lower and the shot of his face progressively closer during the course of the film, but the cigar stays in place throughout his speeches. Even when Ripper is shown from the back, the smoke from his cigar is voluminous.

Ripper's bizarre scheme begins with a lie, telling his second in command, Captain Mandrake, that it "looks like we're in a shooting war" initiated by the Soviet Union, claiming that he received this information from the Red Phone. He orders the base to be shut down and all radios confiscated, thus cutting off any communication from the outside. He ignores Mandrake's information that there does not seem to be any crisis. Ripper instructs the troops guarding the base to "trust no one" and to "shoot first and ask questions later." Obsessed with the need to control, he boasts that he is the only person who knows the recall code and refuses to share it with Mandrake. He locks Mandrake in the office and finally threatens him with a gun. He then reveals his opposition to "communist infiltration, indoctrination, and subversion," culminating in his belief in an "international communist conspiracy to sap and purify all our precious bodily fluids" through the fluoridation of our water supply. He later reveals that he first detected the plot when he suffered a bout of impotence, and he has subsequently avoided women, since he understands that they are all out to "seek our life essence." Jason Sperb, in his analysis of *Dr. Strangelove* as an "aggressive clashing of conflicting narrative constructions," identifies Ripper's paranoid stories as his attempts to gain "absolute narrative order and control over his environment" and "overcompensate for experiences he clearly cannot otherwise come to terms with."[15] Finally, when Ripper realizes that the men defending Burpleson have surrendered, he imagines, in his paranoia, how the invading soldiers will surely torture him. He goes into the bathroom and kills himself with his handgun, controlling even his own death. The authoritative tone of his speeches and his conversation with Mandrake might be reassuring in other contexts, but, in this case, his use of military jargon transforms military readiness and vigilance into paranoia.

Turgidson also makes use of military language to explain the situation to the president. In contrast to Ripper's paranoia, however, Turgidson's tone varies from a matter-of-fact description of all the automatic procedures that go into operation once Code R is initiated to macho enthusiasm when he describes the effectiveness of the U.S. Air Force. He is anything but paranoid. Nelson describes him as "blockheaded," saying the following:

> He chomps down on his chewing gum like a cud, prowls around the War Room with the same grunting intensity he employs in the bedroom, and obscures nuclear war through a mixture of military euphemisms and homespun verbosity (destroying the Russians becomes "catching them with their pants down," and causing the deaths of 20 million Americans as "getting our hair mussed").[16]

Alexander Walker describes Turgidson's remarks as "almost a précis of what has been published in military journals, even to euphemisms."[17]

Turgidson's first "appearance" in the film is actually off-screen, his voice coming from his bathroom as he is taking a break from his lovemaking with Miss Scott (Tracy Reed), his "secretary" who also moonlights as a Playboy centerfold. Kubrick has said, "Confront a man in his office with a nuclear alarm, and you have a documentary. If the news reaches him in his living room, you have a tragedy. If it catches him in the lavatory, the result is comedy."[18] His telephone rings, and Miss Scott gets his permission to answer it. Kagan declares, "What follows is a small masterpiece, the executive secretary running interference in the ultimate emergency."[19] For a minute or so, Miss Scott's dialogue varies from her soft conversation with the caller, a Colonel Buttridge (whom Miss Scott addresses in intimate tones as "Freddy") and her loud relaying of the colonel's message to Turgidson in the bathroom. Once Turgidson comes to the phone, his response to the news that Plan R has gone into operation is filled with military clichés and a casual attitude that he continues to employ throughout the film: "What's cookin' on the threat board? . . . Tell you what you'd better do, old buddy. You give Elmo and Charlie a blast and bump everything up to condition Red." Hanging up the phone, he announces to Miss Scott that he needs to "mosey down to the War Room."

Once in the War Room, Turgidson informs President Muffley of the order to retaliate against Russia in what Kagan describes as a "calm, disinterested, yet vaguely approving voice."[20] He seems determined to treat Plan R as a viable operation, with measurable results in terms of enemy destruction, referring to their options as "two admittedly *regrettable* but nevertheless *distinguishable* postwar environments—one where you got 20 million people killed, and the other where you got 150 million people killed." He departs from his professional, matter-of-fact remarks only rarely in the film. He objects angrily when he is told that the president has invited Russian ambassador de Sadesky into the War Room, where, as Turgidson observes, the "lousy Commie punk" will see everything. He'll see the Big Board!" He switches into a whispered tone in his telephone conversation with Miss Scott when, contrary to his orders, she calls him in the War Room. And he displays an ironic enthusiasm when he is asked if the one plane that has not been recalled can accomplish its bombing mission even if it is damaged, saying, "If the pilot's good—I mean really sharp—well, he can barrel that baby in so low, you just got to see it sometimes! A real big plane like a B-52, its jets' exhaust frying chickens in the barnyard." Only then does he realize that the success of that plane's mission will set off the doomsday machine, which will destroy all human and animal life on the planet, and he stares silently in acknowledgment of the consequences of the situation. Throughout the film, Scott employs facial grimaces, wide-eyed reactions, and bizarre gestures to display how such dedication to military superiority can turn into madness.

Meanwhile, President Muffley tries to deal with the insanity of Turgidson and others as rationally as possible. Many consider Sellers's portrayal of the president to be based on Adlai Stevenson, whose "egghead" persona helped him to lose both the 1952 and 1956 presidential elections to General Dwight Eisenhower but was an asset in his role as U.S. ambassador to the United Nations during the time of the film's release. Muffley's efforts to deal with the situation by rational means are frustrated by the rest of the major players. He first seeks to contact General Ripper, who has blocked all incoming communication. He tries to fathom the depth of the danger by gathering information about Plan R from Turgidson. He invites de Sadesky into the War Room; engages in a man-to-man telephone conversation with the Russian premier, Dmitri Kissov; and finally consults with Dr. Strangelove, all to no avail. Muffley is surrounded by liars and lunatics. Ripper is psychotic, Turgidson is manic, the Russian ambassador is using the opportunity to photograph the War Room and its charts, Kissov is drunk, and Dr. Strangelove is sadistic.

The mild-mannered president's calm, meanwhile, borders on the naive and ineffectual. He seems uninformed about much of the military's nuclear strategy, and his diplomatic conversation with Kissov, with whom he is on a first-name basis, is a masterpiece of understatement not unlike an attempt to break bad news to a child:

> You know how we've always talked about the possibility of something going wrong with the bomb . . . the bomb, Dmitri. . . . Well, now what happened is, one of our base commanders, he had a sort of, well, he went a little funny in the head. . . . And, uh, he went and did a silly thing. . . . He ordered his planes . . . to attack your country.

Muffley describes the telephone contact as a "friendly call," which turns into something like a lover's quarrel:

> Well, listen, how do you think I feel about it? Can you imagine how I feel about it, Dmitri? . . . I'm very sorry. Alright! You're sorrier than I am. . . . I am as sorry as you are, Dmitri. Don't say that you are more sorry. . . . I am capable of being just as sorry as you are.

Muffley's rational approach becomes almost as grotesque as the attitudes of Ripper and Turgidson. As Walker observes, "By his very serious brand of sanity, the president seems as removed from reality as the others," best revealed in his remark when he breaks up a fight between Turgidson and the Russian ambassador by declaring, "Gentlemen, you can't fight in here. This is the War Room."[21]

Dr. Strangelove appears briefly approximately two-thirds of the way through the film but dominates its last five minutes. When he is introduced as the director of military research and development, he praises the automatic nature of the nuclear attack system, which "rules out human meddling." His Germanic accent, confinement to a wheelchair, dark glasses, and incapacitated left arm present him as a monster of human intelligence and aggression. Rasmussen describes his behavior at his first appearance as a "physically frail, emotionally repressed individual who bides his time until circumstances are more congenial to the fulfillment of his desires."[22] He catalogs the activity of Strangelove's hand as it "becomes increasingly unruly. . . . Refusing to release its grip on a chemical chart, periodically jutting out in an inappropriate Nazi salute, turning his wheelchair and therefore him away from the audience, punching him in the chin, rising out of his lap like a rampant penis, and finally trying to strangle him."[23]

Sellers has claimed that the idea of this rebellious gloved hand came from his own improvisation, saying that he began to think "that the hand was a Nazi while the rest of him had made the compromise to live in America. That idea just came to me—it was completely spontaneous."[24] Walker further analyzes the nature of the hand as a "piece of mechanism in collusion with all the other mechanism that rebels against its creators in the film."[25]

Strangelove's madness dominates the film's final scenario. At that point, the nuclear bomb has exploded. The War Room crowd may or may not be aware of this eventuality, but, in any case, they enthusiastically embrace Strangelove's strategy for the preservation of a "nucleus of human specimens." He offers his plan for sending some people down into mineshafts, where the nuclear fallout cannot penetrate, estimating that they will need to stay there for 100 years. Nuclear reactors will provide power, greenhouses will maintain plant life, and animals could be bred and slaughtered. (Strangelove emphasizes the word *slaughtered*, which he clearly enjoys contemplating.) The choice of mineshaft inhabitants could be made by a computer that would be "set and programmed to accept factors from youth, sexual fertility, intelligence, and a cross-section of necessary skills," along with "our top government and military men." The latter group would, of course, include the very men in the War Room who are listening to this extreme example of social planning, all too similar to the Nazi dream of an Aryan nation. Indeed, twice during his narrative his right arm rises in a Nazi salute.

Highlighting the need for the mineshaft inhabitants to "breed prodigiously," Strangelove's plan includes a ratio of ten females to each male; furthermore, the "women will have to be selected for their sexual characteristics, which will have to be of a highly stimulating nature." Sexual relations are reduced to a zoological level in this self-serving plan for the computer-driven survival of the human species. The film ends as Strangelove rises from his wheelchair. His articulation of his plan has somehow empowered him. In the last line of the film's dialogue, Strangelove shouts "Mein Führer! I can walk!" Thus, the dream that Hitler failed to accomplish would be achieved by his ardent admirer. Unfortunately, time has clearly run out, and before the plan can get under way, the War Room personnel are annihilated, along with the rest of all human and animal life on the planet by the nuclear explosions already in progress as they speak.

No less important to the satire is the fact that the captain of the plane that will eventually deliver the fatal nuclear payload, "King" Kong, is a Texas-bred example of the sort of military discipline and obedience to orders that characterized the Nazi regime and was beginning to reappear in the "silent majority" of love-it-or-leave-it Americans unquestioningly supporting U.S. involvement in Southeast Asia. Never second-guessing the orders he has been given, Kong proceeds to follow all the procedures for a nuclear air strike outlined in his manual. In a parody of the many speeches to the troops in World War II movies, Kong attempts to inspire his crew by calling upon them to "remember one thing—the folks back home are counting on you. And, by golly, we ain't about to let them down." In a deeper satirical mode, his speech becomes a parody of Shakespeare's

Prince Hal's appeal to honor to his troops before the battle of Agincourt by predicting that "you're all in line for some important promotions and citations when this thing's over with." Throughout the rest of the film, Kong leads the crew through the routine of aerial warfare, the control of their craft after it is struck by a missile, and finally the hands-on unlocking of the bomb door to release the nuclear payload. Replacing his helmet with a cowboy hat, he acts out his own "private drama with an Old West showdown with civilization."[26]

At first, a similar dedication to military procedures is displayed by Mandrake as he begins to follow Ripper's orders to shut down the communications to and from Burpleson Air Force Base, but, soon realizing that there is no Soviet attack, he tries to reason with his commanding officer to issue a recall order to stop the planes. When Ripper refuses to do so, Mandrake attempts to use his position as executive officer to recall the planes himself, but he is prevented from doing so by Ripper, who locks them both in his office. Although he soon realizes that Ripper is insane, Mandrake continues as calmly as possible in his attempts to convince Ripper to give him the recall code that only Ripper knows. He humors Ripper as he listens to the madman's theory about the Soviet plan to "impurify our precious bodily fluids" by fluoridating the nation's water supply, as he assists Ripper's defense of the base with a machine gun, and as he witnesses Ripper's suicide.

Mandrake's British decorum and understated language serve as a last bastion of sanity against the terror of his absurd situation, but that all crumbles when, after Ripper's suicide, the office door is opened by a member of the "invading army," Colonel "Bat" Guano (Keenan Wynn). Mandrake abandons all of his military decorum, resorting to foul language, insults, and threats in his efforts to call the White House with the numbers of the recall code, which he has managed to decipher. His use of a public pay telephone is hampered by the suspicions of Guano, his lack of the proper change to place the call, and the hesitation of Guano to fire at a Coke machine in the hallway to release the needed coins. Guano's attitude represents both Kong's blind following of orders and, in his suspicion of Mandrake, the paranoia of Ripper and Turgidson.

While the grotesque characters could suffice to create a powerful satire, Kubrick also makes use of visual symbols, settings, and camera angles to reinforce his critique. The famous opening sequence sets the tone with its presentation of an in-flight refueling procedure performed to the tune of "Try a Little Tenderness." The insertion of the top plane's tubular delivery system into the body of the plane below it not only introduces the sexual motif that persists throughout the film, but it also hints ironically at the slogan that was beginning to represent the antiwar movement at the time: "Make love, not war."

There are only four main settings in the film. The first one is Burpleson Air Force Base, presented in the darkness of the night, broken only by the lights of the landing field and the arriving plane. The scene quickly switches to the base command center, where Captain Lionel Mandrake works in an "uncluttered, evenly lit realm of computers, graphs, maps, and uniformed personnel calmly going about their appointed, coordinated tasks."[27] The next scene is set in Ripper's office, which is lit only by a large fluorescent light fixture above his desk. Nelson observes that the sharp focus and depth of field exaggerate its low ceiling and horizontal geometry. He writes, "Kubrick alternates between medium shots that place Ripper within the symmetry of flanked compositions and low-angle close-ups that blur out surrounding space and visually reinforce the madman's verbal muddle."[28] The base's motto, "Peace Is Our Profession," figures prominently in the background.

The setting of the next sequence is the interior of Kong's B-52 bomber. It is a dark space lit only by several narrowly focused spotlights but mainly composed of shadows and filmed with handheld cameras. The crew of the plane is surrounded by a massive amount of dials and switches, making for an extremely crowded space, with the machinery dominating the scene. The close-ups of the captain and the rest of the crew, along with the steady hum of the plane's engines, reinforce the sense of confinement. Much time is spent on close-up views of the cockpit's elaborate control panel. From the moment that Kong trades in his helmet for his Stetson, each sequence inside the plane or in the air is accompanied by music from the ballad "When Johnny Comes Marching Home." The song's original lyrics, which describe a severely wounded soldier returning from war, would offer the film's viewers another satirical message if they were sung, but they are not.

The film's third sequence, set in Turgidson's bedroom, first focuses on the bed on which Miss Scott lies under a sunlamp. The walls are all mirrored and reflect the various lamps in the room. Except for the brief sequence in Burpleson's computer room, where Mandrake works, this is the only scene in the film that is brightly lit. The only action in the scene is the telephone conversation informing Turgidson of the Plan B orders and summoning him to the War Room; however, with Miss Scott in her bikini and Turgidson in his Hawaiian shirt opened to reveal his hairy torso, the mood of the scene is slightly sensual and serves as the film's only appearance of a woman in the narrative. It is the last depiction of any activity other than military and diplomatic involvement, and Turgidson's parting promise to return to his bedroom and Miss Scott is never fulfilled.

Finally, the last of the four setting shows the War Room. The largest percentage of the film takes place in this setting. Like most of the other settings, the edges of the scene are pitch black in contrast to the bright fluorescent lighting above the massive round table, where the majority of the president's advisers occupy their seats but never speak, resembling automatons as mechanical as the B-52's equipment. The room is dominated by the "Big Board" covering an entire wall, showing the position of all the targets in Russia and tracking the progress of all the U.S. planes toward those targets. The speakers, especially Turgidson, are often shown in semidarkness, or, in the case of Strangelove, lurking in the darkness of the room, away from the brightly lit table. There is a large ray of light emanating from an unknown source that beams behind the president and his aides. The camera frequently shows the entire room, often with a high-angle shot showing the entire conference table and the advisers, but most of the time the camera focuses on either Muffley or Turgidson in their debate over military strategy.

Underlying the grotesque characters, absurdist dialogue, and gloomy settings, a motif of sexuality pervades the film, suggesting that nuclear warfare is inspired by the erotic impulse that is not always satisfied in these men's personal lives. The opening sequence portrays the mechanical intercourse involved in the refueling of a plane in flight. The über-male Turgidson promises to return to his lady friend as soon as possible to "blast off." Ripper reveals that his theory about the need to protect our "precious bodily fluids" arose from his failure to perform sexually. The first appearance of Kong shows him reading a *Playboy* magazine (with Miss Scott as the centerfold). The survival kit that is given to each crew member contains prophylactics, lipstick, and a pair of nylon stockings meant to come in handy when the boys land in enemy territory. The nuclear bomb is certainly phallic. And finally, Strangelove's survival scenario includes the hope that the survivors will "breed prodigiously" with the help of women chosen for their "sexual characteristics."

The names of the three major characters continue to express the sexual substratum of the narrative. Jack D. Ripper is, of course, a reference to the notorious British killer of prostitutes; "Buck" Turgidson's name suggests the male of the species, as well as a certain turgid swelling of the male organ in preparation for sexual activity; and Merkin Muffley's name is composed of slang words for female genitalia, which might explain his sissified lack of enthusiasm for warfare. The name of British executive officer Lionel Mandrake derives from the plant that in many cultures has been considered an aphrodisiac, with powers to incite sexual desire and increase male potency and female fertility, suggesting a certain bisexuality. The Soviet premier is named Dmitri Kissov, a term of derision that is mildly sexual. The Russian ambassador Alexi de Sadesky's name recalls Marquis de Sade and his fascination with power and punishment. Major T. J. "King" Kong's nickname conjures up images of the primitive ape threatening to violate the virginal heroine. Dr. Strangelove's name itself may be the mildest of all in merely suggesting that his sexuality is unusual, while his description of life in the mineshafts for the survivors of the nuclear destruction delights in the prospect of "prodigious" sexual activity. Even Colonel "Bat" Guano, who hinders Mandrake from calling the president, accuses the slightly effete British officer of being "some kind of deviated pervert" who is organizing "some kind of mutiny of perverts." The colonel's name, of course, is scatological. Even the bombs that are dropped at the end of the film have sexual messages handwritten on them: "Dear John" on one bomb suggests the breakup of a heterosexual romance, while "Hi There" on another hints at some homosexual flirtation.

Considerable activity also illustrates the sexualization of the entire endeavor. The description of the U.S. aircrafts' "penetration" of enemy territory ties in with Turgidson's suggestion at one point that a surprise attack on the Russians would catch them "with their pants down." The phallic implications of Ripper's large cigar at the beginning of the film are repeated in the image of a phallic weapon being dropped on the Russians, with Kong riding it, waving his cowboy hat, and shouting out in triumphant whoops as if he were on a bucking bronco at a Texas rodeo. The entire film is an overwhelming testimony to nuclear warfare as the male sex drive gone haywire. Female sexual desire, of course, is absent from the picture completely.

A second motif throughout the film is the fascination with technology, which eventually morphs into a complete helplessness in the face of its automatic performance. Almost every aspect of Bergson's analysis of comedy as the presentation of a human body turned into a machine is exemplified in the narrative.[29] Ripper's orders to shut down all of Burpleson's communication with the outside world highlight the dependence of everyone on machines and their helplessness when the machines are not functioning properly. His initiation of Plan B produces automatic behavior on the part of the airplane personnel, and his refusal to share the recall code with Mandrake reinforces the power of technology over any human activity. Mandrake, who in his initial appearance in the film is surrounded by the giant machines in the computer room, at first attempts to obey Ripper's orders and follow standard operating procedure. Even his decision to countermand Ripper's instructions is presented as his rightful duty as chief executive officer. Once he realizes the extent of Ripper's psychosis, however, he struggles to insert some humanity and rationality into the crisis. When he finally ascertains the recall code, his attempts to contact the White House are frustrated by the telephone's irrefutable insistence on correct change for a long-distance call. The long-distance operator, the potentially human element in the transaction, is as inflexible an automaton as the telephone itself. When Mandrake insists that Guano shoot the Coke machine in the hallway to acquire correct change for the telephone, Guano at first refuses to do so, since his ingrained respect for authority carries over into the threat of having to answer to the Coca-Cola Company. In this one instance, however, human behavior defeats machinery when Mandrake succeeds in contacting the president, who is then able to use the recall code.

In the B-52, the crew moves into action that is just as automatic as the machinery, with only one crew member casting any doubt on the validity of the Plan R signal. As they proceed to follow the procedures outlined in their attack profile and engage in what Kong describes as "nuclear combat toe-to-toe with the Russkies," their mechanical obedience to orders illustrates the danger of military discipline when controlled by a madman.

In the War Room, the presidential advisers are seated in a highly organized pattern around the perfectly circular table, lit by the steady, unblinking fluorescent lighting above them, and, in their uniforms, starkly resembling one another in some sort of strategic assembly line. The room is dominated by the Big Board, with its flashing lights tracking the uncontrollable progress of the bombers. De Sadesky and Dr. Strangelove describe Russia's doomsday machine as a series of automatic activity of computers that "rules out human meddling."

The film's ultimate presentation of humanity turned into machinery is, of course, depicted in the person of Dr. Strangelove himself, trapped in his wheelchair, his eyes hidden by his dark spectacles, a fixed smile on his face, burdened with an uncontrollable right arm, speaking with a Germanic accent, and still possessed of an unquestioning devotion to his führer. His plans for the survival of the human species in mineshafts include the operation of computers for the selection of desirable inhabitants, as well as the control of the environment. Nelson's critique speaks of the "relentless logic" of the fail-safe system and the doomsday machine. He writes, "The machine, for the first time, plays a prominent role in Kubrick's work. *Strangelove* . . . remains his darkest vision of what an emerging 'machinarchy' could mean to humanity and human civilization."[30]

Finally, in its own oblique manner, the film suggests that religion has become the handmaid of the military attitude, invoked automatically at times and, in at least one instance, used to support some naughty behavior. At one point, Turgidson refers to Kissov as a "degenerate atheist Commie," employing the usual Cold War appeal to religion to support any military action against the Soviet Union. Shortly before Ripper enters the bathroom to commit suicide, he tells Mandrake, "I happen to believe in a life after this one, and I know I'll have to answer for what I've done. And I think I can," to which Mandrake replies, "Yes, well, of course, Jack, you can. I'm a religious man myself, you know, Jack. I believe in all that sort of thing." The telephone message from Ripper that Turgidson reads to the president confirming that Ripper has issued the "go code" for the attack on Russia ends with, "God willing, we will prevail in peace, freedom from fear, and in true health through the purity and essence of our natural fluids. God bless us all." Turgidson comments, "We're still trying to figure out the meaning of that last phrase, sir." He is apparently referring to the words about the "purity and essence of our natural fluids," but the subtext could be a questioning of the meaning of invoking God's blessings on their military actions. After the recall code is activated and, presumably, all of the U.S. planes have been accounted for, Turgidson is inspired to offer a "short prayer of thanks for our deliverance": "Lord, we have heard the wings of the angel of death fluttering over our heads from the valley of fear. You have seen fit to deliver us from the forces of evil." Indeed, Turgidson advocates the use of prayer for others as well. When he receives a phone call from Miss Scott, after upbraiding her for calling him on his War Room number, he urges her to go to bed and "don't forget to say your prayers."

In this film, which, as already mentioned, Brustein describes as a "nightmare farce,"[31] Kubrick allows reality to intrude only occasionally. Shots of the airplanes flying above the clouds, particularly at the beginning, with the erotic depiction of the refueling process, and specifically the sequence showing the B-52 flying low over the Russian landscape, are at least some objective portrayals of the reality of the situation. The scenes of the army unit that President Muffley has sent to invade Burpleson are filmed in documentary style, the handheld camera often shaking because of the artillery explosions, showing some of the soldiers falling and perhaps dying on the battlefield. And, finally, the depiction of the nuclear explosions that end the film are taken from actual footage of nuclear tests and the only instance of nuclear weaponry employed in actual combat so far in our history, the bombings of Nagasaki and Hiroshima. The insertion of such documentary material only underlines the life-and-death seriousness of the film's satirical critique. The inclusion of the World War II ballad "We'll Meet Again" serves to remind viewers of such destructiveness in history.

True satire is rarely produced in Hollywood, where the "feel-good" mood can insert itself into even the most serious "true-life" dramas (*Norma Rae* [1979], *Erin Brockovich* [2000], *The Blind Side* [2009], *The Fighter* [2010], and so forth). Even as it is presenting itself as a dark and even absurdist fantasy, *Dr. Strangelove* dares to suggest, especially in the film's final moments, that its scenario is quite possible. Laugh all you want, says Kubrick, but work up some anger as well.

A Sampling of Satire

Modern Times (1936)
The Great Dictator (1940)
M*A*S*H (1970)
The Hospital (1971)
Nashville (1975)
Network (1976)
The Life of Brian (1979)
Wag the Dog (1997)
The Truman Show (1998)
Pleasantville (1998)

Notes

1. A. M. Juster, ed., *The Satires of Horace* (Philadelphia: University of Pennsylvania Press, 2008), 4.

2. For a thorough survey of Juvenal's satires and their contrast with the work of Horace and other classic satirists, see Frederick Jones, *Juvenal and the Satiric Genre* (London: Gerald Duckwork & Co., Ltd., 2007) and *The Satires of Juvenal*, trans. Rolfe Humphries (Bloomington: Indiana University Press, 1970).

3. Alexander Walker, *Stanley Kubrick, Director* (New York and London: W. W. Norton & Company, 1999), 114.

4. David Hughes, *The Complete Kubrick*, rev. ed. (London: Virgin Publishing, Ltd., 2001), 108.

5. Joseph Gelmis, *The Film Director as Superstar* (New York: Doubleday, 1970), 309.

6. Norman Kagan, *The Cinema of Stanley Kubrick*, 3rd ed. (New York: Continuum, 2000), 111.

7. Robert Brustein, "Out of This World." In *Perspectives on Stanley Kubrick*, Mario Falsetto, ed. (New York: G. K. Hall & Co., 1996), 136, 140.

8. Hughes, *The Complete Kubrick*, 108.

9. Randy Rasmussen, *Stanley Kubrick: Seven Films Analyzed* (Jefferson, N.C., and London: McFarland & Co., 2001), 6.

10. Kagan, *The Cinema of Stanley Kubrick*, 111.

11. Thomas Allen Nelson, *Kubrick: Inside a Film Artist's Maze* (Bloomington: Indiana University Press, 2000), 83.

12. Hughes, *The Complete Kubrick*, 129.

13. Hughes, *The Complete Kubrick*, 120.

14. Brustein, "Out of This World," 139.

15. Jason Sperb, *The Kubrick Façade* (Lanham, Md.: Scarecrow Press, 2006), 64, 71, 72.

16. Nelson, *Kubrick: Inside a Film Artist's Maze*, 89.

17. Walker, *Stanley Kubrick, Director*, 185.

18. Walker, *Stanley Kubrick, Director*, 176–77.

19. Kagan, *The Cinema of Stanley Kubrick*, 117.

20. Kagan, *The Cinema of Stanley Kubrick*, 120.

21. Walker, *Stanley Kubrick, Director*, 189.

22. Rasmussen, *Stanley Kubrick: Seven Films Analyzed*, 41.

23. Rasmussen, *Stanley Kubrick: Seven Films Analyzed*, 48.

24. Hughes, *The Complete Kubrick*, 112.

25. Walker, *Stanley Kubrick, Director*, 204–5.

26. Nelson, *Kubrick: Inside a Film Artist's Maze*, 90.

27. *Kubrick: Seven Films Analyzed*, 8.

28. Nelson, *Kubrick: Inside a Film Artist's Maze*, 91.

29. "The attitudes, gestures and movements of the human body are laughable in exact proportion as that body reminds us of a mere machine." Henri Bergson, *Laughter: An Essay on the Meaning of the Comic* (New York: Macmillan, 1924), 29.

30. Nelson, *Kubrick: Inside a Film Artist's Maze*, 97, 99.

31. Brustein, "Out of This World," 136.

CHAPTER 7

Parody

YOUNG FRANKENSTEIN (1974)

Parody has deep roots in human history and the human psyche. Relying on some innate instinct for imitation, humorists of all stripes have composed their own literary, artistic, theatrical, and even musical works that broadly mimic another work of art or another artist's characteristic style and hold the originals up for ridicule, which is usually affectionate but may sometimes prove hostile. Aristophanes's *The Frogs* parodied the works of the tragedies of Aeschylus and Euripides. Miguel de Cervantes mocked the heroic novels of his time in *Don Quixote*. Falstaff and the other "low characters" mocked their noble counterparts in Shakespeare's history plays. Thomas More provided a comic critique of Renaissance philosophy in his cynical *Utopia*.[1]

Parody has been Mel Brooks's stock in trade throughout his filmmaking career, not that he hasn't achieved extraordinary success in other forms of comedy. His greatest financial and critical triumph, the musical version of his early film, *The Producers* (1968), won a record-breaking twelve Tony Awards in 2001 and ran on Broadway for five years. *The Producers*, however, includes relatively little parody. It is more of a satirical farce and sex comedy in its own right, with outlandish takeoffs on the culture of the Third Reich, but not a mirror of any other established work. His stand-up sketch with his friend Carl Reiner, "The 2,000-Year-Old Man" (1961), which spawned several highly successful record albums, a book and CD set, and an animated television show, has also remained popular and garnered several awards. It might be considered a parody of a celebrity interview in its format, but most of its humor depends on the sort of skewed view of history that Brooks developed more fully in his film *The History of the World, Part I* (1981).

Brooks's career in films, however, has mainly relied on his talent for parody. Even before his first venture into Hollywood filmmaking, he enjoyed major success on television by teaming up with Buck Henry to create the popular

Dr. Frederick Frankenstein (Gene Wilder) presents his creation (Peter Boyle) to his colleagues in a sophisticated song-and-dance routine that goes awry in *Young Frankenstein* (1974).

television spy spoof *Get Smart* (1965–1970), an absurdist parody of the international double-agent genre that had recently been revived to great acclaim in the iconic James Bond films, beginning with *Dr. No* in 1962.[2] It also drew upon a growing cynicism toward Cold War politics in the 1960s. *Get Smart* earned an Emmy for Outstanding Comedy Series both in 1968 and 1969. Robert Alan Crick remarks, "Even though the number of *Get Smart* episodes Brooks himself actually scripted can be counted on the fingers of one hand, his mania for comic contrasts is all over the series."[3] Brooks's later effort at televised parody did not achieve the same popularity. *When Things Were Rotten*, a Brooksian version of the tale of Robin Hood and his Merry Men, received considerable critical praise for its inventive attempts to bring a certain film-comedy sensibility to television, but it was canceled less than halfway through its first season in 1975, only to reappear almost twenty years later on the big screen as *Robin Hood: Men in Tights* (1993). Meanwhile, Brooks's first two feature-length films, *The Producers* and *The Twelve Chairs* (1970), while zany and sophisticated in their view of Broadway theater and nineteenth-century Russia, respectively, contained few, if any, attempts to imitate popular film genres or literary works.

In 1974, however, two of his finest parodies were released. *Blazing Saddles*, which opened in February of that year, broke new ground in its twisted version of the Hollywood sheriff-saving-the-town Western by making the hero an African American. *Young Frankenstein*, released in December, pays tribute to the entire genre of horror films, specifically the work of James Whale. Brooks's next release, *Silent Movie* (1976), true to its name, contained no spoken dialogue except for one line spoken by the world-famous mime Marcel Marceau and reveled in the standard editing devices and slapstick performances of silent film comedy. *High Anxiety* (1977) pays comic tribute to the films of Alfred Hitchcock, particularly *Vertigo* (1958). *Spaceballs* (1987) recognizes the popularity of Stanley Kubrick's *A Space Odyssey* (1968) and the cultural phenomenon of the Star Wars films with Brooks's own version of intergalactic battles. *Robin Hood: Men in Tights* (1994) offers a hilarious Mel Brooks version of the traditional story, while *Silence of the Hams*, released the same year, flew under the popular and critical radar and proved to be his least successful effort, attempting to spoof the dark thriller *Silence of the Lambs* (1991). Undaunted, Brooks returned the following year with his variation on the numerous vampire films that regularly emerge out of Hollywood, *Dracula: Dead and Loving It*.

According to Brooks's biographer, James Robert Parish, the idea for *Young Frankenstein* originated with Gene Wilder, who told Brooks about his idea after he had written only a two-page treatment. He continued working on his screenplay while he was acting in *Blazing Saddles* and some other projects. Although Brooks was reluctant to work on a film that was not based on his own material, he agreed that he and Wilder would work on a rewritten version of the screenplay, and, if a studio agreed to film it, Brooks would direct.[4] They worked on the script while Brooks was also engaged in the postproduction of *Blazing Saddles*. After Twentieth Century Fox agreed to produce the film, Brooks managed to shoot the entire film in less than two months, in March and April of 1974. When it opened that December, the movie was welcomed with a flood of enthusiastic reviews. Vincent Canby calls it "Mel Brooks's funniest, most cohesive comedy to date."[5]

Young Frankenstein ranks as a brilliant parody for several reasons. First, for a parody to succeed, the original work must be well enough known to its intended audience. It can be even more helpful if the original work is well respected or culturally significant. The original must be dense enough to offer sufficient material to be imitated, especially if the parody runs almost two hours, as does *Young Frankenstein*. The original novel and film versions of the Frankenstein story meet this criterion better than any of the works that inspired Brooks's other film parodies.

As a novel, *Frankenstein* (1818) is a fascinating product of the early nineteenth-century Romantic movement, boasting distinguished as well as scandalous credentials. Its author is eighteen-year-old Mary Godwin, the daughter of the protofeminist writer Mary Wollstonecraft. Her father, William Godwin, was a well-known political thinker whose treatises nourished the revolutionary ideals of the British Romantic poets. At the time that she composed *Frankenstein*, Mary was romantically involved with the renowned English poet Percy Bysshe Shelley, who was married at the time. She had, in fact, already borne him two children. In June 1816, Mary and Percy joined Lord Byron, along with his mistress (Mary's half sister) and his physician, for a vacation at Villa Diodati in Cologny, Switzerland, near Lake Geneva.

Forced to remain housebound by unusually cold and stormy weather, the literary trio challenged each other to write a "ghost story." Mary's imagination had been stimulated by listening to the conversations Percy and Byron were having about the "principle of life" and possible experiments in reanimation of dead matter. Finally, after an unusually long conversation on the topic, she spent a sleepless night haunted by fantasies of a scientist attempting such reanimation. The next morning, Mary began to write her story, which would eventually become the novel. She continued writing when she returned to England, finally finishing the work in April 1817.[6] She subtitled the novel *The Modern Prometheus*, drawing on an earlier, less well-known element of the myth, where the scientist is called "Prometheus Plasticator," because he created human beings.

> The idea of Prometheus as the creator of mankind in general crops up in various Latin authors, including Ovid, Horace, and Catullus, often with the accompanying notion that the work was ill done, or at least that man's imperfections, and especially his "animal nature," are to be blamed on him.[7]

The other source of material for Brooks's film is the classic 1931 horror film *Frankenstein*, directed by James Whale and starring Boris Karloff in his career-defining role, daring to show the monster in a sympathetic light and combining terror and humor in an unforgettable performance. When Whale directed the sequel, *The Bride of Frankenstein*, four years later, he presented the same combination of sympathetic portrayal, humor, and horror, with the added benefit of the high-voltage amp of Elsa Lanchester's white-streaked beehive hairdo, the inspiration for numerous pop culture figures, from Disney's Cruella de Ville to Marge Simpson. Wilder and Brooks also borrowed characters and incidents from the various horror film follow-ups, including *The Bride of Frankenstein* (1935), *The Son of Frankenstein* (1939), and *The Ghost of Frankenstein* (1942), as well as the whole series of monster films produced throughout the 1930s and 1940s by Universal Studios, featuring Frankenstein, Dracula, the Wolf Man, and even the slapstick hit *Abbott and Costello Meet Frankenstein* (1948). The extensive collection of monster films from that era provided more than enough material for Brooks's fertile parodic sensibility.

The look of the film strives to imitate the original. Brooks was fortunate enough to find the actual set for Dr. Frankenstein's laboratory and much of the original laboratory apparatus, which Whale's designer, Kenneth Strickfaden, had saved in his garage. Dr. Frankenstein's über-Gothic castle, which "covered 150,000 square feet and rose to an impressive 35 feet . . . erected by the production designer Dale Hennesy at a cost of $350,000," enabled the environment to loom over the characters in the wide shots that comprised much of the footage inside the castle.[8] In a similar homage to Whale's original, Brooks insisted that the film be shot in black and white. In fact, when Columbia Pictures insisted that it be shot in color (and for a smaller budget), this issue was so nonnegotiable that Brooks and his team took the film to Twentieth Century Fox. (This was no small achievement, since, as Maurice Yacowar observes, no one had processed a film in black and white in more than six years.[9]) The film uses a 1:85 aspect ratio, which was the standard format of 1930s films until it was replaced in the 1950s with the wider 4:3 ratio for theatrical release Hollywood films. Most of the shots are dark and moody, with the ominous play of light and dark typical of the horror film genre. The music also imitates the high-culture sentimentality of the original films. The editing makes use of iris-outs, spins, wipes, and other linking devices typical of 1930s film melodrama. Brooks occasionally varied the formula by filming most of the close-ups in bright lighting, which he found more appropriate for the comic dialogue and asides. Yet, even this cinematography did not stray too far from the period. The Marx Brothers comedies, notably *Duck Soup* (1933) and *A Night at the Opera* (1935), as well as The Thin Man series and many of the screwball comedies of the 1930s, employed high-level lighting and glistening art deco mise-en-scène to enhance the effect of their madcap and sophisticated comedy.

The plot of *Young Frankenstein* centers on the struggles of Dr. Frederick Frankenstein (Gene Wilder), the American great-grandson of Baron Beaufort von Frankenstein. Frederick habitually informs everyone that he pronounces his surname as "Fronk-en-steen" to avoid any connection with his infamous grandfather, Dr. Victor Frankenstein, and his "cuckoo" attempts to create life. When his family's lawyer arrives with a copy of the baron's will, Frederick agrees to visit the family castle, which is presided over by its dour housekeeper, Frau Blucher (Cloris Leachman). Once there, he finds his grandfather's book, *How I Did It*, and becomes obsessed with reenacting his grandfather's reanimation experiments with a buxom German sex kitten named Inga (Teri Garr) as his laboratory assistant. Unfortunately, his servant, Igor (Marty Feldman), steals the wrong brain from the brain depository, and the creature whom the doctor animates is a massive man with an abnormal brain. Various escapades follow, including the monster's escape from the castle; his recapture and transformation into a semirefined creature; a theatrical demonstration of his abilities to an audience of Frederick's scientific peers; and his seduction of

Freddy's frigid fiancée, Elizabeth (Madeline Kahn), who has followed her beloved to the castle only to end up falling in love with his creation. Finally, to save his creature from the rioting villagers, Frederick transfers his own brain into him while he receives a different portion of the monster's body, and all ends happily. In fact, as Crick remarks, *Young Frankenstein* is "probably the first movie version of Mary Shelley's novel ever in which neither scientist nor monster ends up dead."[10]

Wes D. Gehring insists that to "create effective parody one must be thoroughly versed in the subject under comic attack. . . . The spoofing artist is often a fan of the target genre or auteur."[11] The same rule applies to the viewers of this film. *Young Frankenstein*, for all its silliness, cannot be fully appreciated without some awareness of the cultural richness surrounding the original novel, which incorporated numerous themes of the Romantic movement of the early nineteenth century. Following closely on the Enlightenment, this quasi-religious reaction to eighteenth-century rationalism (and atheism) found expression in the revival of Gothic architecture, the interest of Wagner and others in Norse mythology, and many other features of medieval culture.

Some remnants of the Enlightenment carried over into the Romantic movement as well. Inspired by the optimistic view of human nature of Jean-Jacques Rousseau, John Locke, and other eighteenth-century thinkers, the Romantics dared to envision even greater possibilities for human endeavor. Could the human mind and will be capable of divine achievement? For example, could an outstanding human being—a brilliant scientist, for example—perform the ultimate divine act of creating life, as did Prometheus?

Another legacy of the optimism of the Enlightenment was the Romantics' concept of an inherent precivilized nobility in human nature, the "noble savage." This too found its way into the Frankenstein story. The monster's response to music, flowers, children, and acts of human kindness revealed an inner dignity even within this tortured, jerry-built creature.

Yet, lurking beneath this confidence in the limitless possibilities and natural goodness in human nature was the warning that was also part of the Prometheus myth and his stealing of fire from the gods. Would the gods (or God), angered by human hubris, punish the overreaching geniuses by driving them to madness, torture, or even self-destruction? The dark threat of supernatural retaliation pervades much of this Gothic sensibility, from the folk tale of the Sorcerer's Apprentice to Johann Wolfgang von Goethe's majestic rendering of the Faustian bargain with the devil. In American culture, Nathaniel Hawthorne's and Edgar Allan Poe's tales of obsessed scientists explore the same fear that science may overstep its divinely appointed bounds.

The setting of the story in Germany also befits its Romantic character. Nineteenth-century Germany represented the height of Western culture, with the philosophy of Immanuel Kant, Georg Wilhelm Friedrich Hegel, Ludwig

Andreas von Feuerbach, and Friedrich Nietzsche; the music of Ludwig van Beethoven, Richard Wagner, Johannes Brahms, George Frideric Handel, Robert Schumann, Georg Philipp Telemann, Felix Mendelssohn, and so many others; the literature of Johann Wolfgang von Goethe, Johann Christoph Friedrich von Schiller, Heinrich Heine, and Johann Christian Friedrich Holderlin; the Baroque architecture of its centuries-old churches and cathedrals; and the scientific achievements of August Ferdinand Mobius and Max Planck. Meanwhile, a vibrant German folk culture, with its country and village dances, beer halls and drinking songs, rich cuisine of pastries and sausages, wines of the Rhine valley, and folk tales collected by the Brothers Grimm expressed the gemütlichkeit of a proud people of all social classes. It is no wonder that the Romantic writers and artists, especially in Britain and the United States, looked to Germany as evidence of the infinite possibilities of the human spirit.

Such universal admiration of the German character would, of course, be lessened considerably by the rise of Bismarck and the horrors of World War I and then wiped out rather thoroughly by the atrocities of the Third Reich. By the mid-twentieth century, the image of Germany came to be associated with the authoritarianism, sadism, militarism, and ethnic arrogance of the "master race" and their führer.

Yet, even this darker twentieth-century image of German culture provided a certain aesthetic fascination. German expressionistic art and cinema, with its whiff of decadence and danger, greatly influenced Hollywood filmmakers in the 1930s, especially in the Hollywood renderings of the Frankenstein story and other horror films. Whale and others exploited the techniques of Fritz Lang and Erich von Stroheim in the extreme chiaroscuro, distorted camera angles, and technomodernism of the art direction of their films.

Scene after scene of *Young Frankenstein* exhibits Brooks's eagerness to dive into the shadows of German character, especially as it culminated in the figure of Adolf Hitler and all that he represented. The Jewish revenge against Hitler, of course, which had already been evident in Brooks's first film version of *The Producers* (1968), would reappear in his remake of *To Be or Not To Be* (1983) and be fulsomely developed in his Broadway musical version of *The Producers* (2001). Brooks engages in plenty of mockery of the German character throughout *Young Frankenstein*, most notably in the sexual repression and fury of the housekeeper, Frau Blucher, and the brisk officiousness of the inspector of police, Inspector Kemp (Kenneth Mars).

However, much of the material that Brooks had at his disposal—the Romantic content of the original novel, the cinematic look of the horror films of the 1930s and 1940s, and the post–World War II image of the German character—would not suffice for the sustained parody that Brooks and Wilder were creating. In his comparison of the parodies produced by Mack Sennett, Buster

Keaton, and others in the silent film era with more contemporary examples, Gerald Mast observes the following:

> Most of the early comedies were short films, while all of today's are full-length feature films themselves. To extend a parody beyond the fifteen-minute limit causes severe problems for both comic artists and audiences. By definition, a parody is not a new, original, interesting narrative in its own right, but an echo of a previous one. How long can one prolong an echo before it seems empty, boring, trivial, trite, silly, self-indulgent, and superficial? That question becomes the central problem to confront every maker of full-length parodic works, and his ability to answer it successfully determines the artistic and comic success of the result.[12]

Mast suggests four ways of sustaining a full-length parody. First, the work must initially capture the viewers' interest by its own original narrative, situations, and characters. Second, the parody needs to aim at a multiplicity of targets, imitating not only its primary model but including some references to other material familiar to the viewers. Third, it helps to include what Mast calls the "method of anomalous surprise," injecting "some character, situation, or event into the parodic narrative that makes absolutely no sense in that context, producing a devastating and delightful violation of audiences' expectations."[13] Finally, Mast mentions the use of stunts and gags and points to Brooks as the most prominent practitioner of such devices. Indeed, Brooks seems unable to resist the opportunity for a gratuitous gag line or bit of physical slapstick to pump up the hilarity of a scene. A closer look at the film's narrative demonstrates how much the use of these four methods—originality, multiplicity, surprise, and gags—contributes to the comic success of *Young Frankenstein*, as does the basic spoofing of the original novel and film.

The combination of the basic retelling of the Frankenstein story with Brooks's mockery of the German stereotype and his use of the various supporting comic methods might best be illustrated by attention to six selected sequences from the film: 1) the opening fifteen minutes, 2) the unsuccessful and successful attempts to give life to the creature, 3) the monster's adventures when he escapes from the castle, 4) the process of taming the monster through the power of love, 5) the introduction of the creature to the scientific community, and 6) the final effort to save the creature from the villagers' wrath by the "transference" experiment.

1. The Opening

A haunting violin melody plays while most of the film's titles and opening credits are displayed in elaborate Gothic lettering. The Frankenstein castle is revealed at the top of a hill during a particularly vehement thunderstorm. The stone archways and leaded windows of the castle endow it with a medieval atmosphere, while the ancient grandfather clock strikes midnight (which, because this is a Mel Brooks film, chimes thirteen times). The camera slowly closes in on the castle and then pans even more slowly across the sides of the coffin of Baron Beaufort von Frankenstein, Frederick's great-grandfather. The coffin lid opens to reveal a skeleton holding an ornate black box. In the first instance of the gags Brooks seems incapable of resisting, as the family lawyer attempts to remove the box, the skeleton refuses to release his grip. Gothic horror meets vaudeville shtick in the film's first moments.

The next fifteen minutes introduce all of the main characters (except the monster himself) and illustrate the insertion of gags and anomalous material into the narrative. After the brief episode involving the coffin, viewers are transported to a contemporary lecture hall in an American medical school, where the distinguished surgeon Dr. Frederick Frankenstein is delivering a lecture on the human brain and nervous system. It becomes evident within a few minutes that, underneath his composed academic demeanor, Frederick is a bundle of raw emotions, primarily anger and vanity. He becomes increasingly annoyed at a medical student's persistent questioning about his father's work, which Frederick finally declares was "doo-doo" and the activities of a "raving lunatic." He then proceeds to demonstrate for his student audience the difference between voluntary and reflexive nerve impulses.

Perhaps in a nod to the showmanship of the scientist-entrepreneur depicted in *Young Tom Edison* (1940) (which Brooks claims played its part in inspiring this film), the scientific demonstration is presented as a performance. Frederick uses the tone of a stage magician to introduce the pitiable figure Mr. Hilltop (Liam Dunn), who will serve as his human guinea pig for the demonstration, announcing him as someone "with whom I have never worked nor given any prior instructions to." To illustrate an involuntary nerve response, without any warning, shouting, "You rotten yellow sonofabitch," he knees Mr. Hilltop in the groin, causing considerable pain and resentment in the human subject. After a second sadistic demonstration of a similar attack that is not immediately felt by Mr. Hilltop because his nerve impulses have been temporarily blocked but that eventually causes even more pain, the moaning Mr. Hilltop is wheeled away on a gurney, while Frederick whispers to one of the attendants to give Mr. Hilltop an extra dollar. He then engages in an argument with the same persistent student, whom he attempts to one-up with arrogant witticisms. The student goads him even further, asking him, "Doesn't bringing back to life what was once dead hold any intrigue for you?" This drives Frederick into such a rage that, as he vehemently argues that reanimation of dead tissue is impossible and screams, "I am not interested in death; the only thing that concerns me is the preservation of life," he stabs himself in the thigh with a scalpel.

After class is dismissed, the Frankenstein family lawyer, who has been sitting in the back row of the classroom throughout the entire lecture, approaches Frederick to present him with the box from the coffin, which contains the last will and testament of his great-grandfather. Frederick is then off to Transylvania and the family castle, apparently to carry out the wishes contained in the will.

The train trip sequence is filled with gags and stunts. Frederick's attempts to give a good-bye kiss to his wealthy, fashionable, but also virginal and repressed fiancée, Elizabeth, at the train station are frustrated by her concern for not mussing her makeup, hair, taffeta gown, and nails. During the ride to New York City, he overhears an older married couple arguing about their son's masturbatory habits; he then hears the same conversation in German on the European segment of the ride. His arrival at his destination and the appearance of a shoeshine boy, of course, sets up another golden gag opportunity and a slightly anomalous surprise reference to the 1940s Glenn Miller hit song, as Frederick pokes his head out of the train window and shouts, "Pardon me, boy, is this the Transylvania Station?" The boy replies, "Yah, track twenty-nine. Oh, can I give you a shine?"

Upon his arrival, he is greeted at the station by Igor and Inga and, once at the door of the castle, by Frau Blucher. At this point, the gag lines and stunts—all fairly gratuitous and marginal to the plot—become too numerous to mention, but a few of the more egregious examples might provide a sense of the rest. Responding to his new assistant Igor's instructions to "walk this way," Frederick actually starts limping and using a cane as Igor does. Inga, lying in the hay of the wagon that takes them to the castle, invites Frederick to a "roll in the hay," but only in the literal sense of actually rolling around in the hay. When Igor uses the castle's oversized knockers to alert Frau Blucher of their arrival, Frederick, in the midst of helping Inga out of the hay wagon, exclaims, "What knockers!" to which Inga replies, "Thank you, Herr Doktor." When Frau appears at the door, the mention of her name, for some reason, frightens the horses in the castle stable. When Frau leads them up the "treacherous staircase," she lights their way with a large candelabra; the candles, however, are unlit. The film continues to depend on such cheap gags and stunts.

2. Reanimation Attempts

The second sequence worth observing is the attempt to bring the monster to life. The scene makes use of such intricate equipment as pulleys and switches, valves and wheels, and lightning and electric charges to create a scene of bizarre scientific experimentation. Frederick's appearance has been transmogrified by his lab coat and stethoscope, his wildly arranged electro-shocked hair, and finally his protective goggles. Inga and Igor tug on the pulleys that raise the doctor's platform and the monster (Peter Boyle) on an operating table through a skylight to be exposed to the lightning that is flashing outside. His face gleaming with intense lighting from below, Frederick challenges the forces of nature with Promethean audacity. Beginning with an almost prayerful reflectiveness and rising into the skylight space, he resembles a priest presiding over an altar of sacrifice. As his invocation reaches its hysterical crescendo, he proclaims the following:

> From that fateful day when stinking bits of slime first crawled from the sea and shouted to the cold stars, "I am man," our greatest dread has always been the knowledge of our own mortality. But tonight we shall hurl the gauntlet of science into the frightful face of Death itself. Tonight we shall ascend into the heavens, we shall mock the earthquake, we shall command the thunders and penetrate into the very womb of impervious Nature herself. . . . Life, life, do you hear me? *Give my creation life!!!*

When Inga and Igor bring the operating table back down to the laboratory floor, the monster remains lifeless despite the doctor's frantic pounding on his chest. When Inga attempts to console Frederick, he responds, "No, no. Be of good cheer. If science teaches us anything, it teaches us to accept our failures, as well as our successes, with quiet dignity and grace." He pauses, sighs, turns away from the table, and then quickly wheels around to begin choking the monster, screaming, "Sonofabitch bastard, I'll get you for this. What did you do to me? I don't want to live. I do not want to live!" As Inga and Igor drag him away from the table, he moans, "Oh, Momma!," and Igor utters the aside to the audience, "Quiet dignity and grace."

Brooks also resorts to the film's ever-present element of sexuality in this scene. As the moment of experimentation arrives, Frederick turns to Inga, who is standing quite close, and instructs her, "Elevate me." In her preoccupation with sex, Inga misunderstands the instruction and wonders if this is the appropriate place and time for such activity. Frederick corrects her misinterpretation, but then, in his invocation to the gods that immediately follows, employing frank sexual metaphor, Frederick pledges to "penetrate into the very womb of impervious Nature herself" in this attempt to create life. The life force of sexuality that his fiancée uses to tease him and that Inga makes so readily available is being redirected by this crazed scientist into scientific reproductive techniques. (The closing cry for his mother provoked by his own inability to bring forth life adds an Oedipal element to this multifaceted failure to produce life.) Nature—as well as the logic of comedy—opposes a plan based on his egotistical obsessions and driven by a mix of anger and vanity. Dr. Frankenstein has much to learn.

However, after they leave the laboratory, the monster comes to life, and Frederick reacts with his usual barely contained frenzy. Upon observing his creature's movements, Frederick repeats the same hysterical announcement made by Dr. Frankenstein (Colin Clive) in Whale's original film, screaming "It's alive! It's alive! *It's alive!*" This time, however, Brooks's camera captures the monster's suspicious reaction to such an outburst. "What have I gotten myself into?" he seems to be asking the audience.

Frederick slowly approaches the monster, promising to set him free, but also checking with the assistants, whispering, "Is the sedative ready?" When Igor, meanwhile, lights a cigarette, the match's flame terrifies the monster, who proceeds to choke the doctor. Unable to speak, Frederick must resort to a game of charades to order Inga to administer the sedative. Once the monster is calmed down, Frederick calmly interrogates Igor about the creature's brain, promising that he will "not be angry" if Igor tells him the truth. Once he finds out that he has inserted an "abnormal brain into a seven-and-a-half-foot-long, fifty-four-inch-wide gorilla," Frederick explodes in anger and proceeds to choke Igor. So much, once again, for "quiet dignity and grace."

3. The Monster's Escape

The monster is released from his bonds by Frau Blucher, who finally admits to the others that Frederick's father was her "boyfriend" and that she had deliberately lured them into the laboratory for another attempt at making his dream of creating life come true. Two incidents in this sequence are direct imitations of scenes from the original Frankenstein films. As the monster wanders through the woods, he encounters a little peasant girl, who invites him to join her in dropping flowers into a well. When they run out of flowers, she says, "Oh dear, nothing left. What shall we throw in now?" The monster turns to the camera, as he and the audience recall that, at that moment in the original Whale film, the monster threw the little girl into a lake and drowned her. In this case, however, they decide to play on her seesaw, and, as he sits on his end of the board, he catapults her through the air and into the window of her own bedroom, safe and sound.

In the second scene, the monster visits a lonely blind hermit (emphasis on "lonely"), played by Gene Hackman, who is overjoyed to entertain a guest. Because he cannot see the monster, the hermit is not intimidated by his fearsome appearance. As he feels the monster, the mood becomes mildly homoerotic. He calls the visitor, "My joy, my prize from heaven. You must have been the tallest one in your class." Since the monster cannot utter words, the hermit concludes that he is a mute, and, as he continues feeling him over, he adds, an "incredibly big mute." Then, in a series of stunts playing off his blindness, the hermit proceeds to burn the monster with hot soup, shatter the mug holding the monster's wine, and finally light the monster's thumb instead of the cigar he has offered him. The flame, of course, sends the monster fleeing from the hermit's house.

The two sequences are grand illustrations of Brooks's basic technique of imitating familiar material while adding gags—and sexual innuendo—for originality; however, it is worth noting that these two scenes offer the rare moments of poignancy in their original films. Brooks will have none of that. He would rather only hint at the dark topics of drowning, loneliness, and confused sexuality than draw a sympathetic tear from his viewers.

4. Taming the Monster with Love

After the monster is lured back to the castle by the melancholy strains of the film's theme music (played by Igor on some sort of oversized Alpine horn), the entire direction and thematic of the narrative change. In the original film, the scientist and the monster become opponents, and the story reaches an unhappy conclusion. Brooks sees the story differently and aims for a happy ending for all concerned. The process begins with the doctor's landmark decision to rehabilitate the monster through the power of love. This attempt is constantly threatened, however, by Frederick's tendency to resort to hysteria. After they recapture the monster and chain him in a locked cell, Frederick announces his plan to "save" his creation. He heroically proclaims, "Love is the only thing that can save this poor creature. And I am going to convince him that he is loved, even at the cost of my own life." Then, ordering Inga, Igor, and Frau Blucher to lock him in the cell with the creature, he firmly instructs them, "No matter what you hear in there, no matter how cruelly I beg you, no matter how terribly I may scream, do not open this door or you will undo everything I worked for. Do you understand? *Do not open this door!*"

However, within a few seconds of being locked in the room with the screaming monster, who breaks his chains and heads toward him menacingly, Frederick quickly changes his mind and hysterically pleads with them to open the door, saying, "Get me the hell out of here. . . . Open this goddam door or I'll kick your rotten heads in. Mommy!" Of course, following her master's orders, Frau Blucher refuses to open the door, and the doctor faces the raging monster. In what seems to be merely a defense tactic, he resorts to complimenting the monster, uttering, "Hello, handsome. You're a good-looking fellow, do you know that?" He tells the monster that people laugh at him and hate him out of jealousy, envying his "boyish face," "sweet smile," and "sheer muscle." He calls him an "Olympian ideal. . . . You are a god!" As the creature succumbs to the flattery, calming down and smiling sweetly, Frederick even appears to believe his own rhetoric. "You are not evil. You are good," he tells the creature. As the monster breaks down in tears, the doctor cradles his head in his arms, crooning, "This is a nice boy. . . . This is a mother's angel. And I want the world to know, once and for all and without any shame, that *we love him*." Then, promising to teach the monster "how to walk, how to move, how to speak, how to think," he reaches a frenzied peak of hubris, shouting, "Together, you and I are going to make the greatest single contribution to science since the creation of fire!" Finally, in a moment of personal transformation, replying to Inga's question, "Dr. Fronk-en-steen, are you all right?" he corrects her pronunciation and shouts to all the world, "My name is . . . Frankenstein!" In that triumphant moment, Frederick's bonding with the monster allows him to embrace the darkness of his own family history, identity, and destiny.

Yacowar interprets the doctor's self-realization as consistent with the standard formula of the story:

> In the Frankenstein tradition, the monster is the embodiment of the creator's suppressed nature. In Jungian terms, the monster is the shadow, the hidden, repressed, and shameful aspect of the conscious personality. As the ego contains unfavorable or destructive qualities, so the shadow also has good qualities—normal instincts and creative impulses. Traditionally, Frankenstein must accept his monster . . . to accept himself and his own dark nature.[14]

5. Introduction to the Scientific Community

Frederick's presentation of the monster to his fellow scientists returns to the same theatrics that characterized Dr. Frankenstein's lecture at the beginning of the film, only more flamboyantly. On the night of the presentation, the nineteenth-century baroque theater of the Bucharest Academy of Science buzzes with the excitement of an opening night; however, the audience of scientists and neurosurgeons, in formal attire, are a critical bunch. They greet this newest Dr. Frankenstein with suspicion, withholding their applause when he is introduced. They laugh when the doctor—in showmanship mode—announces that he has been experimenting with the "reanimation of dead tissue."

They are even more disturbed when he describes his achievement as "possibly . . . the gateway to immortality." Continuing in this P. T. Barnum style, he offers to present "for your intellectual and philosophical pleasure . . . The Creature!" The women panic, but Frederick reminds them that "we are not children here. We are scientists!" The audience then is forced to applaud as "The Creature" responds to his creator's simple commands to show balance and coordination (and is rewarded with a doggie treat). Frederick then promises to "enter—quietly—

into the realm of genius" and announces, "Ladies and gentlemen, Mesdames et Messieurs, Damen und Herren . . . may I now present a cultured, sophisticated man-about-town." He and the monster then engage in an outlandish imitation of the Fred Astaire-style number "Puttin' on the Ritz," as the monster, in a white tie, tails, and a top hat and using a cane, mumbles the occasional phrase and clumsily performs a tap routine. At one point, Frederick steps behind the dancing monster and mouths to the audience, "I . . . love . . . him."

Unfortunately, one of the footlights explodes, terrifying the monster. Sensing that their performance is heading toward disaster, Frederick frantically tries to complete the dance number. He then berates the monster for "trying to make me look like a fool," displaying the same callousness that he showed toward Mr. Hilltop in his similar showbiz demonstrations in his medical school classroom. The audience turns hostile, throwing fruit at the performers, enraging the monster, who leaps into the crowd only to be captured by the police and placed in chains.

6. Saving the Creature

The final salvation of the monster includes not only Brooks's typical dabbling in sexual humor but also an affirmation of the saving power of love in general. His usual sexual comedy, however, is legitimately prompted in this case by the original 1931 film. In Whale's narrative, a few minutes before their marriage, Dr. Frankenstein's fiancée, Elizabeth, quite nervous, even distraught, does not notice that the monster is perched outside her window and seems ready to enter her bedroom. This portrayal of such an advanced case of "wedding jitters" and the looming possibility of sexual assault can be readily interpreted as symbolic of any virginal bride's fear of her upcoming sexual initiation, wondering whether the apparent gentleman she is about to marry may prove to be a sexual brute. Of course, this sort of Freudian subtext is catnip to Brooks, who proceeds to color the rest of the narrative with sexual ramifications.

Young Frankenstein's sexual reinterpretation of the story begins with the surprise arrival of Frederick's fiancée, Elizabeth. As it happens, Frederick has just finished having sex with Inga on the laboratory table when Frau Blucher, clearly disapproving of such activity, informs them of Elizabeth's imminent arrival. Elizabeth steps out of her carriage in a stunning attire that includes a turban, a white fox fur, and diamond earrings. She is still as romantically flirtatious but sexually repressed as ever, with an added nervousness in the presence of Igor. She is shocked that Frederick suggests that they "turn in" and is also immediately suspicious of Inga's relationship with her fiancée. Igor, aroused at the sight of Elizabeth, violently attacks her fox fur with his teeth and offers his assistance to Frederick, "if you need any help with the girls."

Elizabeth, like her virginal counterpart in the 1931 film, has resisted any sexual activity with her future husband, engaging instead in baby talk with Frederick and convincing him to wait until their wedding night for the sexual satisfaction he so obviously desires. The monster, however, has escaped again, and, as Elizabeth prepares for bed, brushing her hair to the tune of "The Battle Hymn of the Republic," he appears at her bedroom window. This time, there is no ambiguity about the monster–bride encounter. The monster whisks her away for a sexual escapade. Elizabeth is clearly thrilled by the monster and his enormous sexual prowess and ends up singing "Ah, Sweet Mystery of Life" as she and the monster make passionate love. After their lovemaking, Elizabeth, now with her hair streaked in the Bride of Frankenstein mode, echoes Frederick's own sentiments about his creation. As the monster departs, she sighs, "I think I love him." It is also worth noting, as does Yacowar, that to some extent, the monster has also been "detraumatized and humanized by his sexual experience with her." His lighting of their two postcoital cigarettes indicates that he has overcome his primal fear of fire.[15]

Having once again lured the monster back to the castle but fearing the wrath of the villagers, the doctor engages in a "transference" experiment, at the risk of both their lives, in which part of his brain is given to the monster. When the mob breaks into the laboratory, the monster, now endowed with a brain, confronts them with an eloquent tribute to his creator:

> I live because this poor, half-crazed genius has given me life. He alone held an image of me as something beautiful. And then, when it would have been easy enough to stay out of danger, he used his own body as a guinea pig to give me a calmer brain . . . and a somewhat more sophisticated way of expressing myself.

The film ends with a portrayal of the monster, now married to Elizabeth, leading a bourgeois existence reading the *Wall Street Journal* as Elizabeth prepares for bed (once again singing "The Battle Hymn of the Republic" and sporting a complete Elsa Lanchester hairdo). Meanwhile, Frederick is shown on his wedding night with Inga, who discovers that the doctor, in the transference experiment, has received the gift of the monster's sexual equipment.

Yacowar finds a wider significance to the element of love in the narrative. He points, perhaps surprisingly, to the figure of Frau Blucher. Observing the neighing of the horses in the stable whenever her name is mentioned, he observes that "she seems to operate on a more elemental level of existence than everyone else":

> For one thing, her melody plays at the beginning and end of the film, lures Frankenstein to the secret library, and soothes and sum-

mons the monster. . . . Not like the other girls, Frau Blucher seems a preternatural force. She virtually personifies the power of fertile love. Hence the softening in her sinister tone when she first meets Frederick and offers him successive temptations: brandy, coffee, Ovaltine. Though her name arouses the eternal neigh-sayers, she represents an eternal, ennobling passion.[16]

Crick finds another type of love exhibited in Brooks's version of the story. He comments on the following:

Perhaps more than anything, the Frankenstein story may be a tale about parental responsibility. Like many modern fathers, Frankenstein brings into the world a new being, then takes no responsibility for it—creates a child, then abandons it to fend for itself. By contrast, Freddy [sic] is a surprisingly good father, in his way, never forsaking his freakish offspring even when he knows full well he might be murdered by him. . . . Amid his horror, Shelley's scientist can feel pity for his gruesome creation, but he can't bring himself to love him, yet Freddy does whatever he can for *his* monster, tries his best to cure him, dry his tears, boost his self-esteem. . . . Freddy loves his monster no matter how others react.[17]

Thus, the Frankenstein story, 150 years after its creation by Mary Godwin, has a happy ending at last, thanks to the love that Frederick and Elizabeth have felt for the monster, along with the transforming power of sexuality, no longer repressed as it was in the 1931 film version. Love—with the help of sex—conquers all.

A Sampling of Parodies

Blazing Saddles (1974)
The Adventures of Sherlock Holmes' Smarter Brother (1975)
Murder by Death (1976)
The Last Remake of Beau Geste (1977)
The Cheap Detective (1978)
Airplane! (1980)
Zorro: The Gay Blade (1981)
Dead Men Don't Wear Plaid (1982)
The Naked Gun: From the Files of Police Squad! (1988)
Austin Powers: International Man of Mystery (1997)

Notes

1. A solid survey of parody in literary, theatrical, and cinematic terms can be found in Simon Detith, *Parody* (London: Routledge, 2000); A. S. Martin, *On Parody* (New York: Henry Holt and Company, 1896); Dan Harris, *Film Parody* (London: BFI Publishing, 2000); and Wes D. Gehring, *Parody as Film Genre* (Westport, Conn.: Greenwood Press, 1999).

2. *Dr. No* was followed by the hugely popular Bond films *From Russia with Love* (1963), *Goldfinger* (1964), *Thunderball* (1965), and *You Only Live Twice* (1967), providing Brooks and Henry with a rich lode of popular-culture material to parody.

3. Robert Alan Crick, *The Big Screen Comedies of Mel Brooks* (Jefferson, N.C., and London: McFarland & Co., 2002), 6.

4. James Robert Parish, *It's Good to Be the King: The Seriously Funny Life of Mel Brooks* (Hoboken, N.J.: John Wiley & Sons, 2002), 199.

5. Vincent Canby, "Young Frankenstein." *New York Times*, December 16, 1974, p. 48.

6. Christopher Small, *Mary Shelley's* Frankenstein: *Tracing the Myth* (Pittsburgh, Pa.: University of Pittsburgh Press, 1973), 30. Small also includes information that deepens the cultural richness of this event. The Villa Diodati was already well known as the house where John Milton had stayed with a friend. Byron's attempt at a ghost story, somewhat unfinished, was later published and is thought to have been the inspiration for Bram Stoker's *Dracula* (1897). Byron's physician, John William Polidori, eventually went mad and poisoned himself.

7. Small, *Mary Shelley's* Frankenstein, 48–49.

8. Parish, *It's Good to Be the King*, 203.

9. Maurice Yacowar, *Method in Madness: The Comic Art of Mel Brooks* (New York: St. Martin's Press, 1981), 121.

10. Crick, *The Big Screen Comedies of Mel Brooks*, 74.

11. Wes D. Gehring, *The World of Comedy: Five Takes on Funny* (Davenport, Iowa: Robin Vincent Publishing, 2001), 180.

12. Gerald Mast, *The Comic Mind: Comedy and the Movies*, 2nd ed. (Chicago: University of Chicago Press, 1979), 308.

13. Mast, *The Comic Mind*, 310.

14. Yacowar, *Method in Madness*, 126.

15. Yacowar, *Method in Madness*, 131–32.

16. Yacowar, *Method in Madness*, 123.

17. Crick, *The Big Screen Comedies of Mel Brooks*, 76–77.

CHAPTER 8

Neurotic Comedy

ANNIE HALL (1977)

The posters for Woody Allen's comic masterpiece *Annie Hall* (1977) sported the tagline "a nervous romance." Both words in that description deserve attention. While *Annie Hall* represents the peak of Allen's neurotic humor, the film also deconstructs the genre of romantic comedy. Both the beginning and end of the film underline the dual character of the motion picture. The first shot after the titles shows a medium close-up of Woody Allen engaging in what appears to be some stand-up comedy, telling a couple of jokes expressing his neurotic view of life, concluding that life is "full of loneliness and misery and suffering and unhappiness, and it's all over much too quickly."[1] He then morphs into his character in the film, Alvy Singer, a successful stand-up comic who is suffering from a recent romantic breakup with Annie Hall (Diane Keaton), thus setting up the mixture of neurosis and romance.

In its concluding moments, the film comes full circle. Once again, Woody/Alvy speaks to the audience. A lovely montage of earlier scenes from the film depicting highlights of Alvy's and Annie's time together floats by on the screen, and the sound track fills with Annie's sweet-voiced rendition of the nostalgic ballad "Seems Like Old Times," along with a voice-over of Alvy's closing comments on their failed relationship. As he did in the beginning of the film, Alvy tells another joke about neurotic views of life. It's a story about a man who complains to his therapist about his "crazy brother," who thinks he's a chicken. When the doctor asks him why he doesn't have his brother institutionalized, he answers, "I would, but we need the eggs." Alvy concludes, "I guess that's pretty much how I feel about relationships. You know, they're totally irrational and crazy and absurd and . . . but, ah, I guess we keep goin' through it because, uh, most of us need the eggs."

A nervous romance, indeed; the film has entered the list of classic American films, achieving considerable critical and financial success. When *Annie Hall* was

Alvy Singer (Woody Allen) is mystified by the off-beat outfits, comments, and behavior of his new acquaintance, Annie Hall (Diane Keaton), in *Annie Hall* (1977).

released in 1977, it was one of the box-office hits of the year, earning $12 million dollars in the United States alone (twice as much as Allen's most recent hit, *Love and Death*, had earned), along with considerable international profit. It went on to win four Academy Awards (Best Film, Best Director, Best Screenplay, and Best Actress) and a host of other critical accolades from the Directors Guild of America, the Los Angeles Film Critics, the New York Film Critics, the National Board of Review, the National Society of Film Critics, and the Writers Guild of America, among others. In 1979, Swedish and Spanish film critics also gave it the Best Foreign Film Award. The movie probably received more critical attention than any of Allen's films.

Before making *Annie Hall*, Allen had been involved in a dozen films in as many years, as an actor, director, and screenwriter, beginning with his screenplay for the Peter Sellers international spy spoof *What's New, Pussycat?* (1965); his first directorial effort, *What's Up, Tiger Lily?* (1966); the film adaptation of his hit Broadway comedy *Don't Drink the Water* (1969); his noncomic role in a film about Hollywood blacklisting, *The Front* (1976); and his performance as narrator of a documentary about his career, *Woody Allen: An American Comedy* (1977), acknowledging Allen's status as a major comic

writer, stand-up comedian, and filmmaker. However, the movies that solidified the Allen image in the public mind during those years were the gag- and
slapstick-filled products for which he served as either director or writer (or
both): *Take the Money and Run* (1969); *Bananas* (1971); *Play It Again, Sam*
(1972); *Everything You Always Wanted to Know about Sex *but Were Afraid to
Ask* (1972); *Sleeper* (1973); and *Love and Death* (1975). As a main character
in all six of these films, Allen offers variations on the persona he had developed in his years as a successful stand-up comic throughout the early 1960s: a
scrawny, neurotic nebbish, with unruly red hair and black-rimmed spectacles;
a highly literate wit with a perpetually frustrated libido, expressing a New
York Jewish sensibility (although the film might be set in an unnamed Latin
American country, the Middle Ages, twenty-second-century middle America,
or nineteenth-century Russia); and an underachieving outsider who has spent
years in analysis but still wonders about his place in an absurd, godless universe. Out of this Jewish Freudian urban existentialist stew, the Woody Allen
character in each film delivers perceptive wisecracks and one-liners while
(usually unsuccessfully) pursuing beautiful women, fleeing from various life-
threatening situations, and occasionally offering absurdist commentary on
the human condition. In these early years, critics often compared Allen to the
Marx Brothers, Charlie Chaplin, Buster Keaton, and Harold Lloyd, setting
him firmly in the clown tradition of film comedy.

Annie Hall transcended such categorization. Indeed, Allen has described it
as a "turning point" in his filmmaking. In an interview with Stig Bjorkman, he
says the following:

> I had the courage to abandon . . . just clowning around and the
> safety of complete broad comedy. I said to myself, "I think I will try
> to make some deeper film and not be as funny in the same way. And
> maybe there will be other values that will emerge, that will be inter-
> esting, or nourishing for the audience." And it worked out very well.[2]

In many obvious ways, *Annie Hall* was a departure. It was the first of Allen's
films to focus so much attention on the female protagonist (although the film's
viewpoint is clearly that of Allen's alter ego, Alvy). It was also the first film to
celebrate so strongly his love of New York City, which would become a defining
characteristic of the Allen canon for many years to follow. It established Allen's
reputation as a respected screenwriter and one of the foremost directors of his
era. It also initiated the foregrounding of many of the issues that would appear in
Allen's later work. Sander H. Lee enumerates several of these themes, including
Allen's fascination with psychoanalysis; sexuality and gender roles; mortality; the
role of the outsider; and the existential issues of freedom, responsibility, anguish,
guilt, bad faith, and authenticity, among others.[3]

Annie Hall did not emerge full-blown from Allen's brain. It began as a series of lengthy and wide-ranging conversations with his cowriter, Marshall Brickman, who had worked with Allen three years earlier on *Sleeper*. Richard A. Schwarz describes the wildly differing directions taken by the script on its way to final form, writing the following:

> Originally the story was to be a murder mystery in which Annie Hall and her boyfriend, Alvy Singer, prove that the apparent suicide of a life-affirming philosophy professor was actually murder. In the next version, the professor was replaced by a neighbor. . . . Next, the story became a farce set in Victorian England and then a stream of consciousness exploration of Alvy's mind as he turns forty and tries to understand his life. In that version, his relationship with Annie Hall was only one aspect of the story. Allen filmed and edited this version, which he entitled *Anhedonia*—a condition whose symptom, the inability to experience pleasure, is characteristic of Alvy but not Annie. However, test audiences . . . were engaged by the love story between Annie and Alvy, which subsequently became the film's focus.[4]

The suicide and murder material that was deleted from the film's final version showed up later in *Crimes and Misdemeanors* (1989) and *Manhattan Murder Mystery* (1993), but many other comic treasures also fell by the wayside. Julian Fox's documentation of the vast amount of material from these earlier versions that were filmed and then cut from the final product gives a glimpse of the rich comic creativity generated by this project. These sequences include a "French resistance fantasy, a dream sequence set in the Garden of Eden, a run-in between the teenage Alvy and a gang of bikers, as well as a spoof on *Invasion of the Body Snatchers*."[5] The scene in the film where Alvy slips away from a reception of New York intellectuals to watch a Knicks game on television was originally followed by a "fantasy in which Alvy joins in the game, playing on a team alongside Kafka and Nietzsche, but losing the ball to the real life Earl Monroe."[6] The final version also eliminated a fantasy sequence in which "Alvy, Annie, and Rob are transported by the Devil on a guided tour of Hell's nine layers. Level Five, for instance, is for 'organized crime, fascist dictators, and people who don't appreciate oral sex.'"[7]

The shape of the finished product was also determined a great deal by Allen's and Brickman's increasing appreciation of the immense charm of Keaton's personality. According to Fox,

> Incorporated are a number of Diane's own quirks and distinctive speech patterns, though the famous "lah-de-dah" catch-phrase was an invention. But it was Diane's endearing stop-start manner of speaking, apologetic, almost self-effacing acting style, and abrupt embarrassed

giggles which Woody and Brickman found so captivating and indicative of the character. These elements, combined with Diane's real life semi-naive/semi-wise sayings, are duly worked into the screenplay.[8]

Ralph Rosenblum, Allen's cinematographer on the film, provides numerous other examples of the wealth of surrealistic material that he, Allen, and Brickman had to remove to trim the original two hours and twenty minutes down to a ninety-four-minute film and to focus the story on the two main characters and their relationship. Rosenblum describes the setup, saying, "Light-headed, devil-may-care Midwestern girl who grew up in a Norman Rockwell painting meets urban Jewish comedian who has enough awareness for both of them and hang-ups to match."[9]

In its final form, *Annie Hall* manages to imitate, develop, and eventually subvert the genre of the Hollywood romantic comedy. In the meantime, it achieves a particularly inventive type of cinematic narrative. All of this is accomplished because of the fundamentally neurotic character of the protagonists. Fox's description of the romantic plot shows how the film's use of so many technical tricks in its screenplay and editing mirrors the self-consciousness of the main characters and the fitful progress and eventual demise of their relationship:

> The story is largely a series of amusing, often touching, two-handed confrontations between Alvy and Annie, as they meet, become friends, fall in love, quarrel, break up, get back together, and part for good. The film employs flashbacks, flash forwards, split screens, double exposure, instant replay, free association, interior monologue, subtitles, pseudo-documentary, and even animation.[10]

Nevertheless, *Annie Hall* follows the standard romantic comedy formula well enough, sometimes even brilliantly. In her study of the literature, Kathrina Glitre observes that, while the movie basically presents its story from Alvy's viewpoint, it continues to use the "dual-focus narrative" of the typical Hollywood romantic comedy. She writes the following:

> Such a narrative places equal emphasis on the hero and the heroine, alternating between their points of view, leading to patterns of simultaneity, repetition, parallelism, and comparison, rather than cause-and-effect progression. The dual focus usually works to articulate the conflict between male and female. . . . The dual-focus narrative usually involves a process of compromise, not conquest. Where classical narrative privileges the values of the hero by villainizing his opposite in a good-versus-evil conflict, dual focus narrative lends positive weight to both sides of the argument, continually renegotiating the balance of power and creating a more egalitarian structure of desire.

Indeed, this process may include the reversal of the couple's original positions, enabling a degree of mutual self-education to take place and suggesting the potential for change.[11]

Tamar Jeffers McDonald, in her defense of the genre, sardonically insists that "even *Annie Hall*, possibly the most radical film in choosing to deny the audience an ending with the couple's union, does not suggest that the goal of finding one's true love is no longer desirable, merely impossible."[12]

Annie and Alvy's romance certainly seems to provide a "mutual self-education" for both of them, but especially for Alvy. Graham McCann observes that Annie's vitality "breathes life into Alvy's meticulously ordered existence." The first time they make love (which occurs unusually early for the typical romantic comedy formula), Alvy confesses, "That was the most fun I've ever had without laughing." McCann remarks that the "scene is probably the single occasion in which Alvy's intellectual and sensual interests truly complement each other," enabling their relationship to deepen into something quite profound and vital:

> When Annie asks Alvy if he loves her, Alvy refers directly to the inadequacy of language when expressing genuinely unique, intimate feelings: "I-uh-love is, uh, too weak a word for what I . . . I *lerve* you. You know, I *lo-ove* you, I-I-I *loff* you." . . . In the amorous passages of our lives, we lose the purchase on our states of mind that the categories of everyday language exert. The more vividly alive we are, the less able we are to commit ourselves to words worthy of that feeling.[13]

However, when Annie decides to move in with Alvy, he is clearly uncomfortable with the arrangement. McCann sees this as stemming from Alvy's awareness of the mutability and evanescence of life, embodied so obviously in Annie's particular ability to adapt and evolve. While Alvy has clearly taken on the task of changing and molding Annie to his own ideals, her very ability to grow unnerves him:

> To love her is to accept that she will at some time be otherwise. Alvy seems to sense the death that lurks beneath the love affair. He prepares himself, almost from the first day, for that moment when he will discern, on the skin of the relationship, a certain minute stain appearing there as the symptom of a certain death.[14]

Such a dire development of the romance finally leads to the end of the relationship, prompting McDonald to label the film a "radical romantic comedy . . . aware of the difficulties of modern love":

The film notes that sexual attraction fades, people have serial romances, Alvy himself has two failed marriages, Annie loses interest in sex and cannot relax without taking marijuana, puts Alvy off, or, giving in, endures the act by detaching her attention. The film's bravery in confronting the realities of modern love culminates in its ending, which insists that the couple, though meeting again and enjoying each other's company, does not ultimately reform.[15]

In the end, although their romance has died, a genuine love and peculiar beauty survives. McCann concludes the following:

> Alvy is left with his art, his seductive fantasies, to fill the space where Annie once was. Death, the first question, is also the final question: The movie began with an admission of the aging process and the death of a love affair, and it closes with a haunting montage of memories from that affair. Only now, in her absence (a death of a kind) can Alvy love her: He is the projectionist, he conjures up the images. Alvy, having struggled to overcome the mind/body conflict for so long, belatedly comes to appreciate that this conflict is, perhaps, the grit that makes the pearl.[16]

Despite all the failure, the film concludes in a wave of romantic nostalgia at least, if not an even deeper commitment to continue searching for love, no matter how unreachable it seems to be.

Lee's study of the film offers a direct connection between the film and psychotherapy, observing that the "organization of *Annie Hall* may be viewed as a series of therapy sessions, with Alvy as the patient and the audience as analysts."[17] The film's opening sequence establishes the motif of neurosis with some inventive techniques. This was the first time that Allen used what would become his familiar title presentation, the white lettering on a black background with no musical score. The film then begins abruptly with a medium close-up of a figure who appears to be the stand-up comedian, Woody Allen, dressed as if he had just walked onto the set, in his familiar tweed jacket, plaid shirt, and black-rimmed glasses, speaking directly to the camera and beginning a monologue, as if the audience were his therapist. His opening comments include a reference to Sigmund Freud's *Wit and Its Relationship to the Unconscious* (1916) and to Groucho Marx and the Catskill resorts, thus reminding everyone of the similarity between stand-up comedy and the "talking cure" known as psychotherapy. After a bit of verbal throat-clearing with a couple of jokes, Woody morphs into his character, Alvy, who seems to be using this particular therapy session to deal with two issues, the crisis of his recently reaching the age of forty and the ending of his romantic relationship with Annie Hall. He says, "I still can't get my mind around that. . . . I keep sifting the pieces of the relationship through my mind . . . tryin' to figure out . . . where did the screw-up come." Alvy, as a successful stand-up comedian, seems to illustrate Freud's own opinion of the therapeutic value of humor. Quoting Freud, Mary Nichols comments on the connection of neurosis and comedy, saying the following:

> "The program of becoming happy, which the pleasure principle imposes on us," Freud writes in *Civilization and Its Discontents*, "cannot be fulfilled," for "life as we find it is too hard for us," and "brings too many pains, disappointments, and impossible tasks." "In order to bear it, we cannot dispense with palliative measures" such as those [that] "cause us to make light of our misery." Comedy, laughter, jokes, for Freud—and for Alvy at the beginning of *Annie Hall*—serve as lies that make life bearable, ways of "making light" of what is not light, a forgetting necessary for life. Life's miseries, presumably, are why anhedonist Alvy is a comedian.[18]

The narrative then develops, first of all, by the typically therapeutic method of recalling one's childhood. Alvy claims that he was a "reasonably happy kid," but the childhood instances that are recalled in flashbacks are anything but happy. His mother took him to the family doctor because he was depressed and refused to do his homework after he had read that the universe was expanding and would someday explode. "What's the point" of doing homework in such a universe, the young Alvy asks. His family home is shown in its tremulous condition under the continuous rattling of the Coney Island roller coaster. He is shown at his father's bumper car concession, letting out his aggression by deliberately bumping into the other drivers. Six-year-old Alvy is shown kissing the girl at the neighboring desk, disgusting her but expressing what he claims to be a "healthy sexual curiosity." He remembers when his teacher compared him unfavorably with his classmates but then imagines where they have all ended up as he and they all turn forty years old (one of them is a methadone addict, another is "into leather"). Finally, his mother is shown symbolically castrating both the young and the grown-up Alvy as she peels carrots and offers a list of his psychological failings, saying, "You always only saw the worst in people. You never could get along with anyone in school. You were always out of step with the world. Even when you got famous, you still mistrusted the world."

The film then moves closer to the present and the narrative of Alvy's and Annie's year of living romantically, but in the course of the story, numerous references to psychotherapy continue. In his first meeting with Annie, Alvy tells her that he has been in analysis for fifteen years, with little apparent progress. "One more year," he says, "and I'm going to Lourdes." His years of analysis are mentioned several times. At one point, when Annie invites Alvy to smoke some marijuana with her, she says, "Oh come on. You've been seeing a psychiatrist for fifteen years. You should smoke some o' this. You'd be off the couch in no time." At an Easter dinner at the Halls' home, Annie's mother's first words to Alvy are, "Ann tells us that you've been seeing a psychiatrist for fifteen years." In his stand-up performance at the University of Wisconsin, Alvy confesses that at one point in his life he was so depressed and suicidal that "I would have killed myself but I was in analysis with a strict Freudian, and if you kill yourself . . . they make you pay for the sessions you miss."

Later, Alvy convinces Annie to start seeing a therapist. In her first session, she achieves significant psychological breakthroughs, talking about her feelings toward men, her relationship with her brother, and her guilt around issues of marriage and children. She recalls her experience of the classic childhood trauma of coming upon one's parents having sex. She breaks down in tears (something Alvy claims he has never been able to do in the fifteen years of his therapy), and then she recounts her dream of Alvy suffocating her and the possibility of her castrating him. "All of this in the first hour!" Alvy exclaims. Later, Allen uses a split screen to show Alvy's and Annie's therapy sessions (with two-thirds of the screen devoted to Alvy). Annie is seated in an Eames chair, in a brightly lit and decorated office, speaking with her female therapist about her realization that, after six months of sessions, she has a right to her own feelings and she need not feel obliged to have sex with Alvy. Meanwhile, Alvy is reclining on the traditional leather therapy couch in what looks like a nineteenth-century wood-lined office, complaining to his elderly—and apparently bored—therapist that he is paying for Annie's therapy and she is making progress while "I'm the one who's getting screwed." While still in the split-screen mode, when asked how often they have sex, Alvy replies, "Hardly ever . . . maybe three times a week." Annie says, "Constantly! I'd say three times a week!"

But Alvy does not depend only on his therapist for counseling. When Annie, fed up with his jealousy, breaks up with him and hops in a cab, Alvy turns to people on the sidewalk for some answers. One older woman walking by tells him that he hasn't done anything wrong. She tells him, "It's never something you do. That's how people are. Love fades." Another older character tells him of the large vibrating egg that he and his wife use to improve their love life (causing Alvy to reflect, "I ask a psychopath; I get that kind of an answer"). He asks an attractive couple who look "very happy" for the secret of their successful relationship, and they tell him that they're both "shallow and empty . . . have no ideas and nothing interesting to say." He then walks into the street to share his feelings with a horse belonging to a mounted police officer. This version of group therapy only affirms Alvy's generally pessimistic view of life and relationships, while suggesting that the unexamined life might well be the only life worth living and that a horse might be as helpful a listener as humans.

Near the end of the film, after Annie has definitely ended their relationship, Alvy once again engages in some sidewalk therapy. As he leaves a movie theater complaining about how deeply he misses Annie and feels that he has made a terrible mistake, a couple overhears him—cleverly subverting the technique of the interior monologue that the audience has become accustomed to by this point in the film—and informs him that Annie is living in California with a new boyfriend, whom, they add, is not the "jerk" that Alvy thinks he is. An elderly woman then walks up and asks Alvy why he doesn't go out with other women. When he replies that he has tried, but "it's very depressing," she throws up her hands and walks away. The neurotic implication is that not only the film's audience, who has served as his therapist from the film's opening monologue, but everyone else is aware of his problematic love life.

Alvy's suave friend Rob (Tony Roberts) appears several times in the film to react to Alvy's habitual whining and offer advice, focusing mainly on the idea of moving out to California and enjoying a sexually liberated life, but he does his most direct counseling when he, Annie, and Alvy (whom, for some reason, he always addresses as "Max") drive out to Brooklyn to visit the "old neighborhood." When the three of them visit Alvy's childhood home, they somehow participate in a group flashback. In one sequence, they witness Alvy's parents arguing; then they observe them hosting a party for their eccentric relatives and friends. As the parents argue, Alvy screams at them, "You're both crazy," to which Rob responds, "They can't hear you, Max"; however, when they watch Alvy's mother at the party bragging about her sister, Tessie, as the "one with personality," Rob manages to make them hear him, as he asks Tessie about her personality and the many men who were interested in her in her younger days. She replies that she was a great beauty and good dancer. Rob's easygoing, pleasure-seeking attitude seems to have no trouble relating to people, even if it involves time travel. In his reminding Alvy that the people in Alvy's past can't hear him (although they hear and respond to Rob) and that Aunt Tessie's portrayal of herself as a "great beauty" is "hard to believe," Rob might—at least in contrast to the neurotic Alvy—represent the reality principle essential to good analysis.

While Alvy is plagued by numerous neuroses, the film focuses mainly on his anhedonia. Annie—and, to a lesser extent, Rob—provide alternative attitudes. Ironically, as Richard Blake points out, the creepy chain-smoking Dr. Flicker in the film's first flashback, offers the "solution that summarizes Allen's [and Alvy's] own attempts to reach reconciliation with his hostile world, when he advises him to enjoy life as much as he can while he has it."[19] Alvy claims that "I am not the morose type. I'm not a depressive character." Yet, his obsession with death, which brought him to Dr. Flicker in the first place and which is expressed in his preference for "books with death in the title," provides the basic underpinning of his many other phobias. His basic attitude is well summarized in his first joke in the film about the elderly woman dining in the Catskills resort who complains that the food is terrible, only to have her companion respond, "Yeah I know . . . and such small portions." Alvy remarks, "That is essentially how I feel about life . . . full of loneliness and misery and suffering and unhappiness, and it's all over much too quickly." This attitude appears again in the life lesson he offers to Annie early in their relationship, that "life is divided up into the horrible and the miserable." Alvy considers the "horrible" to be terminal cases and blind and crippled people, and the "miserable are everybody else."

This combination of a fear of death and a view of the journey toward death as "divided between the horrible and the miserable" is linked with a fundamental hostility bordering on misanthropy. The child crashing his bumper car into the other rides at Coney Island is father to the man. The list of people Alvy dislikes is quite extensive. He resents his incompetent schoolteachers; his fellow grade-school classmates; the fans outside the Beekman movie theater who recognize him as the "guy on television"; the pompous media professor in another movie line expounding on the theories of Marshall McLuhan; the intellectuals whom his second wife fawns over at a literary reception; the "pathetic" comedian who hires Alvy to provide him with material; Annie's former boyfriends, especially the flaky actor; the literature professor in Annie's adult education course; the "asshole" Joey Nichols who always came to his parents' parties; "Grammy Hall," whom he calls a "classic Jew hater"; Tony Lacey, the award-winning singer-songwriter who woos Annie away from him; and the *Rolling Stone* reporter who, when he goes on a date with her to a Maharishi Yoga concert, sings the praises of Bob Dylan and Mick Jagger and other stars of the rock music world as she declares the Maharishi event to be "transplendent."

It is worth noting that his first conversation with Annie, after a terrifying ride up the F. D. R. drive with Annie at the wheel, consists mainly of put-downs and expressions of disapproval of her. When Annie slams on the brakes, turns the car sharply, and awkwardly backs into a parking space, Alvy declares, "That's okay, you . . . we-we can walk to the curb from here." He then pronounces her the "worst driver I've ever seen in my life." He only gets more hostile once inside her apartment. When she tells him that her tie is a gift from her "Grammy," he responds, "My Grammy . . . n-never gave gifts, you know. She-she was too busy getting raped by Cossacks." When Annie comments that some of Sylvia Plath poems "seem neat," Alvy says, "Uh, I hate to tell yuh, this is 1975, you know that 'neat' went out, I would say, at the turn of the century."

He shows himself unwilling to indulge in anything that might be too enjoyable and resents other people's enjoyment of life. Annette Wernblad observes the following:

> Most importantly, Alvy is not only unable to enjoy himself, but he is distracted and inhibited when other people do so, as is brilliantly illustrated in the early scene where as a child he is all but incapable

of eating his borscht because hedonists are riding the roller coaster above his house.[20]

Throughout the film, Alvy consistently begs off opportunities to indulge in pleasurable activities and social activities. In his second marriage, he slips away from the reception for the New York intellectuals whom his wife (Janet Margolin) finds so exciting, ostensibly to watch a Knicks game on television, but actually to opt out of the gathering. Out at his Long Island beach house, he opposes Annie's suggestion that they go to a party with friends. When he and Annie receive another invitation from Tony (Paul Simon) to join him in a drink with "Jack [Nicholson] and Angelica [Huston]," Alvy makes up a story about "that thing" that he and Annie are supposed to take care of. When Tony assures them that the gathering would be "mellow," Alvy responds, "I don't think that I could take a mellow evening. I don't respond well to 'mellow.' I have a tendency, if I mellow, I get too ripe and then I rot." Just as he had declined Annie's invitations to join her in smoking some marijuana, when offered a chance to try some expensive cocaine, he sneezes into the powder, scattering it to the winds.

Alvy's anhedonia expresses itself most particularly in his animosity toward California and his preference for and identification with New York City. Rob, having constantly encouraged Alvy to move out to California, finally does so himself. Annie also eventually moves out there to advance her singing career and move in with Tony. It must be mentioned that, at the time of the film's release in 1977, the popular perception of New York City was quite negative. Coping with fiscal collapse; awash in street crime; and dealing with a large homeless population, abandoned neighborhoods, and the drugs and sex of Plato's Retreat and Studio 54, New York City was seen as the very embodiment of social and moral decay. The year of the film's release was also the Summer of Sam, the serial killer, and the two-day power outage that paralyzed the overheated city and led to major looting and other criminal activity. Rob's recollection of working in the city likely struck a chord with many in the audience at the time. "I did Shakespeare in the Park, Max. I was mugged. I was playing Richard the Second and two guys with leather jackets stole my leotard." Even Alvy is forced to acknowledge the city's problems. As he tells Rob, "The rest of the country looks upon New York like we're-we're left-wing communist, Jewish, homosexual pornographers. I think of us that way, sometimes, and I-I live here." Yet this is the city that Alvy clearly prefers.

Woody himself describes his sense of the contrast between the two cities:

> Los Angeles is fine. It's just not to my taste. . . . I just don't like that kind of light. I don't like sunshine. And I don't like it where everything is spread out and you need a car to go to every place. It doesn't have a cosmopolitan feeling or a cosmopolitan quality,

the type that I'm used to, like London or Paris or Stockholm or Copenhagen or New York. There it's more of a suburban feeling. So I'm not comfortable. I like to be able to walk out of my house and have the whole city around me, pavement to walk on and stores and places to go. . . . Also between the television industry and the film industry so much of what comes out of there is in bad faith. It's done for the sake of exploitation.[21]

Much of that description—and more—is rendered visually in the film's two sequences depicting Alvy's visits to Los Angeles. On the first visit, Alvy arrives at Christmastime, and, while it is remarked that it's snowing in New York City, the holiday in Los Angeles looks completely plastic, with statues of Santa and his reindeer sitting on green lawns underneath rows of palm trees, while canned Christmas carols blare on the sound track. A movie marquee announces its double feature, *House of Exorcism* and *Messiah of Evil,* as if to question the carolers' reassuring words that "Christ our Savior was born . . . to save us all from Satan's power."

Rob, now living there, reports that he has "never been so relaxed" and that he lives next door to Hugh Hefner and gets to use Hefner's Jacuzzi. Alvy, of course, responds with several hostile observations. While Annie notices that the city is so clean, Alvy says that it's because "they don't throw their garbage away. They make it into television shows." When Rob reminds him that there's no crime or muggings in L.A., Alvy answers, "There's no economic crime, you know, but there's-there's ritual, religious-cult murders, you know, there's wheat-germ killers out here."

Alvy is disgusted by Rob's need to use a laugh-track machine while editing his hit situation comedy to make up for the fact that the show doesn't inspire any genuine laughter from its live audience. Alvy experiences a psychosomatic fit of dizziness and nausea at the prospect of appearing on television to give an award—the reason for the trip in the first place. Once he finds out that they have found a substitute for him on the show, his health returns immediately. Tony's lavish Christmas party is filled with L.A. types conversing in Hollywood jargon about "taking a meeting," developing something from a "notion" into a "concept" and later "an idea" (if "I can get money"). One of the guests needs to call someone because "I forgot my mantra," while other partygoers brag about watching *Grand Illusion* in Tony's private screening room while stoned. All of this drives Alvy's party chatter into hypercritical mode, with comments about his feet not having touched pavement since they've been in Los Angeles; the need for a road map to find the bathroom in Tony's mansion; and references to such trendy L.A. items as food-tasters, est, shock therapy, and the psychic Uri Geller.

Later, after Annie has moved in with Tony, Alvy, realizing how much he loves and misses her, makes the admirable sacrifice of a return trip to Los Angeles to ask Annie to move back to New York City and to marry him. Again, Los Angeles is bathed in sunlight as Alvy actually dares to drive a car to meet Annie at an outdoor health food restaurant, where he orders the "alfalfa sprouts and, uh, a plate of mashed yeast." Annie appears to have adjusted well to L.A. lifestyle, having traded in her androgynous thrift shop New York City wardrobe for a white linen sundress and sunglasses and a schedule of meeting new people, going to parties, playing tennis, and accompanying Tony to the Grammy Awards. Above the annoying sound of the Sunset Boulevard traffic, Annie rejects his marriage proposal. Alvy abruptly leaves the restaurant; manages to crash into other cars in the restaurant's parking lot (reenacting his childhood bumper car activities); and experiences a meltdown in the presence of an intimidating Aryan-type traffic cop, ending up in the Los Angeles County jail. When Rob arrives to bail him out, he informs Alvy that his phone call from jail interrupted his make-out session with sixteen-year-old twins. (Dark humor alert: Roman Polanski had been arrested for similar activity earlier in the very year of the film's release.) Rob then puts on an elaborate helmet and goggles for driving in his convertible, explaining that the outfit "keeps out the alpha rays, Max. You don't get old."

On the surface, Alvy's anti-California stance might appear to be simply another expression of his aversion to physical pleasure and his resentment of other people's enjoyment. Annie even accuses Alvy of such an attitude, saying, "L.A. is perfectly fine. . . . You're incapable of enjoying life . . . your life is New York City . . . like this island unto itself." However, the rejection of the pleasurable California lifestyle is more than a knee-jerk attack of anhedonia. As Nichols observes, it is a fundamental life choice:

> Unlike Rob and Annie, Alvy loves New York, even if, as the self-righteous Californians claim, it has become such a dirty city. Alvy, after all, is "into garbage." Nor does he share Rob's and Annie's infatuation with what he calls Munchkin land. . . . Rob should be doing Shakespeare in the Park, he urges, not Hollywood sitcoms. In California, he thinks, people simply watch movies all day and eventually get old and die. It is a lifestyle that no thinking person could choose. The complete self-satisfaction that California represents to Alvy leaves no room for thought. Nor does it leave room for striving. . . . We begin to see "civilization and its discontents," even New York City garbage in a different light, if canned laughter and thoughtless satisfaction is its alternative. . . . There would be something good about alienation itself, and even a wholesome discontent, if alienation were the condition for thought, and discontent the condition for striving.[22]

Fox's description of the difference between the two cities for Alvy is both succinct and comprehensive. He says that "for Alvy, as for Woody in real life, the West Coast is an environment where artistically, intellectually, and in this case, emotionally, he cannot function."[23] He quotes a British critic's commentary on the New York City audience's reaction to *Annie Hall* as "something of a shared perception . . . that someone has managed to articulate, for the first time, the distinctive ways in which many people survive the bizarre rigors of social and erotic life in New York."[24]

Alvy is also hindered from enjoying life and achieving romantic success because of his confusion about the relationship between art and life. He even admits in his opening monologue that "I have some trouble between fantasy and reality." In the very telling of the story, audiences and critics alike appreciated the film's inventive use of what Peter J. Bailey calls "antimimetic devices," which "establish a visual representation of Alvy's subjective reality."[25] When, for example, infuriated by the pontifications on the work of Fellini and the theories of Marshall McLuhan made by a pompous film professor standing behind him and Annie in a movie theater line, Alvy manages to bring McLuhan himself into the scene to roundly refute the professor, telling him, "You know nothing of my work." Alvy then turns to the camera and exclaims to the audience, "Boy, if life could only be like this!" Bailey remarks the following:

> Only in artistic wish-fulfillment is Marshall McLuhan available to serve our yearnings for revenge against the outrages reality inflicts. . . . The disparity between mental projections of reality and actuality is the pedal chord of *Annie Hall*, and its antimimetic emblems are the notes comprising that chord.[26]

This is definitively displayed at the end of the film, when Alvy once again turns to the audience as therapist. Observing a rehearsal of a scene from a play he has just written, a scene that re-creates his encounter with Annie in the health food restaurant but that ends with the Annie character inexplicably changing her mind and agreeing to marry the Alvy character, Woody semiapologizes to the audience, saying, "Tsch, whatta you want? It was my first play. You know, you know how you're always tryin' t' get things to come out perfect in art because, uh, it's real difficult in life."

The narrative form of the film itself relies on this reality-fantasy dilemma. Allen presents the entire story as a series of flashbacks about a failed romance narrated by the jilted lover himself. The film is thus structured as an associative act of self-reflexivity so that the story is not told in chronological order and is frequently interrupted by subjective interpretations bordering on pure fantasy. Even in what would otherwise be straightforward passages in the film's narrative track, Allen permits elements of fantasy to intervene. He provides subtitles for Annie and Alvy as they self-consciously engage in what begins as a realistic bit of flirtatious small talk in their first conversation in her apartment:

> ALVY: Photography's interesting, 'cause, you know, it's a new art form, and, uh, a set of aesthetic criteria have not emerged yet.
>
> *(I wonder what she looks like naked?)*

ANNIE: Aesthetic criteria? You mean, whether it's, uh, good photo or not?

(I'm not smart enough for him. Hang in there.)

ALVY: The-the medium enters in as a condition of the art form itself. That's-

(I don't know what I'm saying—she senses I'm shallow.)

At Easter dinner at Annie's family home, Allen presents Alvy as he imagines he must appear to the Halls—especially the "Jew-hater" Grammy—as an Orthodox Jew, dressed in a long black coat and hat, with a mustache and beard. Alvy once again addresses the film audience directly, commenting on how "American" and healthy the Halls look, "nothing like my family." The screen splits to show the two families, the Halls eating quietly and politely in an elegant family dining room, the Singers at a crowded kitchen table, eating frantically, interrupting one another loudly, and arguing. The Halls's and the Singers's dialogue overlap, and they eventually address each other across the split screen to talk about how the Singers spend the Jewish holidays (fasting for their sins).

Numerous other elements of fantasy bordering on theater of the absurd occur throughout the film. These include Alvy's various discussions of his love life with strangers on the street; the transition to animated film with Annie, Rob, and Alvy as characters in a cartoon version of *Snow White*; the flashback-within-a-flashback when they visit Alvy's childhood home in Brooklyn and another similar device when Annie and Alvy watch her interact with two of her earlier boyfriends; the double exposure when Annie steps outside of her body while she and Alvy are having sex because she feels distant from him; the split-screen portrayal of Annie and Alvy's therapy sessions; Alvy's appeal to the film audience in the middle of an argument when he needs them to verify that Annie said, "Will it change my wife?" (he says to the audience: "You heard that because you were there, so I'm not crazy"); and the on-screen presentation of Alvy reverting to his childhood bumper car behavior as he crashes into cars in the health food restaurant's parking lot. Fantasy and reality collide regularly throughout the film.

But, as Bailey observes, while these "self-reflective cinematic devices . . . constitute ingenious filmic means of . . . distilling the distinction between the world mentally constructed and reality," they raise the question of the relative validity of either realm:

> The irony of such scenes is that they distort the surface cinematic reality of a situation (Alvy and Annie's conversational sparring over the aesthetics of photography) . . . to express its underlying reality (the subtitles manifesting the truth [that] they're scrutinizing each other as prospective sexual partners).[27]

Bailey also averts to the real-life background of the film, which was widely understood to be based somewhat on the actual romantic relationship of Allen and Keaton:

> The roman à clef aspect of *Annie Hall* adds yet another layer of art/life ambiguity to the movie, reminding the attentive viewer that, for all its pretensions to documentary veracity, *Annie Hall* too is aesthetic artifice, another creator's deliberately fabricated effort to "get things to come out perfect in art."[28]

In his study of the film as a modernist tale told by an "unreliable narrator," Thomas Schatz describes it as an elaborately constructed comedy routine, saying the following:

> Through the framing device of the stand-up comedy routine, which is sustained throughout the film by means of various cinematic devices, Allen establishes a pretext for authorial intervention and character aside. . . . The comedy routine presents itself as the primary narrative level, with the courtship story as essentially another comic bit within the routine—albeit one that is developed at considerably greater depth and length than the other bits. In fact, until the courtship story begins some time later in the film . . . the organizing principle is the comic narrator's life, with the sequences following an associative rather than a chronological pattern.[29]

This "stand-up routine," however, with its technical and narrative devices, represents more than just a play on fantasy versus reality or a more sophisticated set of visual and verbal jokes that simply up the ante of Allen's comedy. Wernblad describes this film's change in Allen's comedy as an examination of the conflict between the heart and the brain, writing the following:

> The central dichotomy in Allen's work so far has been between the mind and the body, a dichotomy [that] could be seen as a reflection of the fantasy/reality distinction: the mind as the pursuer of fantasy and the body as the performer of reality. Also, the two forms of humor used in these works, slapstick and verbal, are closely connected with the division: slapstick as the comedy of the body and verbal humor as that of the intellect. Likewise, the basic situation of the Allen persona in the three films *Bananas*, *Sleeper*, and *Love and Death* is rooted in this dichotomy. Because the *schlemiel* is physically weak and placed in a hostile environment [that] threatens his body, he is forced to rely entirely on his oral rapidity and the ingenuity of his wits . . . to escape.
>
> In *Annie Hall* and most of Allen's subsequent films, the emphasis has shifted. The Allen persona is no longer displaced, but right in the

middle of his natural habitat, New York City. . . . Even though the
universe may be expanding . . . the body part of the earlier dichotomy
is of no real interest, and, accordingly, the slapstick gradually disappears from Allen's films. . . . The central dichotomy is between the
heart and the brain, the emotional and the intellectual.[30]

The heart, of course, finds its expression in the beauty and spontaneity of
Annie. When they first speak to one another, after a doubles tennis match with
Rob and, presumably, Rob's current girlfriend, Annie appears in an androgynous outfit—a floppy homburg, a loosely fitting pair of khakis, and a white dress
shirt with a vest and tie—and begins one of the most awkward and disjointed
dialogues in film history:

> ANNIE: Hi. Hi, hi.
>
> ALVY *(Looking over his shoulder)*: Hi. Oh, hi. Hi.
>
> ANNIE *(Hands clasped in front of her, smiling)*: Well . . . bye.
>
> *She laughs and backs up slowly toward the door.*
>
> ALVY *(Clearing his throat)*: You-you play . . . very well.
>
> ANNIE: Oh yeah? So do you. Oh, God, whatta—whatta dumb
> thing to say, right? I mean you say it, "You play well," and right away
> . . . I have to say well. Oh, oh . . . God, Annie. *(She gestures with her
> hand)* Well . . . oh, well . . . la-de-da, la-de-da, la-la.
>
> *She turns around and moves toward the door.*

This is followed by the terrifying ride in Annie's car to her apartment, Alvy's
demeaning comments about her driving and her Midwestern naiveté, and the
terribly self-conscious conversation in her apartment. Yet, as McCann observes,
in the two encounters at the tennis court and Annie's apartment, Alvy "seems
to be vaguely aware that this nervous, gauche woman possesses something that
he lacks: the ability to enjoy oneself."[31] Her very nervousness and awkwardness
express her vitality and spontaneity. McCann further remarks:

> Annie is the Other: not so much because she is a woman or a Gentile,
> but because she seems uninhibited and ever-changing. She can ex-
> press the emotions that Alvy keeps inside himself: she can sing, she is
> artistic, she is receptive to new ideas and images. . . . Annie embraces
> change, Alvy closes himself to it.[32]

However, when they first meet, as Lee points out, Alvy is older, more experienced, and more professionally successful than Annie:

Annie has little confidence in her abilities in the areas in which she "dabbles"—acting, photography, and singing. Thus the scene is set for Alvy to move completely into his favorite role, that of the romantic mentor taking in hand his younger, less sophisticated female protégé.[33]

Annie has her own neuroses, but they are the opposite of Alvy's. Wernblad describes the difference succinctly, mentioning the following:

While Annie too is neurotic, her neuroses manifest themselves not in depression and paranoia, but in a tendency to babble, make silly sounds, and occasionally laugh out of context. The most illuminating example of this is when, laughing hysterically, she tells a horrified Alvy the story of Grammy Hall's brother George, who suffered from narcolepsy and died while standing in line to get his free Christmas turkey from the union.[34]

Alvy attempts to change Annie by passing on to her his view of life as a mix of "the miserable and the horrible," giving her books to read on death, paying for her to see a therapist, dragging her to depressing films like Marcel Ophuls's Holocaust documentary *The Sorrow and the Pity* (1969), and encouraging her to take adult education classes. Foster Hirsch describes the process and its ultimate failure by writing the following:

They're equally neurotic. And indeed their anxieties, insecurities, and social terrors draw them together in the first place. Alvy, though, begins to take advantage of Annie's lack of self-confidence. . . . Treating Annie like an appendage to his own life and career, making her feel bad because she is not as bright as he is, generally reinforces her insecurities rather than trying to counteract them, he is the Svengali to her Trilby. Alvy is attracted to her precisely because she is someone he can mold. . . . Their relationship is based on the premise that Annie is an idiot; once she begins to question that, once she begins, however tentatively, to strike out on her own, cultivating friends and developing interests, the affair is doomed.[35]

Maurice Yacowar offers a similar observation, locating it in the myth of Pygmalion: "It is the story of an artist who falls in love with his own creation and loses her when she blossoms into full life."[36]

At the same time, Annie also attempts to change Alvy, even suggesting, when she offers to get together with him again after their first breakup, "Maybe I could help you have more fun, you know?" While she seems to be a willing student of Alvy's life lessons, engaging in every exercise he suggests and moving in with him even though she accuses him of thinking that she's "not smart enough," her deep-seated joie de vivre keeps hindering her best efforts to conform to Alvy's way of life. She cannot repress her laughter when she, Rob, and Alvy observe the flashback to Alvy's parent's arguments. She is always the one who is eager to accept invitations to parties or even cocaine. Eventually, she even takes up Tony's offer to move out to sunny California (and in with him), which represents everything Alvy resents. Ultimately, Annie's deep-seated joy wins out. As Wernblad describes it, "Despite all of Alvy's efforts . . . Annie persists in wanting to enjoy life, to be happy, and to smoke marijuana before making love. Ultimately, Annie's insistence on holding on to her own carefree and babbling personality is what breaks up their relationship."[37]

In general, Annie finds herself moving away from Alvy's mentoring and growing into a life of her own. She begins to "understand the references" in Alvy's stand-up comedy act; starts reading *National Review* because "I like to get all points of view"; makes significant progress in therapy; and even develops into a smooth, sophisticated cabaret singer. Sam B. Girgus observes that Annie's progress in personal independence and career growth, partly because of Alvy's influence on her, become obvious in her ability to use language more effectively":

> Annie's acquisition of more developed and coherent speech often evidences itself in rebellious exchanges with Alvy. . . . This relationship of language, power, and dependence is clear when Annie furiously responds to catching Alvy spying on her. She uses Alvy's own language against him: "Yeah, well, you wanted to keep the relationship flexible, remember? It's your phrase." . . . Returning to school at Alvy's suggestion, she angrily corrects Alvy's childishly jealous attempts to belittle her when he misstates the title of her adult education course: "'Existential Motifs in Russian Literature'! You're really close."[38]

In Annie's use of sarcasm and a sense of intellectual superiority, one can even feel that Annie has learned her lessons all too well, acquiring some skills that her Svengali may not have planned on passing on to her. Schwarz notes how even the very comedy of the film changes as Annie's character grows, stating the following:

> Because both Annie and Alvy are neurotic at the beginning of the film, their obsessions and insecurities make easy comic targets. However, as Annie begins to overcome her neuroses and become a stronger, more centered person, she becomes less the butt of the humor, and Alvy becomes more so. Thus, when he flies out to unfamiliar Los Angeles to try to retrieve her at the end of the movie, the jokes are entirely at Alvy's expense, or at California's, but never at Annie's. Their roles have become emphatically reversed; Annie now seems

cosmopolitan and mature, and Alvy is whiny and infantile. When Alvy, a notoriously poor driver, creates mayhem in a parking lot and then loses his composure before a policeman because figures of authority intimidate him, he is reduced to a farcical figure.[39]

In the end, both Annie and Alvy have grown. Blake summarizes their mutual progress beautifully:

> As she gains independence . . . Annie, who has received her life from Alvy, gradually seems to outgrow him. . . . During their separation scene in the health food restaurant, Annie acknowledges her debt to Alvy by reminding him that he was influential in helping her to grow emotionally and continue with her singing career. . . . The gift, however, is mutual. Because of Annie, Alvy has gotten over his severe case of anhedonia. . . . In the final monologue, he recounts the moments with her that he will cherish forever. After their lunch, he recalls how much he enjoyed simply knowing her. He no longer needs intellectual solutions to the problem of the "expanding universe" as he did while a child, nor does he need pleasures that will last beyond death. The transient, simple joys of life are enough to keep him going. But even more, Alvy as a playwright has been able to translate his experiences into art. In a rehearsal, young actors closely resembling Annie and Alvy discuss their breakup. . . . Alvy interrupts the scene to explain that it is only his first play. Life has made its way into Alvy's art and pushed back his limits of being a clever one-line comedian. Loving Annie has made Alvy a richer artist; loving Alvy has made Annie a richer person.[40]

The last few minutes of the film provide something of a coda to the story. In his closing monologue, Alvy describes how he had encountered Annie only recently. He states, "She had moved back to New York. She was living in SoHo with some guy. And when I met her she was, of all things, dragging him in to see *The Sorrow and the Pity*, which I considered as a personal triumph." They are then shown meeting for lunch at a restaurant in the Lincoln Center area. Since the scene is shot through the glass window of the restaurant, none of their conversation is heard, but they are clearly enjoying themselves as they "kick around old times," and a visual montage illustrates the sort of reminiscing in which they are engaged. They then leave the restaurant, and—this time with the camera inside the restaurant looking out through those same glass windows—the audience sees them shaking hands, engaging in a friendly kiss, and, as Annie crosses the street and moves out of the shot, Alvy is seen standing there watching her walk away. He turns and walks out of the frame as Diane Keaton sings the last note of "Seems Like Old Times." Then, in the final voice-over, Alvy recalls how great it was to see Annie again. "I realized what a terrific person she was and-and how much fun it was just knowing her."

In his explanation of the popularity of the film, especially with New York filmgoers, Fox observes that, "In the nervous romance of Alvy and Annie, they saw something of themselves and their environment, and attained through these two kindred spirits a warm insight into their own insecurities, plus the comfort to be derived from meaningful relationships."[41] Schatz's analysis of the film is less upbeat, claiming that the search to find out "where did the screw-up come," which Alvy poses at the beginning of the film, is never really answered. Yet even he concedes that the film seems to be saying that "human relationships are both an elemental necessity . . . 'we need the eggs' . . . and also a practical impossibility due to the general self-conscious alienation suffered by contemporary American culture—or at least by characters in Woody Allen's films."[42] Lee believes that the film's ending shows that "Alvy has overcome his anger at Annie and accepted the fact that romance often confuses and disappoints us. But, as with life itself in the opening joke about the Catskills resort, we cling to the magic of love in dread of the alternative."[43]

The film's conclusion also represents a more authentic resolution of Annie's conflicts and signifies true maturity on her part. Wernblad notes that Annie's life in California "could hardly be called independence. Instead of going to bookstores, movies, and delicatessens with Alvy and staying home from parties because he wanted to, she now goes to Grammy Awards with Tony because *he* is nominated.[44] She also points out that no mention is made of any advancement in Annie's singing career out in California. Annie's eventual return to New York and her preference for Alvy's movie choices is a personal victory, not just for Alvy, but also for Annie. "For all her delusive self-confidence in the Beverly Hills scene, Annie Hall had a preeminent personal style and was a much more exciting and energetic woman when she was confused and agitated in disconcerting New York City."[45]

The film's ending also comments on the role of art—particularly comic art—in one's efforts to deal with love and the meaning of life itself. Yacowar remarks:

> In this respect Annie is like life itself. Alvy loses her but learns to hold her in his memory and in his emotion. And through the art of film, Allen can hold her in yet another dimension; he can triumph over time and loss by transforming his experience into art. Alvy's treasuring homage to his lost love becomes Allen's melancholy homage to lost life and time. Annie Hall is a character as charming, as absurd, and as elusive as life itself. She embodies Alvy's denial of death through romantic love, and Allen's through art.[46]

Nichols also sees the ending as a reconciliation of several of the story's issues and conflicts: anhedonia versus joy, California versus New York, reality versus fantasy:

> Annie does return to New York from Los Angeles, but not with Alvy. . . . Although Allen does not romanticize the ending of *Annie Hall*, as Alvy does in his play, he does show that the former couple can meet as friends. . . . Friendship is neither the self-forgetting hedonism of sunny California nor the self-reflective alienation of New York intellectualism. It is something more than either. . . . Art can reflect happiness as well as sadness. . . . Alvy's first play, with its purely imaginary reunion of Alvy and Annie, unlike Allen's movie, is purely fiction. But then, Alvy asks the audience, "What do you want? It was my first play." If Woody Allen, stand-up comic, merges at the beginning of the film into Alvy Singer, who tells us about his relationship to Annie, perhaps Alvy Singer in the end can develop into an artist who, like Woody Allen, discovers a new kind of comedy, whose vision of life permits him to be funny in a different way.[47]

Nichols even suggests that the film offers a new way of looking at the function of comedy itself as a way of dealing with life's difficulties and the neuroses they create, positing the following:

> Do jokes, and comedy more generally, simply help to make life livable, as Freud suggests, or is comedy among the things that make life worth living? That is, is life not so miserable after all, and is comedy an indication of this? Is comedy not only a forgetting of what we must forget . . . to live but a reminder of why life is good? Comedy surely comes in a variety of forms, just as people laugh for different reasons. If one sort of comedy makes life livable by hiding its miseries, might there be another sort that expresses life's goodness?[48]

Annie Hall, then, might constitute an authentic, if neurotic, romantic comedy, after all. In the dual narrative that Glitre considers typical of the genre, this becomes not only an expression of Alvy's fear of life and love, but a celebration of Annie's appreciation of life's joys. She promises Alvy, "Maybe I could help you have more fun." Maybe, indeed, she can help us all.

A Sampling of Neurotic Comedy

Harold and Maude (1971)
The Jerk (1979)

Arthur (1981)
All of Me (1984)
What about Bob? (1991)
Benny & Joon (1993)
Rushmore (1998)
The Royal Tenenbaums (2001)
About Schmidt (2002)
I Heart Huckabees (2004)

Notes

1. All quotations from the film are taken from Woody Allen, *Four Films of Woody Allen* (New York: Random House, 1982).

2. Woody Allen, *Woody Allen on Woody Allen* (New York: Grove Press, 1993), 75.

3. Sander H. Lee, *Eighteen Woody Allen Films Analyzed: Anguish, God, and Existentialism* (Jefferson, N.C., and London: McFarland & Co., 2002), 35.

4. Richard A. Schwarz, *Woody, from* Antz *to* Zelig: *A Reference Guide to Woody Allen's Creative Work, 1964–1998* (Westport, Conn., and London: Greenwood Press, 2000), 17.

5. Julian Fox, *Woody: Movies from Manhattan* (Woodstock, N.Y.: Overlook Press, 1996), 14–15.

6. Fox, *Woody: Movies from Manhattan*, 15.

7. Fox, *Woody: Movies from Manhattan*, 15.

8. Fox, *Woody: Movies from Manhattan*, 92.

9. Ralph Rosenblum and Robert Karen, *When the Shooting Stops* (New York: Viking Press, 1980), 282.

10. Fox, *Woody: Movies from Manhattan*, 92.

11. Kathrina Glitre, *Hollywood Romantic Comedy: States of the Union, 1934–1965* (Manchester, U.K., and New York: Manchester University Press, 2006), 15.

12. Tamar Jeffers McDonald, *Romantic Comedy: Boy Meets Girl Meets Genre* (London and New York: Wallflower Press, 2007), 13.

13. Graham McCann, *Woody Allen* (Cambridge, UK: Polity Press, 1990), 108.

14. McCann, *Woody Allen*, 109.

15. McDonald, *Romantic Comedy*, 74.

16. McCann, *Woody Allen*, 112, 113.

17. Lee, *Eighteen Woody Allen Films Analyzed*, 35.

18. Mary Nichols, *Reconstructing Woody* (Oxford, UK, and Lanham, Md.: Rowman & Littlefield, 1998), 34.

19. Richard Blake, *Woody Allen: Profane and Sacred* (Lanham, Md.: Scarecrow Press, 1995), 67.

20. Annette Wernblad, *Brooklyn Is Not Expanding: Woody Allen's Comic Universe* (Cranbury, N.J.: Associated University Press, 1992), 65.

21. Allen, *Woody Allen on Woody Allen*, 90.

22. Nichols, *Reconstructing Woody*, 41.

23. Fox, *Woody: Movies from Manhattan*, 95.

24. Fox, *Woody: Movies from Manhattan*, 96–97.

25. Peter J. Bailey, *The Reluctant Film Art of Woody Allen* (Lexington: University Press of Kentucky, 2001), 35.

26. Bailey, *The Reluctant Film Art of Woody Allen*, 37.

27. Bailey, *The Reluctant Film Art of Woody Allen*, 37.

28. Bailey, *The Reluctant Film Art of Woody Allen*, 35.

29. Thomas Schatz, "*Annie Hall* and the Issue of Modernism." In *The Films of Woody Allen*, Charles L. P. Silet, ed. (Lanham, Md.: Scarecrow Press, 2006), 127–28.

30. Wernblad, *Brooklyn Is Not Expanding*, 69–70.

31. McCann, *Woody Allen*, 107.

32. McCann, *Woody Allen*, 107.

33. Lee, *Eighteen Woody Allen Films Analyzed*, 44.

34. Wernblad, *Brooklyn Is Not Expanding*, 64.

35. Foster Hirsch, *Love, Sex, Death, and the Meaning of Life: The Films of Woody Allen* (Cambridge, Mass.: DaCapo Press, 2001), 86.

36. Maurice Yacowar, *Loser Take All: The Comic Art of Woody Allen* (New York: Frederick Ungar Publishing Co., 1979), 172.

37. Wernblad, *Brooklyn Is Not Expanding*, 64–65.

38. Sam B. Girgus, *The Films of Woody Allen*, 2nd ed. (Cambridge, UK: Cambridge University Press, 2002), 56.

39. Schwarz, *Woody, from* Antz *to Zelig*, 17

40. Blake, *Woody Allen: Profane and Sacred*, 70–71.

41. Fox, *Woody: Movies from Manhattan*, 97–98.

42. Schatz, "*Annie Hall* and the Issue of Modernism," 130.

43. Lee, *Eighteen Woody Allen Films Analyzed*, 54.

44. Wernblad, *Brooklyn Is Not Expanding*, 67.

45. Wernblad, *Brooklyn Is Not Expanding*, 67.

46. Yacowar, *Loser Take All*, 184–85.

47. Nichols, *Reconstructing Woody*, 45–46.

48. Nichols, *Reconstructing Woody*, 35.

CHAPTER 9

Dionysian Comedy

NATIONAL LAMPOON'S ANIMAL HOUSE (1978)

The fall 1978 cover of *Newsweek* magazine displays a picture of John Belushi as John "Bluto" Blutarksy, the ringleader of the "animals" of Delta House in the major hit comedy of the year, *National Lampoon's Animal House*. Proudly overweight, smiling smugly with his right eyebrow mischievously arched, and crowned with a garland of vine leaves and the top of a toga visible on one shoulder, Bluto was the very reincarnation of Dionysius, the Greek god of wine, fertility, ecstasy, overindulgence, and anarchy.[1] A larger version of the portrait has gone on to grace the walls of college dorm rooms ever since. The magazine cover's headline reads, "College Humor Comes Back," and the five-page feature article by Tony Schwartz begins with a description of one of the most memorable scenes in the film:

> Lunchtime in the cafeteria at Faber College. As Bluto, the lovable glutton in *National Lampoon's Animal House*, John Belushi is making an astonishing trip down the cafeteria line. He gobbles down a goocy éclair, stuffs sandwiches into his pockets, inhales half a hamburger, and slides a huge slab of Jell-O down his throat, all the while piling food on his tray. Full up, he plops down at a table where his fraternity mate Otter is baiting some of the archenemies from the upstanding Omega House.
>
> "See if you can guess what I am now," he says, and stuffs mashed potatoes and gravy into his mouth until his cheeks bulge. Without warning, he slaps both cheeks, spraying the mess all over his horrified onlookers.
>
> "I'm a zit," he announces merrily, "Get it?"[2]

Everyone, critics and audiences alike, definitely got it. *Animal House* was a box-office phenomenon, the first Hollywood comedy to gross more than $100 million, having cost only $2.7 million to make.

John "Bluto" Blutarsky (John Belushi) leads his fraternity brothers in the destruction of Faber College's homecoming parade in *National Lampoon's Animal House* (1978).

Animal House is often cited as the ur-dumb-and-dumber film, or "slob comedy," or "frat boy comedy," creating a subgenre dear to the hearts of the twelve-to thirty-nine-year-old male demographic that keeps multiplexes in business and has created careers for the likes of Chris Farley, the Wayans Brothers, Adam Sandler, Jonah Hill, and many others; however, the film rises above its successors in its portrayal of college life as the closest most middle-class Americans will ever get to Dionysian frenzy. The situation and plot take on mythological proportions, and the hero of the myth is the Greek demigod Dionysius.

The comic situation is revealed in the film's opening sequence. Two "loser" freshmen, the dorky Larry Kroger (Tom Hulce) and the pudgy Kent Dorfman (Stephen Furst), make their way to a rush party during Pledge Week at the most prestigious fraternity on the Faber College campus, Omega House, populated by clean-cut student leader types who are quickly shown to be snobbish, condescending, and ambitious preppies with bubblehead girlfriends. Feeling distinctly unwelcome at Omega House, Larry and Kent next visit the "worst fraternity on campus," Delta House (officially Delta Tau Chi Fraternity) and are greeted by an intoxicated Bluto Blutarsky (John Belushi), who, as he turns to greet the newcomers, mindlessly urinates on their shoes. Entering the frat house, Larry and Kent are welcomed into an adolescent male wonderland of sex, alcohol, crude language, and other expressions of ungentlemanly conduct. The spontaneity and honesty of the group, however, sharply contrast with the hypocrisy of Omega House.

Animal House garnered critical raves for two reasons. First, reviewers picked up on and enjoyed the film as a tribute to the frat boy lifestyle. In his critique in *Time* magazine, Frank Rich admits, "At college, I halfheartedly admired the guys who tore themselves apart on Saturday night, but I never wanted to join their revels." The film apparently won Rich over to the fraternity code completely. After describing the scene in which Bluto perches on a ladder outside the window of a sorority house and "blissfully watches a gorgeous but prissy coed undress and fondle herself," Rich concludes, "At that point I realized that Belushi was right and that resistance to the movie's crudity was hopeless. . . . Anyone who won't join the fun is a prig."[3]

In *Newsweek*, David Ansen describes the boys of Delta House as a "raunchy band of misfits, degenerates, and social untouchables" whose goal is the "noisy pursuit of anarchy at all costs." Ansen goes on to describe the activities of the fraternity as a "panty raid on respectability," and he admires the film as "low humor of a high order."[4]

Roger Ebert was particularly impressed with the comic genius of *Animal House*. He writes:

> The movie is vulgar, raunchy, ribald, and occasionally scatological. It is also the funniest comedy since Mel Brooks made *The Producers* . . . because it finds some kind of precarious balance between insanity and accuracy, between cheerfully wretched excess and an ability to reproduce the most revealing nuances of human behavior. . . . It's like an end run around Hollywood's traditional notions of comedy. It's anarchic, messy, and filled with energy. It assaults us. Part of the movie's impact comes from its sheer level of manic energy . . . the anarchy is infectious.[5]

Even the reviewer in the usually sober *Christian Century* appreciates the anarchic humor and acknowledges that the "film has uproarious moments that are genuinely insightful." Describing the seduction by Eric Stratton (Tim Matheson) of a college girl by pretending to be the fiancé of her recently deceased roommate, the critic writes that the "ruse is both despicable and hilarious, and like several other incidents, it approaches the complex nature of American morality in a way that moralizing films never seem to approximate";[6] however, the critic also appreciates the film as an exercise in baby boom nostalgia, turning the clock back sixteen years to 1962 at fictional Faber College. *Animal House* was described as a "reverie about the golden age of college . . . a time when morality was less complex, when the demands of a rationality imposed by the educational process were counterbalanced by an outlandish irrationality."[7]

Schwartz offers a similarly nostalgic description of the college setting as a time and place for relatively safe rebellion before adulthood sets in:

> Smart-ass, gloating, salacious, everything but uptight, this is good old college humor—brought back with a vengeance. The enemy in *Animal House* is not so much Faber College dean Vernon Wormer [John Vernon], who wants to ban the appalling Delta House from campus, or even the goody-goodies of Omega House. It's the far more revolting prospect of growing up—which is to say, settling down. This is your last chance, *Animal House* says, to be alive and kicking.[8]

The Christian Century calls *Animal House* an "exercise in past, present, and future nostalgia," saying the following:

> *Animal House* plays on these fantasies, and theaters are filled with teenagers who gleefully look forward to bursting the bonds of parental restrictions, by college students who revel in the dramatization of these stories, and by graduates whose college experiences have become golden memories.[9]

In other words, *Animal House* offers a mythology, and the presiding deity of the myth is the god of wine, fertility, revelry, and excess: Dionysius. In true Dionysian fashion, the film attacks the bourgeois values guiding middle-class mores and, at the same time, Hollywood's traditional depiction of college life as both the playground and testing ground for middle-class American males.

The film acquires its Dionysian credentials and other connections to classical culture honestly. The writers were all postcollegiate types from distinguished universities founded on the tradition of classical liberal education. Douglas Kenney worked on the staff of the *Harvard Lampoon* as an undergraduate and later founded *National Lampoon* magazine with his friend Henry Beard. Chris Miller, during his time as contributing editor to the *National Lampoon* in 1974, began writing a series of short stories based on his own fraternity days at Dartmouth. Harold Ramis graduated from Washington University in St. Louis. College fraternities are often referred to as the "Greek system" because of their title letters, but do they perpetuate the tradition of the Athenian academy or the rural fertility rites? Meanwhile, other elements of ancient Greek literature find their way into the narrative of *Animal House*. The fraternity's resident lothario, Eric

Stratton, seduces the wife of Dean Wormer (Verna Bloom), who tells him that she is old enough to be his mother, an act that can be seen as a variation on the Oedipus story; the insertion of Delta House's "Eat Me" cake-shaped float into the homecoming parade repeats the stealth technique of the Trojan Horse. Beware these particular Greeks bearing gifts.

Schwartz may have erred, however, in hailing *Animal House* as the "comeback" of college humor. It would be more accurate to describe the film's anarchic view of college life as a distinct turning point in the history of college comedies coming out of Hollywood, going all the way back to the silent era. Portrayals of campus life and college students were comic fodder for many film comedians, with the films' plots usually focusing on the college years as a test of manhood. One of Harold Lloyd's biggest hits was *The Freshman* (1925), the story of a water boy for a collegiate football team who gets to play in the big game and wins. In *College* (1927), Buster Keaton portrays a bookworm working his way through college determined to become a star athlete to impress his new girlfriend. A year later, in one of his most admired films, *Steamboat Bill Jr.* (1928), Keaton again portrays an effete young man returning from college who tries to impress his rough-and-tumble steamboat captain father and win the heart of the rival steamboat captain's daughter. The lesser-known comedy team, the Ritz Brothers, starred in their own college romp, *Life Begins in College* (1937), in which the brothers help the school team win the big game. Dean Martin and Jerry Lewis starred in *That's My Boy* (1951), with Lewis as the athletically challenged son of the college football legend and Martin as the current star of the team hired by the father to coach Lewis. Several years later, Lewis returned to campus in one of his most successful films, *The Nutty Professor* (1963), which presented Lewis as an awkward, unattractive, and social inept chemistry professor who discovers an elixir that transforms him into a suave ladies' man. Almost all of these comedies sent the same message: Even in academia, athletic achievement or other signs of male prowess win the day.

A new pattern emerged in some of Hollywood's musical comedies of the 1930s and early 1940s, with college life mainly serving as a popular framework for the presentation of youthful exuberance. The formula made a lot of sense to the studio bosses. These loosely plotted comedies provided their star comedians with a vehicle for their standard routines, while also introducing audiences to some of the studios' attractive newcomers in the roles of energetic students. One of the early musical hits of the sound era was MGM's film version of a 1927 Broadway hit musical, *Good News* (1930), which features the "roaring twenties" dance number "The Varsity Drag," as well as the song "Football," which is sung three times during the course of the film. *College Humor* (1933) stars Bing Crosby as a college professor and George Burns and Gracie Allen as members of the faculty. Burns and Allen show up again a few years later in *College Holiday* (1936), a musical that also features Jack Benny and Martha Raye in the cast. Bob Hope joins the gang in another musical, *College Swing* (1938), along with Betty Grable, Jerry Colonna, Martha Raye, and—once again—George Burns and Gracie Allen. Judy Garland makes her feature film debut in another college musical, *Pigskin Parade* (1936), which stars Betty Grable and a young Alan Ladd. Another musical, *College Rhythm* (1934), stars the hunky Jack Oakie as an All-American football player who finds himself unemployed and underappreciated after graduation. One of MGM's all-star musicals, *Best Foot Forward* (1943), starring Lucille Ball, June Allyson, Gloria DeHaven, and others, turned a college pep rally into a major production number, "Buckle Down, Winsockie." Pleased with *Best Foot Forward*'s popularity, MGM brought back Allyson in another coed role in a remake of its 1930 hit *Good News* (1947). Playing the role of a shy student librarian, Allyson was teamed up with another of the studio's up-and-coming stars, Peter Lawford, as the college quarterback. The remake was one of the studio's biggest hits that year.

During the 1940s and 1950s, film comedies set in college took yet another turn, playing with a fish-out-of-water formula, as older characters—some of them already familiar to movie audiences—attempted to enter the academic world. (*Best Foot Forward* included this formula with Ball as a movie star returning to her old hometown.) This string of comedies about older students, *Blondie Goes to College* (1942), *Mr. Belvedere Goes to College* (1949), and even *Bonzo Goes to College* (1952), may well have been a nod to all the servicemen and women entering college on the GI Bill. In 1946, America's favorite teenager of the 1930s, Andy Hardy, returned from wartime military duty and enrolled in college in *Love Laughs at Andy Hardy*. Even Oscar winner Loretta Young dabbled in light comedy as she portrayed a mother returning to college, along with her daughter, in *Mother Is a Freshman* (1949). The formula heated up a bit with *She's Working Her Way through College* (1952), in which a burlesque star, played by Virginia Mayo, attempted to pursue a college education, with Ronald Reagan as her favorite professor. The pattern reached its logical/absurd conclusion in the near-pornographic premise of the film *Sex Kittens Go to College* (1960), featuring Mamie Van Doren as an ex-stripper turned chairman of the college's science department.[10]

Through all the variations, one pattern consistently held. Whether as vehicles for popular comic stars to pursue alpha male status, as lighthearted musical romps for carefree faculty and students, or as fish-out-of-water explorations of post–World War II issues of age and gender-appropriate behavior, these college comedies are consistently conservative. They do little or nothing to challenge the common understanding of college as a world of established customs and expectations that tolerate youthful exuberance, romantic experiences, and general foolishness but eventually socialize students into responsible citizens.

Few successful comedies attempt to present any alternative view of college life. In the classic *Horse Feathers* (1932), the Marx Brothers turn almost every college tradition on its ear, with Groucho as the president of Huxley College and Chico and Harpo as overage students. *The Male Animal* (1942), a more sophisticated comedy written by the acerbic James Thurber and starring Henry Fonda as a college professor, goes firmly against the grain with its critique of the athletic hegemony prevailing in the American collegiate environment.

Animal House, however, ventures far beyond Thurber's critique, gleefully reversing almost every feature of Hollywood academia. There is no football game; in fact, no athlete even appears in the film—the captain of the swim team is mentioned as an Omega House man but is never seen. Replacing the genial gentlemen professors Bing Crosby, Henry Fonda, and Ronald Reagan of previous film faculties, Donald Sutherland plays the failed novelist-cum-English teacher, Dave Jennings, who confesses to being bored by Milton's poetry, introduces his students to the joys of marijuana, and sleeps with one of his students. The college coeds are no longer shy June Allyson types, but snobbish sorority girls who are not above cheating on their boyfriends with the studs of Delta House. Instead of the precise and perky choreography of "The Varsity Drag" and other musical sequences of the earlier college comedies, *Animal House* features the spontaneous gyrations of intoxicated frat party animals singing and dancing to "Louie, Louie."

In its revolutionary view of college life, *Animal House* reaches into a deep mythological vein for its inspiration. The film's guiding spirit is the demigod Dionysius, the son of Zeus and the beautiful mortal Semele. A child of darkness, passion, and disorder, Dionysius also presided over the mystery of life itself, often appearing as the deity who could confer life after death. His character can best be understood by contrasting him, as Friedrich Nietzsche does, with Apollo, the god of light, reason, and order. In enumerating the features of the Dionysian worldview, the influence of this deity on the inhabitants of Delta House becomes obvious.

Dionysius dances at the heart of comedy. The word *comedy* itself has its roots in the *Komos*, a primitive rite of spring honoring Dionysius as the god of fertility. Francis MacDonald Cornford's classic study *The Origins of Attic Comedy* maintains that "comedy sprang up and took shape in connection with Dionysiac or Phallic ritual."[11] He continues:

> We shall argue that attic comedy, as we know it from Aristophanes, is constructed in the framework of what was already a drama, a folk play, and that behind this folk play lay a still earlier phase, in which its action was dramatically presented in religious ritual.[12]

Cornford later describes the conclusions of Aristophanes's comedies as the most direct connection to the earlier fertility rituals:

> The plays usually end with a procession in which the chorus marches out with the orchestra, conducting the chief character in triumph. . . . The hero, moreover, is accompanied in this *Komos* by . . . a nameless courtesan, sometimes an allegorical figure. She is the temporary partner of the hero in what is, in fact though not always in the legal sense, a marriage. . . . This marriage with its *Komos* ends almost every play of Aristophanes, no matter what its subject may be. . . . If we are right in supposing that this is the survival of a ritual marriage, little doubt can remain as to the further point that, in that case, the protagonist in comedy must originally have been the spirit of fertility himself, Phales or Dionysius. Who else, indeed, can lead the *Komos* from which, in all probability, comedy (i.e., *kom-odia*) derives its name?[13]

Several features of the ancient *Komos* ritual are essential elements of the comedy of *Animal House*. The following seven elements of Dionysian celebration can be found throughout the film:

1. a connection between humans and animals
2. an excessive consumption of food and drink
3. a delight in ecstatic music and dance
4. a search for sexual satisfaction
5. rebellion against authority
6. a tendency toward chaotic and destructive behavior
7. association with the demonic

The Animal Connection

It was customary at the *Komos* and similar primitive rituals for participants to dress up in animal skins; wear horns as headdresses, beaks as mouthpieces, and claws for hands; and generally imitate animal behavior, often exaggerating the physical features of their totems, especially the genital areas. The Deltas, for their part, don horns, headdresses, and other animal attire for the fraternity's induction ceremony and bestow such animal names as "Flounder," "Pinto," and "Weasel" on the pledges. The comedy of *Animal House*, in its very name, hearkens back to the animalistic roots of the genre.

Excess

Dionysius is the enemy of moderation, especially in terms of eating, drinking, and consuming mind-altering substances. Friedrich Nietzsche's study of the Dionysian spirit in his 1870 essay *The Birth of Tragedy* observes the "Dionysian rapture, whose closest analogy is furnished by physical intoxication." He contemplates

> the glorious transport [that] arises in man, even from the very depths of nature, at the shattering of the *principium individuationis*. . . . Dionysiac stirrings arise either through the influence of those narcotic potions of which all primitive races speak in their hymns, or through the powerful approach of spring, which penetrates with joy the whole frame of nature. So stirred, the individual forgets himself completely.[14]

Nietzsche later contrasts this spirit with the wisdom of Apollo, who traditionally represented the alternative to Dionysian ecstasy:

> As a moral deity, Apollo demands self-control from his people, and . . . to observe such self-control, a knowledge of self. And so we find that the aesthetic necessity of beauty is accompanied by the imperatives "Know thyself" and "Nothing too much." Conversely, excess and hubris come to be regarded as the hostile spirits of the non-Apollonian sphere, hence as properties of the pre-Apollonian era—the age of Titans—and the extra-Apollonian world, that is to say the word of the barbarians. It was because of his Titanic love of man that Prometheus had to be devoured by vultures; it was because of his extravagant wisdom [that] succeeded in solving the riddle of the Sphinx that Oedipus had to be cast into a whirlpool of crime: In this fashion does the Delphic god interpret the Greek past.[15]

Bluto's cafeteria gluttony and the frat boys' shoplifting visit to the local supermarket express the Delta House's Dionysian excess in the acquisition and consumption of food. Much more attention, of course, is given to the consumption of alcohol in several of the film's sequences. Delta House's rush party that begins the film, their meeting to select the new pledges, the initiation ceremony, the toga party, the road trip and its aftermath, and even the fraternity's gathering after they have been expelled from the college all involve considerable amounts of beer and other alcoholic beverages. In one scene, Bluto manages, in one long swallow, to consume an entire bottle of Jack Daniels whiskey. Larry and his friend Boon (Peter Reigert), along with Boon's girlfriend, Katy (Karen Allen), are even treated to some marijuana when they visit their English professor. The spirit of Dionysian excess reigns on the Faber College campus.

Ecstasy

Dionysius is always associated with ecstatic music, which differs distinctly from the harmonious melodies of Apollo. Nietzsche devotes a considerable portion of his study to the Dionysian mode of music. He describes Apollonian music as a "regular beat like that of waves lapping the shore . . . a Doric architecture of sound—of barely hinted sounds such as are proper to the cithara."[16] Dionysian music, on the other hand, aims at ecstasy by means of the

> heart-shaking power of tone, the uniform stream of melody, the incomparable resources of harmony. . . . In the Dionysian dithyramb man is incited to strain his symbolic faculties to the utmost: Something quite unheard of is now clamoring to be heard: the desire to tear asunder the veil of Maya, to sink back into the original oneness of nature; the desire to express the very essence of nature symbolically. Thus an entirely new set of symbols springs into being. First, all the symbols pertaining to physical features: mouth, face, the spoken word, the dance movement [that] coordinates the limbs and bends them to its rhythm. Then suddenly all the rest of the symbolic force—music and rhythm, as such, dynamics, harmony—assert themselves with great energy.[17]

In such a description, Nietzsche has in mind the gargantuan compositions of Richard Wagner and other hyper-Romantic composers of his age, but his description just as certainly applies to the rock and roll of the 1950s and the rock music of the 1960s. The Apollo–Dionysius distinction is well illustrated by the moment at the Delta House's toga party when Bluto descends the stairs and silently stands by as another student—who is obviously not from Delta House—serenades several young ladies with a rendition of the gentle folk ballad "I Gave My Love a Cherry." Bluto tolerates the performance for half a minute, then slowly and firmly grabs the young singer's guitar and smashes it to bits over the singer's head. (It is worth noting that the singing student is played by Stephen Bishop, who not only wrote the movie's theme song but went on to a successful career as a composer and singer of many Oscar-nominated songs. He was given the remains of the smashed guitar, signed by the film's cast, and is reported to have hung it in his home.) Bluto then continues down the stairs to the dancing area, where he joins in an orgy of atavistic writhing to the unintelligible words and tribal rhythms of the frat boy anthem "Louie, Louie."

In this brief sequence, *Animal House* enacts the meeting of two modes of music that competed for the baby boomers' attention during the Kennedy era. In 1962, the folk ballad had already entered the scene with a mix of work songs, like Harry Belafonte's Caribbean banana boat songs or the Kingston Trio's railroad worker ballads of John Henry and their urban folk song about the Boston MTA. Peter, Paul, and Mary; Joan Baez; Bob Dylan; and others were bringing the folk music of Odetta, Pete Seeger, and others into the mainstream. Their early hits, however, tended toward romantic nostalgia with such songs as "Michael, Row the Boat Ashore" and "Puff, the Magic Dragon," offering only hints of the protest music they would later perform in the more turbulent years to come. Such innocent, nonthreatening, and fairly sexless music was fervently embraced and sung by guitar-strumming upwardly mobile college students throughout the land. Meanwhile, the rock and roll of Elvis, Chuck Berry, and others that had swept over the teenage landscape in the mid-1950s was morphing into something more raw and exciting, much more expressive of the sexuality and physical abandon of African American rhythm and blues. The folk music craze of the early 1960s soon gave way to the psychedelic frenzy of hard rock, throbbing with sexual energy and political fury. The orderly melodies of Apollo yielded to Dionysian ecstasy.

Sexual Adventures

Indulgence in sexual activity also prevails at Faber College. Smooth-talking Eric, otherwise known as Otter, has reason to boast of his many conquests, including the girlfriend of archenemy Greg Marmalard (James Daughton) of Omega House and the wife of Dean Wormer. Even the naive newbie Larry manages to deflower the underage daughter of Mayor Carmine DePasto (Cesare Danova). Bluto engages in some major voyeurism, peeking into the windows of a sorority house and peeking up the skirts of cheerleaders by lurking under the bleachers. Eric seduces a young lady from the nearby women's college during the Delta House road trip. Even Boon's otherwise responsible girlfriend, Katy, engages in an affair with Professor Jennings. In retrospect, the film's exhibition of naked female breasts in several scenes and Professor Jennings's naked posterior must be considered quite daring for a comedy in 1970s Hollywood. The fraternity's toga party is a raucous orgy of alcohol, sexual coupling, and rock and roll frenzy.

Women are generally treated as sexual objects throughout the film, an attitude that may represent the gender relations prevalent in colleges in 1962 but that borders on the insensitive for a film released in 1978. The cruelest treatment of women in the film occurs when the Deltas, having taken some female students from a neighboring college to a roadside establishment populated by a black clientele, run out of the bar at the first threat from one of the patrons, leaving the ladies to their ominous fate. Fortunately, the female students are later seen walking back from the roadhouse unscathed.

Rebellion against Authority

True to the spirit of Dionysius, the men of Delta House instinctively oppose authority and regimentation of any kind. The film's comic plot, such as it is, revolves around the enmity between the Deltas and the Omegas and the crusade of Dean Wormer to have the Deltas thrown off campus. The Delta House men, on their part, fill their days and nights with mischievous, anarchic, and rowdy adventures. Many of the film's sequences have become classics of the genre. In one episode, Bluto and others take revenge on both the dean and the rival fraternity by sneaking the favorite horse of Doug Niedermeyer (Mark Metcalf), the sadistic Omega House ROTC captain, into the dean's office late at night and, in a prank that goes awry, giving the horse a fatal heart attack. Finally, when Dean Wormer expels Delta House members from college, the fraternity brothers wreak their revenge in the form of a "really futile and stupid gesture," which involves major disruption of the homecoming parade. Anarchy rules!

The boys' rebellious attitude, however, presents itself as a more humane alternative to the tyrannical behavior of Dean Wormer, who is determined to destroy the Delta House fraternity and all their free-spirited antics. The rules of comedy dictate that such a humorless tyrant should also be exposed as a hypocrite. Dean Wormer is eventually shown to be a liar, an administrator who will bend the rules to suit his purposes, who is not above bribing the town mayor, playing loose with the university's budget, and other illegal or immoral activity. The director claims to have chosen John Vernon to play Dean Wormer because of his resemblance to "Tricky Dick" Nixon, whose Watergate cover-up activity and resignation in disgrace occurred only three years before the film's release.

The misbehavior of Delta House also seems ethically preferable to the military regimentation and discipline encouraged by the ROTC officers of Omega House, whose fascination with things military readily slips into sadism in their initiation ceremonies, military exercises, and bullying treatment of some of the Delta men who fall into their hands, especially the hapless Kent and even the suave Eric. Various Omega men are revealed to be sexually incompetent and confused, sycophantic, academically dishonest, and the sort of ROTC officers who could easily morph into SS troopers. Compared to the Nazi behavior of the Omegas and the Nixonian qualities of Dean Wormer, the horny, raucous Delta House men's pranks and assorted mischief seem innocent and almost healthy. They may not be angels, but they may be Greek demigods.

Chaotic and Destructive Behavior

Dionysian energy, however, can be destructive, and anarchy can descend into chaos. Property damage occurs throughout the film. Kent's brother's expensive car is totaled on the Delta House's road trip to a nearby women's college. Various pieces of furniture in Delta House are smashed, thrown out of windows, or otherwise mistreated. The folk-singing student's guitar is demolished. There is even loss of life in the case of Doug's horse's fatal heart attack. But nothing compares to the snowballing chaos that ensues when the Deltas disrupt the homecoming parade in the film's final sequence.

During the course of the melee, most of the parade floats are dismantled; the reviewing stand, holding the dean, the mayor, their wives, and other dignitaries, comes tumbling down; a runaway float crashes through the display window into the showroom of the mayor's automobile dealership; and various other pieces of property, large and small, are destroyed. One of the Omega men attempting to maintain order throughout the outburst (played by a newcomer named Kevin Bacon) is reduced to a cartoon-flattened figure as he is trampled over by the panic-stricken onlookers he was trying to calm down. Much more is destroyed in this revolutionary attack on the homecoming parade, however. Physical property is only the most visible victim of the Dionysian fury unleashed on Delta House's enemies. The dignity of the cuckolded Dean Wormer, the authority of the likely mob-connected mayor, the reputation of the college in the eyes of returning alumni, and the prestige of the Omega fraternity men are all severely wounded in the chaos of the parade.

Association with the Demonic

Finally, the animal behavior, the excessive consumption of food and drink, the sexual indulgence, the ecstatic music, the antiauthoritarian attitude, and the chaotic destruction of life and property all hint at a darkness that has often been associated with the diabolical. The iconography of Western art has often associated Dionysius with the devil of the Judeo-Christian tradition, portraying Satan as a horned creature with a tail or hooved feet. (It is worth noting that there is no biblical basis for such a depiction of the devil.) *Animal House* alludes to this tradition in its only scene set in a classroom, a lecture on Milton's *Paradise Lost.* The decadent Professor Jennings informs his bored students that, while generally not a fan of the Puritan poet, he, like many other Milton critics, considers Satan the most interesting character in the poem. He then asks the class if, in fact, "Milton is trying to tell us that being bad is more fun than being good." He follows this question by biting into an apple, the customary image of the forbidden fruit of Paradise.

The conclusion of the comedy is not only faithful to its Dionysian character, but it also offers some political humor. Instead of ending with a Mack Sennett chase, a wedding or other romantic fulfillment, or a resolution of misunderstandings, *Animal House* ends with a Dionysian *Komos*, a parade that wreaks chaotic revenge on Delta House's enemies. The fraternity, having all been expelled from college by Dean Wormer (who has taken the trouble to notify their draft boards of the loss of their student deferments and new availability), has decided that their only remaining weapon in the battle is a "really futile and stupid gesture." Disruption of the political order has, in fact, a long history as a final weapon of the politically powerless, either as civil disobedience (the Boston Tea Party, sit-ins in the segregated South, Poland's Solidarity movement) or guerrilla terrorism (IRA car bombs, Palestinian suicide bombs). Senseless mayhem can serve the same purpose in any society that is perceived as repressive, and so Delta House decides to sabotage the Faber College homecoming parade.

In this final sequence, the film offers retrospective commentary on the political and social hypocrisy of mainstream 1960s America. The portrayal of the homecoming parade as a public relations event meant to impress the alumni already offers opportunity to ridicule administrative hypocrisy. The satire develops in numerous details worthy of Dionysius's ongoing defiance of the Olympian hegemony.

Some of the parade's floats represent the idealism of the early 1960s, which was later severely challenged by many events during the rest of the decade. Omega House's float is dedicated to the New Frontier of the Kennedy White House, with sorority girls dressed (anachronistically) in the pink dress suits and pillbox hats that Jacqueline Kennedy went on to wear a year later in Dallas, when the dream of Camelot came to an end. Another float, titled "Togetherness," praises the racial harmony that the new decade promises, with two giant hands, one black and the other white, joined in a handshake. The tension in an earlier episode in the film, when the Deltas and their dates from the nearby women's college step into an all-black roadhouse tavern, illustrates how far the races were from such pleasant interaction at the time. The subsequent inner-city violence and assassinations of Malcolm X and Dr. Martin Luther King Jr. as the decade progressed also bear testimony to the fatuousness of such a premature vision of racial equality in America.

American militarism is also mocked. Doug, Omega House's reigning fascist, leads the ROTC drill team in the parade. Their disciplined display of rifle twirling is disrupted, however, when Kent rolls out 10,000 marbles under their feet and they all tumble to the ground. The leader of the Faber College marching band is captured and replaced by a Delta House brother, who promptly leads the players down a blind alley, a move that could be interpreted as a commentary on the U.S. military's blind and stubborn march into the quagmire of Vietnam.

Other jaundiced views of the era are expressed in another float, on which is written "When Better Women Are Made, Faber Will Make Them." What seems like a possible (even if ambivalent) tribute to the emerging feminism of the era turns retrograde when the women on the float are revealed to be dressed in Playboy Bunny outfits. Another float even suggests that some of the darker political forces of the century are still operative. One fraternity, Sigma Sigma, sports a giant head of what appears to be Genghis Khan. Is this meant to salute the barbarian ethos of Nazi SS storm troopers as a viable ideal for college graduates? If so, it is appropriate that this float is thoroughly dismantled in the ensuing chaos.

The destruction of the parade is completed when the Delta House float, a large cake decorated with the Lewis Carroll invitation "Eat Me," opens up to reveal the "Deathmobile." Kent's brother's car, seriously damaged during the Deltas' road trip, has been reconstructed into a James Bond mobile weapon that makes mincemeat out of the other floats (neatly dividing the two hands of the "Togetherness" float and sending the Jackie Kennedy look-alikes into the open air) and finally storms the bastille of the parade reviewing stand to dethrone Dean Wormer and his wife, the mayor, and the rest of the ruling elite. The Deathmobile, driven by the scariest Delta House brother, D-Day (Bruce McGill), also contains the great Bluto himself, who arises out of the vehicle dressed as a pirate, a classic romantic outlaw. Imitating some of the gestures and actions of Douglas Fairbanks Jr. and other silent screen antiheroes, Bluto presides over the chaos and, his work done, finally drives off into the sunset, having won the hand of Mandy Pepperidge (Mary Louise Weller), the sweetheart of Omega House. The Dionysian *Komos* is complete, as the demigod takes his bride into the future.

But what of the other revelers, rebels, and villains? In its comic coda, *Animal House* informs viewers of the subsequent careers of the film's main characters, offering a version of comic resolution in tune with the comedy's nostalgic perspective. It is interesting to note that Dean Wormer is forced to take Delta House off double-secret probation, and almost all of the characters eventually graduate from Faber College. Robert Hoover (James Widdoes), the Delta House president, becomes a public defender. Larry, the naive newbie, becomes an editor of *National Lampoon*. Kent, the overweight schlimazel, becomes a sensitivity trainer. Boon and Katy get married the year after they graduate but are divorced five years later. The ladies' man Eric fittingly ends up as a gynecologist in Beverly Hills. All that is said about the fearsome D-Day, however, is "whereabouts unknown."

Darker fates await the film's villains. The sadistic militarist Doug is killed by his own troops in Vietnam. Greg, the sexually confused pretty boy of Omega House, becomes a Nixon White House aide and, apparently convicted of criminal activity in his government service, is eventually raped in prison.

The two most prominent coeds find happiness. Babs Jansen (Martha Smith) finds good use for her chipper personality as a tour guide at Universal Studios, while Mandy becomes half of the team of Senator and Mrs. John Blutarsky.

In this account of the characters' futures, *Animal House* expresses the ethos of carnival. The college period, which, at least for Bluto, amounted to seven years, is depicted as a long raucous holiday from responsibility that will eventuate in a reentry into normal society, where even these apparent social misfits will find their own place and perhaps even slightly expand the definition of normalcy.[18] They are, when all is said and done, basically white middle-class young men enjoying relative social privilege and entitlement. Rich's review of the film expresses this comic optimism in his description of Delta House's pranks:

> They are probably the only form of rebellion available to square college boys. (Hip kids tend not to join fraternities, i.e., they get laid off campus.) In a few years, those boys will be doctors, lawyers, businessmen, but at nineteen they can make outrageously cruel and infantile jokes and no one will give them too hard a time.[19]

And wasn't it Thomas Jefferson who opined that every democracy would benefit from a revolution every twenty years or so?

A generation or two of college comedies have followed in the wake of *Animal House*. As the titles often reveal, many of the film's heroes are misfits of one sort or another (*Accepted* [2006], *Slackers* [2002], *Real Genius* [1985], *Revenge of the Nerds* [1984–1994]), or they are party boys repeating Bluto's pattern of spending seven years in college presiding over orgiastic fraternity parties (*National Lampoon's Van Wilder* [2002], *Road Trip* [2000], *PCU* [1994]). Two of the most successful of these comedies tweak the earlier pattern of an adult returning to college (*Back to School* [1986], *Old School* [2003]) by starring such clownish grown-ups as Rodney Dangerfield and Will Ferrell. The administration and faculty tend to be the heroes' nemesis, repeating Dean Wormer's attempts to stifle the students' Dionysian lifestyle (with the one notable exception of the English professor Rodney Dangerfield falls for in *Back to School*, played by the eternally sexy Sally Kellerman). In a few of the films, the college athletes are also the comic antagonists, but only one of the films reverts to the 1930s plotline of the weakling who turns out to be a star football player in the successful Adam Sandler vehicle *The Waterboy* (1998).

All of these post–*Animal House* comedies concentrate on male protagonists, with the young women as distinctly secondary characters. Finally, however, two recent college films have featured free-spirited young women who manage to turn the tables on their critics. *Legally Blonde* (2001) stars Reese Witherspoon as the bubbly California girl who follows her boyfriend to Harvard Law School and ends up at the head of the class, and *The House Bunny* (2008) presents

Anna Faris as an ex-Playboy Bunny who educates a group of nerdy sorority girls in the ways of sexual gamesmanship while otherwise enlivening their campus. These mildly feminist comedies, however, hardly approach the Dionysian chaos of *Animal House* and its male-dominated successors. They might, on the other hand, be announcing the admittance of a new student to Hollywood University. Her name is Aphrodite.

A Sampling of Dionysian Comedy

Up in Smoke (1978)
Wayne's World (1992)
American Pie (1999)
Road Trip (2000)
Dude, Where's My Car? (2000)
Old School (2003)
Superbad (2007)
Pineapple Express (2008)
The Hangover (2009)
Bridesmaids (2011)

Notes

1. While the proper spelling of his name, since he originated in Greek mythology, would be Dionysis, the Latin word has emerged as the more popular name in modern times and, if only in a spirit of mild rebellion, is used throughout this study.

2. Tony Schwartz, "College Humor Comes Back." *Newsweek*, October 23, 1978, p. 88.

3. Frank Rich, "Cinema: *School Days.*" *Time*, August 14, 1978, p. 87.

4. David Ansen, "Gross Out." *Newsweek*, August 7, 1978, p. 85.

5. Roger Ebert, "*National Lampoon's Animal House.*" *Chicago Sun-Times*, January 1, 1978, p. 53.

6. "Current Cinema: *Animal House.*" *Christian Century*, December 6, 1978, p. 1,186.

7. "Current Cinema: *Animal House*," p. 1,186.

8. Schwartz, "College Humor Comes Back," p. 88.

9. "Current Cinema: *Animal House*," p. 1,186.

10. Two very informative surveys of the depiction of college life in Hollywood films are John E. Conklin, *Campus Life in the Movies* (Jefferson, N.C., and London: McFarland & Co., 2008); and Wiley Lee Umphlett, *The Movies Go to College* (Teaneck, N.J.: Fairleigh Dickinson University Press, 1984).

11. Francis MacDonald Cornford, *The Origin of Attic Comedy* (Ann Arbor: University of Michigan Press, 1993), 5.

12. Cornford, *The Origin of Attic Comedy*, 6.

13. Cornford, *The Origin of Attic Comedy*, 55.

14. Friedrich Nietzsche, *The Birth of Tragedy and the Genealogy of Morals* (New York: Doubleday, 1956), 22.

15. Nietzsche, *The Birth of Tragedy and the Genealogy of Morals*, 22.

16. Nietzsche, *The Birth of Tragedy and the Genealogy of Morals*, 27.

17. Nietzsche, *The Birth of Tragedy and the Genealogy of Morals*, 27–28.

18. See the discussion of the connection between the carnivalesque and social norms in Robert Stam, *Subversive Pleasures: Bakhtin, Cultural Criticism, and Film* (Baltimore, Md.: Johns Hopkins University Press, 1989), 96–106.

19. Rich, "Cinema: *School Days*," p. 87.

CHAPTER 10

Mockumentary

WAITING FOR GUFFMAN (1996)

In relatively recent film history, American audiences have been introduced to a new genre, a set of films that claim to document the careers of rock music groups (*The Rutles* [1978], *This Is Spinal Tap* [1984]), student filmmakers' encounters with terror (*The Blair Witch Project* [1999]), a senatorial campaign (*Bob Roberts* [1992]), the production of a community theater group's pageant in honor of their town's sesquicentennial (*Waiting for Guffman* [1996]), the competition in a national dog show (*Best in Show* [2000]), a reunion of 1960s folk singers (*A Mighty Wind* [2003]), a tour of the United States by a foreign correspondent (*Borat: Cultural Learnings of America for Make Benefit Glorious Nation of Kazakhstan* [2006]), and other purported reportage. The common feature of these films is that, while the style of the films suggests that they are documenting reality, they are all fictional. The main characters or situations are not real, but they are presented as such. These films have created something new in film comedy: the mockumentary.

While the films in previous chapters can trace their roots in comic history to preceding eras, some as far back as ancient Greece and Rome, the mockumentary, as a latecomer to American cinema, enjoys the advantage of using a variety of elements to create its comedy: the documentary format, parody, and occasional ventures into satire. First, as its name implies, mockumentary can make use of the techniques of documentary film familiar to modern film audiences. It borrows the techniques of cinemaverité with the handheld camera, unscripted and spontaneous action and dialogue, and nonprofessional actors. It can include archival material, eyewitness footage of an event, and on-camera interviews of significant people. As Jane Roscoe and Craig Hight describe it,

> Mock-documentary's agenda is ultimately to parody the assumptions and expectations associated with factual discourse. . . . Deliberately

Dr. Allan Pearl (Eugene Levy), Libby Mae Brown (Parker Posey), and Sheila and Ron Albertson (Catherine O'Hara and Fred Willard) are directed and inspired by Corky St. Clair (Christopher Guest) in creating their hometown's bicentennial pageant in *Waiting for Guffman* (1996).

appropriating the documentary codes and conventions, mock-documentary filmmakers more specifically seek to offer some form of commentary on aspects(s) of contemporary culture—it may be to parody affectionately the cultural status of popular icons, or to incorporate a specific political critique, or to comment more pointedly on the nature of the documentary project.[1]

Second, this genre can count on a certain sophistication in its audience. As Roscoe and Hight also point out, there is the presumption on the part of the filmmakers that their viewers will recognize the text as a spoof because of their familiarity with both the format and the subject matter. In his study of *This Is Spinal Tap*, Ethan de Seife remarks that a "knowledge of the conventions of the documentary (as well as those of the rockumentary) provides an essential backdrop against which the film must be understood."[2] The comic premise might arise from the triviality of such events as dog shows and community theater productions, the mediocrity of the featured personalities, or the unstated comparison with genuine documentaries of more noteworthy matters or people. The audience can appreciate *The Rutles* as a parody of the phenomenal success and fan worship of a certain rock group from Liverpool; or *This Is Spinal Tap* as apathetic imitation of the tour and concert documentaries of *Don't Look Back* and *Gimme Shelter*; or *Best in Show* as a gentle commentary on the triviality, egotism, and obsessiveness of show-dog owners and the general American fascination with every type of contest and competition.

However, while most of these mockumentaries are affectionate spoofs, the parody can quickly turn into a critique. Several sequences in *Borat* expose the darker sides of American patriotism, religious practices, sexism, celebrity worship, and other issues. De Seife observes that the "shallow glory of the MTV-era rock star, as well as that of the music industry itself, receive some of *This Is Spinal Tap*'s sharpest barbs."[3] And Tim Robbins's liberal political viewpoint colors *Bob Roberts*'s critique of the American political process, the news media, and especially conservative politicians.

The British spoof of the Beatles, *The Rutles*, created by Eric Idle and other members of the Monty Python troupe, in collaboration with cast members from its newly created American counterpart, *Saturday Night Live*, is generally considered the originator of the mockumentary form. Although highly regarded, it did not inspire any immediate imitators. Six years later, another partnership of British and American talent produced a similar comedy. *This Is Spinal Tap* was directed by Rob Reiner and written by Reiner, Christopher Guest, Michael McKean, and Harry Shearer, who also acted in the film. Reiner had already written for several television comedy series (*The Smothers Brothers Comedy Hour* [1967–1970], *Happy Days* [1974–1984], *Saturday Night Live* [1975–], and *All in the Family* [1968–1979] [in which he also starred as Archie Bunker's live-in son-in-law and nemesis, Mike "Meathead" Stivic]) and had some experience in directing films for television, but *This Is Spinal Tap* was his first foray into directing a Hollywood film for theatrical release. His job was surely made easier by the zany personalities in the cast: Michael McKean plays the lead guitarist, David St. Hubbens; Christopher Guest plays the *other* lead guitarist, Nigel Tufnel; Harry Shearer plays the bassist, Derek Smalls; R. J. Parnells is Mick Shrimpton on drums; and David Kaff is Viv Savage on keyboard.

The band, as the film briefly displays, had experienced previous incarnations in almost every phase of rock music from the 1960s to the 1980s, first as a folk group, then as Beatles imitators, for a while as religious rockers, later as flower children engaging in psychedelic mini-extravaganzas, until eventually diving into heavy metal with a bit of Satanism and punk. The film documents the band's U.S. tour as they attempt a comeback and promotion of their latest album, *Smell the Glove*, with little success and a good deal of hostility arising among the band members as they proceed from one disastrous performance to another until a final triumph in Japan. The grandiosity of the band is matched by the promotion of the actual film. The tagline in the advertisements proclaimed, "Does for rock and roll what *The Sound of Music* did for hills." De Seife succinctly summarizes the approach of the film:

> [The band] *Spinal Tap* is not intended to be dreadful or unlisten-able; the band and its music are meant to be mediocre, yet pompous. This strategy allows the film to ridicule the band while maintaining a significant degree of sympathy for its members. Similarly, Marty DiBergi [the fictional documentarian following the band] is shown to be a bit of a buffoon, but not an unlikable or incompetent man. . . . DiBergi, too, is rather mediocre at his chosen art, a fact [that] complicates and enriches *This Is Spinal Tap.*[4]

Critics got the joke. Roger Ebert comments that the "rock group does not really exist, but the best thing about this film is that it could," and he dubs the film as "absolutely inspired in the subtle way it establishes Spinal Tap's bad-ness."[5] Janet Maslin calls it a "witty, mischievous satire . . . obviously a labor of love" and comments that the "most appealing thing . . . aside from the obvious enthusiasm of all concerned, is the accompanying lack of condescension."[6] And Richard Corliss describes the film as the "newest send-up . . . of pop culture's twin inanities: inept musicians and their earnest hagiographers." He compares the film to the two Richard Lester films starring the Beatles: "*A Hard Day's Night* is in part a joke documentary, while *Help!* functions as both parody and prophecy of MTV's slick surrealism. *This Is Spinal Tap* forfeits the good will associated with the Beatles for something far more bizarre and desperate."[7] *This Is Spinal Tap* needed to do little to morph into a mockery of the entire rocku-mentary scene.

After his success in this genre, however, Reiner went on to direct a series of distinguished films in a wide variety of genres, including *Stand by Me* (1986), *The Princess Bride* (1987), *When Harry Met Sally* (1989), *Misery* (1990), *A Few Good Men* (1992), *The American President* (1995), and *Ghosts of Mississippi* (1996), among others. But Christopher Guest continued to be fascinated by the genre and created a series of mockumentaries, starring what turned out to be something of a repertory company, many of whom appear in his first film of the series, *Waiting for Guffman*, in 1996.

With its allusion to Samuel Beckett's absurdist masterpiece, *Waiting for Guffman* presents its story of small-town dreams as something of a (perhaps pretentious) parable for the vague fulfillment of our hopes and dreams. The film purports to document the activities of the citizens of Blaine, Missouri, as they plan to conclude their celebration of the town's sesquicentennial with a pageant titled *Red, White, and Blaine*. As Blaine residents see it, there is much to dramatize in the town's history. It was founded in 1845 by a group of settlers, led by Blaine Fabin, who mistakenly thought that they had reached California. When President

William McKinley's train made a whistle-stop in Blaine in 1898, the townspeople presented him with an elegant footstool. The publicity generated by the event created a considerable demand for such footstools and a thriving industry for Blaine, which deservedly gained its reputation as the "stool capital of the world." The other historical event was the visit of extraterrestrials in 1946.

The film's narrative is divided into three sections: the planning and casting of the show, the rehearsal period, and the actual performance. Part one sets the off-kilter tone of the film in its interviews with the townspeople: the mayor, Glen Welsch (Larry Miller), who wants the sesquicentennial celebration to be a model for all the other towns in Missouri; Phil Burgess (Don Lake), the town historian and director of the Blaine Museum, who cheerfully recounts the stories of the town's accidental founding and the visit of extraterrestrials as equally credible historic events; councilman-pharmacist Steve Stark (Michael Hitchcock), who cannot audition for the show since that day is scheduled for "stocking" at the pharmacy; a UFO expert (David Cross), who proposes (incorrectly) that the extraterrestrials visited Blaine because the name of the town has five letters just like the home planet of the alien visitors; and an actual direct descendant of Blaine Fabin, Gwen Fabin-Blunt (Deborah Theaker), who feels the burden of being a "Fabin" in the town. "I can certainly understand how the Kennedys felt," she confesses.

Some of the aspiring actors are also interviewed. Ron and Sheila Albertson (Fred Willard and Catherine O'Hara) run the Magic Carpet Travel Agency, although they have never left the town itself, except for a "medical procedure" in Jefferson City. As viewers soon discover, the Albertsons have been involved in other theater productions in Blaine. The interview with Libby Mae Brown (Parker Posey), held during a break from her job at the local Dairy Queen, consists of her description of the various food products provided there. In his interview, Dr. Allan Pearl (Eugene Levy), the town dentist, explains that he probably got the "entertaining bug" from his grandfather, who had starred in Yiddish theater in New York. His grandfather's most famous role, Dr. Pearl tells us, was in the "sardonically irreverent" revue *DybbukShmybbuk—I Said More Ham.*

The highlight of this section of the film, however, is the interview with the man who has been chosen to direct the pageant, the flamboyant Corky St. Clair (Christopher Guest). As Corky tells us, he came to Blaine after spending twenty-five years as an actor, director, and choreographer in the Off-Broadway theater scene. He muses that he actually thought that, moving to Blaine, he might get a job as a construction worker. Instead, he became the drama teacher at Blaine High School and founded the Blaine Community Players. According to Corky, his first production, *Barefoot in the Park*, was an "absolute smash." His second production did not go as well. He wanted his theatrical version of the fire department film *Backdraft* to come across as "in your face theater."

To achieve that effect, he had someone burn newspapers backstage so that the smell would enhance the audience experience, but the theater burned down. Despite his mixed success, the mayor and the city council still hold Corky in great respect. Councilman Stark, in fact, expresses more than usual enthusiasm for him.

Part two moves from the primary use of interviews to documentary footage of the auditions and the rehearsal for the pageant. Corky is joined by the high school's music teacher, Lloyd Miller (Bob Balaban), who is mildly upset that, after fifteen years of directing plays "completely by myself," he will serve only as the musical director in support of Corky, the "professional from New York." The auditioners include a middle-aged man singing an off-key, off-beat version of "Lightning Striking Again"; another fellow juggling ping-pong balls with his mouth, finally choking on one of them; and an older gentlemen reciting the scene of an argument between Robert De Niro and Joe Pesci from *Raging Bull,* playing both roles. His recitation includes the movie script's four-letter words but lacks the New York-Italian accent and appropriate emotion. Libby Mae, in a short schoolgirl jumper, offers a seductive song and dance of the 1950s hit "Teacher's Pet." Dr. Pearl makes a favorable impression on the judges with his slightly off-key medley of Stephen Foster songs. The Albertsons, dressed in matching tracksuits, perform a nonerotic version of "Midnight at the Oasis." While Lloyd seems unimpressed, Corky had worked with them in his previous shows and sees them as the "old stand-bys, the workhorses" of community theater, or, as he calls them, the "Lunts of Blaine."

Corky also goes out of his way to recruit a hunky young garage mechanic, Johnny Savage (Matt Keeslar), although Johnny has no acting experience and his father is clearly suspicious of Corky's intentions. Corky offers to ease Johnny into the world of theater, providing him with his private telephone number, which he asks Johnny not to share with anyone.

In the midst of the rehearsal period, Corky reads the cast a letter from a New York producer's office informing them that, in response to Corky's invitation, they are sending a representative, Mr. Mort Guffman, to see the show and report on it. Corky is quick to interpret the letter to mean that "We may be goin' to Broadway." In Corky's view, this means that the stakes have been raised, and he decides to request $100,000 from the city council to produce a "beautifully wrapped, glossy, sweet-smelling show."

The council finds the request laughable, causing Corky to go into a rant, calling them "bastard people." Corky resigns from the show, and Lloyd, happily but briefly ("It's my play!"), is put back in charge. The city council begs Corky to return to the show. Councilman Stark calls him a "genius" and begs him to "wave his magic wand" on the show, even with the tiny budget. Corky returns.

Part three takes place on the day of the show. It begins badly, with a phone call from Johnny telling Corky that his father won't allow him to appear in the show. The furious Corky shouts into the phone, "I hate you, and I hate your ass-face," and he is forced to take over Johnny's part as the sexy youngster, a role for which Corky is clearly unsuited.

As the audience gathers, a front-row seat reserved for Mr. Guffman remains empty, but someone finally arrives to take the seat. With song-and-dance routines, the play recounts the main historical events of Blaine: the founding of the town, President McKinley's visit, the subsequent "stool boom" of the town's footstool production in a factory sequence that alludes to the similar scene in Charlie Chaplin's *Modern Times*, and the UFO visit. The audience is thrilled, especially Councilman Stark, who cannot contain his enthusiasm for Corky, comparing him to the "only other person in the world" with an equal level of talent, Barbra Streisand. Corky's romantic duet with Libby Mae, in fact, brings Stark to tears. The show's grand finale features a display of U.S. flags and red, white, and blue balloons.

Red, White, and Blaine is an unqualified crowd-pleaser; however, after the show, Corky invites the man he assumes to be Mr. Guffman to come backstage to meet the cast. The visitor informs them that he is not Mr. Guffman, and Corky reads the telegram message received during the show explaining that Guffman was stuck in New York because of a snowstorm and could not make it to Blaine. Corky and the cast are crushed, their hopes for a Broadway run dashed.

The film ends with a conventional documentary coda, interviews with several of the featured people three months later. Dr. Pearl, confessing, "I *have* to entertain," has moved to Miami, where he performs Yiddish songs at senior citizen centers; the Albertsons are pursuing their Hollywood dreams with non-speaking bits in films; and Libby Mae has moved to Sipes, Alabama, to live with her father, who had been released from prison and is working at another Dairy Queen, hoping to develop a "healthy, low-fat blizzard." They have not given up on their dreams.

And Corky has returned to New York. Inexplicably wearing a bandleader's jacket straight out of *The Music Man* (another musical about small-town America and the magic of a charismatic leader), he reports on his meeting with the real Mr. Guffman. Guffman has hinted that he might want Corky to appear in his upcoming revival of *My Fair Lady*. Corky presumes that he will be asked to play Henry Higgins, so he is, illogically, working to perfect his Cockney accent. And, in what Corky describes as the "cake and eat it too" part of his story, he has opened a shop in Times Square for all his theater memorabilia, featuring *My Dinner with Andre* action figures, a set of figurines of the Brat Pack actors of the 1980s, *The Remains of the Day* lunchboxes, and similarly obscure cinematic references. The shop appears to be attracting no customers.

An analysis of the comedy of *Waiting for Guffman*, as with *This Is Spinal Tap*, begins with the mediocrity of the performers and, in this case, the director, combined with their inability to acknowledge their lack of talent. As John Kenneth Muir describes it:

> One of the big ironies of *Waiting for Guffman* is a self-reflexive one. This is a film about nonprofessional actors putting on a show made by professional actors making a movie. This accomplished ensemble renders the people of Blaine so colorfully and truthfully that viewers never feel an ounce of condescension either from the actors or the man directing them. . . . Instead, everybody behind the camera and in front of it really gets into the spirit of the show and into the heads of these quirky characters . . . by modulating or tuning their talent level (some might say lowering it) to the level of the people they are depicting: enthusiastic amateurs with a flair for performing, but no real talent to speak of.[8]

Perhaps the best examples of this trick are the performances of Fred Willard and Catherine O'Hara as Ron and Sheila. As the most experienced and confident members of the troupe, the "Lunts of Blaine," they take the trouble to perform their audition piece, a rendition of "Midnight at the Oasis," within the framework of a flirtatious conversation, which Muir describes as a "bizarre nightclub act that played like a Taster's Choice coffee commercial."[9] In their on-camera interview, Ron offers his poor impersonation of Humphrey Bogart with the misquote, "Here's looking at you, babe," and an even more unrecognizable imitation of Henry Fonda. While Sheila loyally laughs at his routines, Ron has to admit that he always has to tell her who he is imitating. Their constant cheerfulness and enthusiasm mask their slightly darker sides; Sheila drinks too much during their night out with Dr. Pearl and his wife, and Ron's humor tends toward the hostile. When Ron and Sheila meet up with Dr. Pearl at the auditions, Ron remarks that the doctor would recognize Sheila "from previous bills." When Dr. Pearl says that he is going to "take a shot" at being cast in the show, Ron says, "I hope it doesn't make Corky numb like your other shots," and he observes that getting a discount from the dentist is "like pulling teeth," along with other similar mild attempts at humor.

Levy also lowers his talent level to portray Dr. Pearl. In his interview, he offers an equally poor impersonation of his hero, Johnny Carson. He also attempts a bit of showmanship in his audition by some painfully bad arrangements of his Stephen Foster songs, complete with segues and a key change. Levy makes good use of his oversized eyeglasses, which, when removed, reveal his "lazy eye."

Posey, whose career in independent films has usually featured her in more sophisticated roles, dives into the role of Libby Mae, a gum-chewing small-town girl who has nothing to share in her interview other than descriptions of the Dairy Queen products. She offers an inappropriately sexy version of the old Doris Day hit "Teacher's Pet" for her audition, which nevertheless impresses the judges enough to land her a role in the pageant. When she hears the news about the possibility of *Red, White, and Blaine* moving to Broadway, she has to look up New York City in an atlas, where she is surprised to find that "it's an island." She is excited about the variety of New York City's residents and hopes that she can meet an "Italian" boy there. Libby Mae not only lacks talent, she is also fairly uninformed about the outside world.

The mediocre talent of the troupe, however, seems to go unnoticed by the townspeople, and the film becomes as much a commentary on the extreme provincialism of the town. There is little to no reference to any outside cultural influence on the citizens of Blaine and no mention of television programs, CDs of popular music, touring theater troupes, or other material that might serve as artistic standards by which the talents of Corky and the others could be judged. In this cultural vacuum, the town's sesquicentennial is a major historical milestone and, as the town historian Phil says, "It's about time the world knew more about Blaine." Of course, the very fact that a film crew is making this documentary serves to foster the townspeople's sense of self-importance bordering on delusion.

The authenticity of the small-town setting was achieved by the crew's twenty-nine days of filming in Lockhart, Texas, with a population of just more than 11,000, approximately thirty miles from Austin. The town provided the perfect atmosphere, with its elaborate county courthouse, its town square, and an actual town celebration. The film's production designer, Joseph T. Garrity, reports the following:

> They were having some kind of event that they do every year, so we got in there and made a banner for Blaine that we put in the foreground, and we shot this event as it was going on . . . they got girls singing and all this other good stuff, and a few of those things made it into the movie. We got real close to those people.[10]

The crew even hired some of the locals for small roles, most of which, however, did not make the final cut. The auditions were held in one of Lockhart's high schools. The genuine bond between the film crew and the citizens of Lockhart surely influenced the film's affectionate attitude toward all the Blaine folks.

Two sequences that diverge from the film's basic concentration on the pageant's preparations and performance are the dinner at the Chop Suey Chinese Kitchen and the interview with the Blaine resident who was visited by extraterrestrials. Ron and Sheila observe that, since they work in the "glamour profession" of a travel agency, Dr. Pearl and his wife are probably intimidated by them and perhaps by the whole glittering world of show business that the dentist and his wife are now experiencing. In an attempt to make them more comfortable, the Albertsons meet the Pearls for dinner at the Pearls' favorite Chinese restaurant. Ron begins the dinner conversation with the appetizing observation that "in China they'll kill a monkey at the table and split its brains open and eat right out of it." Sheila, having consumed too much wine, asks the Pearls (since they are Jewish) about circumcision, which leads to the mention of Ron's penis reduction surgery, which prompts Ron to stand up to show the doctor the results of the operation. While the interaction hardly succeeds in making the Pearls more comfortable, the scene is perhaps the most hilarious bit of improvised dialogue in the film, performed by three of the world's most talented improvisers, Levy, O'Hara, and Willard. With such lunacy, who cares how this scene furthers the plot of the film?

The other interruption is the interview with the Blaine resident who was abducted by the interplanetary visitors during the course of their memorable 1946 visit to the town. The abductee (Paul Dooley) recounts his experience in the most matter-of-fact manner, describing how they "put me on a big white table" and "probed me" for more than three or four hours. Different space visitors would come into the room, and "all of them probed me. Not all at once, you know . . . at different times." He then volunteers the information that ever since then, even now, "on every Sunday, about the time I was taken aboard that ship, I find I have no feeling in my buttocks."

Perhaps these two sequences serve some purpose in the film's presentation of the main characters' social awkwardness, or perhaps it is the film's nod to the traditional literary fascination (e.g., the work of Stephen King, Shirley Jackson, or Ray Bradbury) with the dark secrets of an otherwise uninteresting small town. But they may simply be enjoyed as examples of what Gerald Mast calls the "anomalous surprise" when a filmmaker "injects some character, situation, or event into the parodic narrative that makes absolutely no sense in the context" but adds to the general lunacy of the film.[11]

At the heart of the film is Corky. Variously described as "fey," or "flamboyant," he certainly stands out from the crowd in Blaine as a recent arrival from New York City and as being more artistically gifted and experienced. The mayor and the town council, while not acceding to what they consider Corky's ridiculous demands for financial backing (after he sees the possibility of a move to Broadway), all agree that only Corky's direction can pull off the pageant as the climax of the town's sesquicentennial celebration. His obvious toupee with its blond bangs defines his character as much as Guest's shoulder-length rockstar hairpiece did for him as Nigel Tufnel in *This Is Spinal Tap*. His lisping delivery, effeminate gestures, and total devotion to theater suggest that he may be gay. His occasional angry outbursts, with such bizarre epithets as "bastard people" and "I hate you, and I hate your ass-face" come across as ineffectual hissy fits. This perception is further supported by his past service in the navy; his description of his long-ago arrival in New York City with just a "dance belt and a tube of Chapstick"; his reference to getting one's legs waxed; his resort to a bubble bath after the city council's refusal of his request for more funding; and his habit of doing the shopping for all his wife's clothes, including her panty hose and pants suit.

In fact, no one in the town has ever seen Corky's wife, Bonnie, and he appears to live alone in his second-story apartment. Even Councilman Stark, clearly smitten with Corky, never seems to entertain thoughts about Corky's, and indeed his own, sexual orientation. In an interview with *Advocate* magazine, Guest seems to sidestep the issue, saying that the film "is not about Corky's sexuality. The heart of the movie is about Corky as a person. . . . If I didn't like him and was making fun of him, it wouldn't ring true."[12] The silence surrounding Corky's sexuality seems consistent with the rest of the characters' lack of self-awareness, especially their grandiose evaluations of their level of talent and the amateur quality of the production that they are perfectly willing to believe is capable of being produced on Broadway.

While *Red, White, and Blaine* never makes its way to Broadway, it turns out to be a major hit with its target audience. The townsfolk in the audience are perfectly thrilled with the pageant. Inspired by the American flag and balloons finale, they rise to give a standing ovation, led by the ecstatic cheers of Councilman Stark. Muir points out the following:

> One of the overlooked things in *Waiting for Guffman* is the recognition that the acting company actually succeeds, at least to some modest extent. Yes, their show is corny and amateurish, but who can deny that this group of actors really pleases the townspeople who attend the show. . . . Really, when you think about it, isn't that the ultimate goal, the ultimate success of any performer, on any stage? To make your audience happy? To elicit hoots of approval from the crowd seated before you?[13]

While Roscoe and Hight comment that "there is a kind of pathos to the fact that such a terrible show can elicit feelings of excitement and recognition," the filmmakers refuse to criticize the audience's taste.[14] Also, as Muir observes, the pattern of mainstream comedy is "that something terrible would have certainly happened in the last act": stage lights falling or exploding, an actor falling over a set piece, or some other calamity, but the "films of Christopher Guest don't play that game."[15] And the coda shows that Corky and the cast have moved on, inspired by their experience of such a major crowd-pleaser.

The film itself did not enjoy an equally enthusiastic audience reception, but the reviews were quite appreciative. In *Newsweek*, David Ansen captures the spirit of the film quite accurately as a "savvy satire of small-town boosterism and an affectionate salute to the performing spirit."[16]

The future of mockumentary films as a comedy genre may well be threatened by the rise of more serious documentaries that combine angry indictment with dark humor. Michael Moore's *Roger and Me* (1989) goes after the auto industry; *Bowling for Columbine* (2002) explores the American fascination with guns and the encouragement of fear and bigotry that fosters the gun culture (and managed to win an Academy Award for Best Documentary); *Fahrenheit 9/11* (2004) attacks the administration of George W. Bush for exploiting the 9/11 attacks to plunge America into wars in Iraq and Afghanistan; and *Sicko* (2007) compares the American profit-driven health-care system to its counterparts in other countries, especially France and Canada, and includes a sequence in which Moore took some 9/11 first responders to Cuba to get better care for their respiratory conditions caused by their rescue work at Ground Zero. Moore's use of outlandish but deadly serious pranks; his device of ambushing politicians, business executives, and other bigwigs with embarrassing questions; and the inclusion of equally embarrassing archival footage can be as comic as anything Guest and company present.

Morgan Spurlock's exposé of the fast-food industry, *Super Size Me* (2004), builds on the outrageous premise that the writer/director spends a month eating food only from McDonalds and documents the resultant damage to his health. Spurlock served as producer for an even more comic documentary, *What Would Jesus Buy?* (2007), which criticizes the commercialization of Christmas by following the Reverend Billy and his Stop Shopping Gospel Choir in their cross-country tour of shopping malls (and even Disneyland) as he warns people of the coming "Shopacolypse." The film indicts the role of multinational corporations and sweatshop industries and looks at the landfills and credit-card debt created by American consumerism. Reverend Billy (performance artist Billy Talen) makes comic use of religious-revival techniques and rites of exorcism to spread his anticonsumerism gospel. The *Chicago Tribune* calls the film a "witty, abrasive, and hugely entertaining romp," and *Mother Jones's* review mentions that the choir's "hymns and carols are silly and sarcastic but surprisingly critical."[17] The mockumentary films' subtle and affectionate spoofs and parodies seem to have given way to more angry critiques that make effective use of a more biting humor of satirical attack. Meanwhile, the genre has made its way into television with the documentary style of such popular situation comedies as *The Office* (2005–), *Parks and Recreation* (2009–), and *Modern Family* (2009–).

From big screen to small screen, mockumentaries have attracted some serious cult followers. Who knows where the mockery will show up next?

A Sampling of Mockumentaries

The Rutles (1978)
Zelig (1983)
This Is Spinal Tap (1984)
Bob Roberts (1992)
The Return of Spinal Tap (1992)
An Alan Smithee Film: Burn Hollywood Burn (1997)
Drop Dead Gorgeous (1999)
Best in Show (2000)
A Mighty Wind (2003)
For Your Consideration (2006)

Notes

1. Jane Roscoe and Craig Hight, *Faking It: Mock-Documentary and the Subversion of Factuality* (Manchester, U.K., and New York: Manchester University Press, 2001), 47.

2. Ethan de Seife, *This Is Spinal Tap* (New York: Wallflower Press, 2001), 6.

3. De Seife, *This Is Spinal Tap*, 7.

4. De Seife, *This Is Spinal Tap*, 47.

5. Roger Ebert, "*This Is Spinal Tap*." *Chicago Sun-Times*, March 1, 1985, p. 57.

6. Janet Maslin, "Movie Review: *This Is Spinal Tap*." *New York Times*, March 2, 1984, p. 14.

7. Richard Corliss, "*This Is Spinal Tap*." *Time*, March 5, 1984, p. 35.

8. John Kenneth Muir, *Best in Show: The Films of Christopher Guest and Company* (New York: Applause Books, 2004), 117–18.

9. Muir, *Best in Show*, 101.

10. Muir, *Best in Show*, 100.

11. Gerald Mast, *The Comic Mind: Comedy and the Movies*, 2nd ed. (Chicago: University of Chicago Press, 1979), 310.

12. "Screen Queen," *Advocate*, March 18, 1997, n.p.

13. Muir, *Best in Show*, 120–21.

14. Roscoe and Hight, *Faking It*, 126.

15. Muir, *Best in Show*, 120–21.

16. David Ansen, "*Waiting for Guffman*." *Newsweek*, February 10, 1997, p. 66.

17. Jessica Reaves, "Movie Review: *What Would Jesus Buy?*" *Chicago Tribune*, November 29, 2007, p. 22; Gary Moskowitz, "*What Would Jesus Buy?*" *Mother Jones*, November 22, 2007, n.p.

CHAPTER 11

Animated Comedy

SOUTH PARK: BIGGER, LONGER & UNCUT (1999)

At the very end of the twentieth century, film animation took a daring leap forward with the release of a controversial import from cable television, Trey Parker's and Matt Stone's *South Park: Bigger, Longer & Uncut.* The very title announces that the goal of the film is to break many taboos. It features four foul-mouthed third-graders whose devotion to two Canadian film comedians—the mindless, vulgar, and flatulent Terrance and Phillip—prompts their parents to declare war against Canada. It was a far cry from the days of Mickey Mouse, Bambi, or even Shrek and Buzz Lightyear. The film is rife with swearing, offensive remarks and gestures, and acts of violence, all of which earned it an R rating.

This new development, however, was not without precedent in the history of the genre. In many cases over the years, it was as if the use of cartoon characters and settings freed up their creators to dip into unknown territory in comedy. It all started in 1910, when a popular comic strip artist for the *New York Herald,* Winsor McCay, responding to a bet from his fellow cartoonists, drew some 4,000 pen-and-ink drawings and photographed them on film so that they could follow one another at sixteen frames per second, the same rate used at that time in the projection of live-action films. The result was a five-minute cartoon with moving characters that starred his already popular comic strip character, Little Nemo. Vitagraph Studios distributed the film, which debuted in theaters on April 8, 1911. A few years later, sixteen-year-old Walter Lantz, who went on to create Woody Woodpecker, started creating film cartoons for William Randolph Hearst's studio, International Film Service. In 1919, William Messmer introduced the first cartoon star, Felix the Cat. By 1920, Paul Terry, another New York illustrator and photographer working at Bray Studios in New York City, using a rural character, Farmer Al Falfa, upped the ante in terms of cartoon production. Stefan Kanfer, in his history of film animation, *Serious Business: The Art and Commerce of Animation*

Cartman, Stan, and Kyle lead a children's crusade against parental foolishness in *South Park: Bigger, Longer & Uncut* (1999).

in America from Betty Boop to "Toy Story," describes the process and the demand, saying the following:

> Terry, like his boss, John Randolph Bray, brought the techniques of Henry Ford into the field of animation. The artists and their assistants worked on what amounted to an assembly line, simplifying costumes, drawing only what was absolutely necessary, and suggesting the rest with an outline or a brushstroke. Output increased; costs were dramatically reduced. The only casualty was quality: At a time when exhibitors demanded "product" to round out the movie program, Terry had little reason to improve or enliven the adventures of Al Falfa.[1]

Bray's real breakthrough came with his series of cartoons based on Aesop's Fables, and a significant understanding of cartoon comedy and its characters was the result:

> The fables underlined what Aesop and LaFontaine and other fabulists had found long ago and what Messmer was in the process of

rediscovering: People who behave like animals get ostracized; animals who behave like people become immortals. . . . The fables, like the adventures of Felix, demonstrate to filmgoers that mammals, birds, reptiles, and amphibians could sustain a picture all by themselves. . . . The Animal Powers, so prevalent in ancient societies, were reasserting themselves in clown costumes.[2]

Then a young man from Kansas City appeared on the scene. Barely out of his teens, Walter Elias Disney built an art studio, learned about animation from a book he borrowed from the library, and formed a company called Laugh-O-Gram Films, Inc. In July 1923, as his company in Kansas City went broke, Disney moved to Hollywood and set up Disney Studios. It is worth noting for the purpose of this study that Disney's first cartoon success, starring a rabbit named Oswald, dabbled in naughty material. Kanfer describes the development, writing the following:

> By the fourth adventure, "Great Guns," Oswald had acquired a hyperactive libido and a rabbity girlfriend, later to be named Fanny. . . . Cannons would fire and then grow flaccid; Oswald's ears also assumed a phallic quality, and Fanny got a lot of laughs when she became excited over Oswald's prowess with a bayonet.[3]

When he encountered problems with his New York distributor in 1928, Disney dropped the Oswald character, who was immediately adopted by the animation division of Universal Studios, and he invented a new one whose physiognomy varied only slightly from the rabbit: a mouse whom Disney's wife, Lillian, named Mickey.

Although *South Park: Bigger, Longer & Uncut* might be the most shocking title ever given to an animated film, there are precedents for daring material even in the most mainstream examples of the genre. From their earliest years, cartoon films dabbled in the risqué. A Disney artist once commented that "Mickey is made out a series of circles . . . but circles are things we have fun with: babies, women's behinds, breasts," while a psychologist suggested otherwise, observing that the "symbolic meaning of Mickey's figure is obvious. Symbolically, we should have to call it a phallus but a desexualized one," and his actions and adventures "demonstrate his lack of genital interest."[4] Many of Felix the Cat's cartoons showed him in a drunken state. Betty Boop's behavior was even more shocking. As Kanfer describes her, "Betty's wardrobe had a mind of its own. Garments opened up or flew off when she least expected it to reveal her bra, panties, and signature garter."[5]

Other material that would be considered shocking and offensive today showed up in animated film. Karl Cohen observes that "racial stereotypes in cartoons date back to the silent era; by the early sound era, unflattering caricatures of almost every nationality had appeared in animated cartoons."[6] The Motion Picture Production Code, which went into effect in 1934, brought much of the sexual naughtiness to an end, but not all of the ethnic stereotypes. Maureen Furniss's study of representation in animated film includes Cohen's report that Paramount's cartoon division "continued to distribute racist imagery until about 1958."[7]

Meanwhile, Disney emerged as the leading provider of good, clean fun, not only producing some of the most famous short cartoons, but soon the full-length stories of Snow White and the Seven Dwarfs, Pinocchio, Cinderella, Bambi, Winnie the Pooh, and many others before his death in 1966. Yet even these full-length animated films were capable of shocking audiences. The first full-length animated film to come out of the Disney Studios, *Snow White and the Seven Dwarfs* (1937), frightened many children in its audience with its graphic presentation of the Evil Queen and the sequence showing Snow White lost in the dark forest. One factoid about the film claims that when the film had its debut at Radio City Music Hall, some of the children were so frightened that they wet their pants, requiring the replacement of many of the stained velvet seats. When the film was released in Britain, considerable controversy arose because the British Board of Film Censors gave the film an A rating, requiring children to be accompanied by their parents (a requirement that was largely ignored by local censors and theaters). All of this concern did not prevent *Snow White and the Seven Dwarfs* from becoming Hollywood's highest-grossing film up to that time. Disney's second animated feature film, *Pinocchio* (1940), also caused controversy for its violent action. The August 1993 edition of *Playboy* magazine cited twenty-three instances of battery, nine acts of property damage, three uses of the word *jackass*, three acts of violence involving animals, and two shots of male nudity. And the sequence in Disney's *Bambi* (1942) in which Bambi's mother is killed by hunters was found to be quite disturbing to children in the audience.

Almost nothing about *South Park* reminds audiences of Disney's work, except for the parodies of songs from the Disney Studios' *The Little Mermaid* and *Beauty and the Beast.* For one thing, it's a good deal funnier. For another, it blends satire with transgressive humor to make its point. And it offers an original story, bearing no resemblance to Aesop's fables or Brothers Grimm fairy tales.

After a few minutes of introduction to the town and the main characters, the plot begins. After four boys—Stan, Cartman, Kyle, and Kenny—leave a movie theater displaying the Canadians Terrance and Phillip, whose only humor consists of crude language and flatulence, in a vulgar and mindless film, *Asses of Fire*, the boys proceed to swear compulsively. School officials become concerned, and Kyle's mother, Sheila Broflovski, forms a group called Mothers against Canada, blaming the country for all of the ills of American society. She is eventually appointed secretary of defense. Terrance and Phillip are captured and condemned to execution. Because, as is shown in a special meeting of the United Nations Security Council, the entire economy of Canada depends upon the popularity of Terrance and Phillip, Canada retaliates by bombing the Baldwin brothers' Hollywood home, and war is declared between the two countries.

Meanwhile, Kenny dies and goes to hell, as his mother predicted he would when he chose to attend the movie rather than go to church. There he finds a muscle-bound Satan involved in a gay relationship with a recent arrival, Saddam Hussein. While in hell, Kenny finds out that the execution of Terrance and Phillip will be the seventh sign of the Apocalypse, when Satan will arise and take over the world. Kenny manages to appear in a vision to Cartman to inform him of this eventuality. The boys join in an underground movement called La Resistance, which intends to disrupt a USO show that is scheduled to end with the comedians' execution.

After considerable military carnage among Canadian and U.S. armies results in utter confusion, Sheila takes matters into her own hands and kills Terrance and Phillip, bringing about, as predicted, Satan's return to earth. In his fondness for Kenny, however, Satan grants him one final wish before Kenny returns with him to hell. Kenny wishes for everything to return to the way it was before the war. His wish is granted, and Kenny, who died before the war and is therefore still dead, is taken up into heaven, while the town of South Park returns to its normal peaceful state.

At its release in the summer of 1999, the film received quite favorable reviews from the leading critics, often with something of a disclaimer. Roger Ebert, for example, writes, "I laughed. I did not always feel proud of myself while I was laughing, however." His summary evaluation praises the film as a "signpost for our troubled times" and urges his readers to see the film: "Just for the information it contains about the way we live now, thoughtful and concerned people should see it. After all, everyone else will."[8] Stephen Holden of the *New York Times* concurs, saying that the film "cannily zeroes in on some essential contradictions in American culture."[9]

Ebert was correct in his predictions of the film's popularity. Even with its R rating, the film grossed more than $83 million worldwide (not bad for a film with a $21 million budget). Mick LaSalle of the *San Francisco Chronicle* offers one of the best descriptions of the film's humor:

> *South Park: Bigger, Longer & Uncut* is an eighty-eight-minute wallow in nonstop crudeness, vulgarity, and unpleasantness. It's without any redeeming social value whatever. And it's funny from beginning to end. . . . A satire on contemporary America. . . . The songs are incredibly profane, and that's what makes *South Park* more hilarious spoof than wallow. The world it depicts is only slightly more crude than our own. Parker's comic imagination is unrestrained and irreverent.[10]

LaSalle's colleague at the *San Francisco Examiner*, Wesley Morris, focuses on the contribution of Parker's and Stone's style of primitive animation:

> One of the elements often overlooked is its multitextured, arts-and-crafts look, which is *a key to its subversiveness* [emphasis mine]. On a big screen, laid out in all its pop-collage glory, *South Park* is a bracing aberration. . . . The inhabitants look as if they were conceived from a still life done on a Technicolor Etch-a-Sketch with an assortment of Peanuts and Fisher-Price roly-poly people for models. Parker and Stone use their movie as an opportunity to imbue *South Park* with computer effects that jab at movie digitalization.[11]

South Park manages to be a combination of three modes of comedy: transgressive humor, delighting in the breaking of taboos; parody of other animated films and some film musicals; and satire of various features of the American culture and the media. An examination of each of these three threads, which often intersect, reveals the richness of this comedy.

Transgressive humor is not to be confused with satire, although they often coexist in one joke or movie plot. While satire attacks its target, transgression plays with it. Satire originates from a sense of outrage against whatever the satirist considers foolish or even immoral behavior or attitudes, declaring war on human folly with the hope of reform.[12] Transgression aims only at breaking society's taboos and shocking its audience without necessarily arguing for any change. Most of *South Park*'s comedy fits under this rubric; in fact, almost all of the comedy in the first season or so of the television version was merely transgressive, seeking only to shock its viewers with extremely inappropriate language and behavior, with no particular social criticism intended. Yet, it turned into something of a guilty pleasure for its viewers. The presentation of third-graders indulging in vulgar language and obscene expressions certainly violates society's standards and taboos. Stan's habit of vomiting whenever he tries to speak to his love object, Wendy, is simply a crude indulgence in some generally disapproved behavior.

In the film, the very titles of some of the film's songs, for example, "Uncle Fucka" and "Kyle's Mom Is a Bitch," are outrageous taboo-breakers. The idea that Stan's mother once made a pornographic film involving a Nazi and some defecation offends political, ethnic, and feminist sensibilities. Sexual taboos are constantly shattered with disparaging remarks by the boys' teacher, Mr. Garrison, about the female menstrual cycle; explicit references to gay sexual activity by Saddam Hussein; the suggestion at one point during the USO show that Winona Ryder is shooting ping-pong balls out of her vagina; the actual appearance of a giant clitoris with the voice of Glinda the Good Witch; and even the appearance of the naked female angels who welcome Kenny when he finally makes it into heaven. Similarly, the brief appearance of Mahatma Gandhi and George Burns as inhabitants of hell is surely not meant as a criticism of these admirable figures but merely a mischievous conjecture. The idea that Conan O'Brien would conspire with the army to capture Terrance and Phillip by inviting them on his show is hardly an attack on him. None of these personalities is treated with any sense of disapproval. Parker and Stone are simply playing in the mud, wallowing in forbidden territory, with no suggestion that any of it is wrong or should be stopped.

Paul Wells's treatment of animated comedy proposes that much of this transgressive humor arises almost by the very nature of the genre, claiming that "animation in the United States has been characterized by a desire to express *difference* and *otherness.*"[13] Furthermore, Wells analyzes the function of animated comedy for adult audiences as the "indulgent regression into an adolescent state or in the opportunity to relive the freedoms of a child's uninhibited imagination."[14] In this film, at least, the boys, while often frustrated by the strictures of their parents and other authority figures, ultimately would agree with Kyle's wish at the end of the film that "everything would go back to the way it was." Neither they nor their creators are arguing for change in their lives in South Park. (American culture at large, however, is another matter.)

Second, the film provides some clever parodies of other animated films and various cultural artifacts. The musical numbers provide the best examples; and, indeed, the musical score won the most awards that the film received: Best Original Score from the Chicago Film Critics, Best Music from the Los Angeles Film Critics, and Best Musical Performance (given to both Parker and Stone) from the MTV Movie Awards. Parker teamed with one of the most successful songwriters in the business, Marc Shaiman, who started his career on *Saturday Night Live* (1975–) and went on to win a Tony for Best Original Score for the Broadway production of *Hairspray* (2002–2009). The first song in the film, "Mountain Town" at first resembles the opening song of Belle in Disney's *Beauty and the Beast* (1991), except while Belle enjoys the friendliness and compliments of her fellow townspeople, Kyle describes his town of South Park, Colorado, as a "whitebread redneck podunk white-trash" little town. Kyle's mother sings "the world is such a rotten place" as the reason why she has moved to "this meshugana" town. Another Disney movie is spoofed in Satan's song, "Up There," in which he compares life on earth, mostly on a gay cruise, to his lonely life in hell, much as Ariel, the mermaid, dreams of life on land in *The Little Mermaid* (1989). The children's military anthem, "La Resistance," parodies the similar anthems in the musical *Les Miserables* (1935); and Big Gay Al's big production number at the USO show, "I'm Super," turns into a Busby Berkeley extravaganza. Even Saddam Hussein's love song to his satanic inamorata, "I Can Change," echoes the anthem "And I Am Changing" from the Broadway and Hollywood musical *Dreamgirls* (2006). When Kyle encounters the giant clitoris, it speaks to him in the voice of Billie Burke as Glinda the

Good Witch from *The Wizard of Oz* (1939), with the inspirational message, "Believe in yourself, and others will believe in you," almost the same words as those in Glinda's song near the end of the stage and film version of the story, *The Wiz* (1978).

Other elements of the narrative are parodies. The young French boy who leads them in the resistance against the plan to kill Terrance and Phillip is a poor man's atheistic existentialist. Morris's review remarks that the film's depiction of hell "looks like the cover art of any metal record come to satanic life."[15] The gay cruise ship that Satan dreams of when he fantasizes a life "up there" on Earth is not too different from the advertisements for actual cruises aimed at the gay-lesbian-bisexual-transgender demographic. Satan and Saddam's lovers' quarrels borrow from television shows and many a manual for communication between couples. Late-night television and television news are spoofed as well. Early in the film, the nightly news features a male midget wearing a bikini (anything for ratings) for his report from the "scene of the crime," the theater showing *Asses of Fire*. Later, amid threats of war between the United States and Canada, the Emergency Broadcast System goes into operation, transmitting the message from President Bill Clinton that "in a day that will live in infamy," the Canadians have bombed the Hollywood home of the Baldwin brothers, a clear "act of war." War is declared. Even Satan and Saddam Hussein watch television in hell; their special favorite is *War News*. In the most absurd television segment, Terrance and Phillip are guests on *The Tonight Show with Conan O'Brien*, only to be ambushed and captured, thanks to a bribe Sheila gave Conan.

While transgression and parody abound, this film offers some satire as well. While most of the film's comedy is merely playful and naughty, Parker and Stone clearly disapprove of several elements in American culture and argue for some change. Their initial target of criticism is the hysteria of controlling parents who, shocked by their own children's behavior, invariably hasten to scapegoat influences other than their own negligent parenting. As usual, the first corrupting influence to be blamed is the media, in this case, Terrance and Phillip's film *Asses of Fire*. And, not surprisingly, because the film was made in Canada, it is inevitable that foreign influences are also seen as dangerous and, in fact, must be opposed by our military might. Sheila leads the Mothers against Canada in the anthem of their crusade, "Blame Canada." The parents' desire to control their children's habit of bad language first gets assistance from the school counselor, Mr. Macker, who gently suggests that they use other words as substitutes for the offensive language, for example, "buns" for "ass," "poo" for "shit," and "rich" for "bitch." The efforts at control go so far as to submit Cartman to aversion therapy to cure him of his penchant for crude language, introducing a V-chip into his brain that administers an electric shock every time he utters a naughty word. Meanwhile, as Holden remarks, the film's "argument is distilled in a single, short speech pointing out that movies allow almost unlimited violence while remaining petrified of anything reeking of smut."[16]

A second target of satire is the military. As the United States enters into war with Canada, the army places anyone of Canadian origin into "death camps" and arranges that the "first attack wing," otherwise known as "Operation Human Shield," is composed completely of African American soldiers. The highlight of the USO show is an execution. The battle against Canada, with its tanks and planes, gets pretty bloody. The military serves as the instrument of the public hysteria over the foul language in the media, while neither the citizens nor the military exhibit any concern about violence. Near the end of the fighting, Kyle first confronts his military commander by maintaining that their crusade is "about more than just fart jokes. This is about freedom of speech and censorship . . . and stuff." He then addresses his mother, Sheila, with the film's basic "message," saying, "Mom, you never took the time to talk to me. Whenever I get in trouble, you go off and blame everybody else. But I'm the one to blame, you and me. You keep going off and fighting all these causes. But I don't want a fighter; I want my Mom."

Animation, almost by its very nature, provides a welcoming space for satire. Wells observes, "Ultimately, animation . . . has the capacity to subvert, critically comment upon, and redetermine views of culture and social practices," and it praises its "omnipresent significance as a potentially radical art form."[17] Meanwhile, since almost all animated films are comedies, Wells also remarks the following:

> The very language of comedy, like animation, is an intrinsically alternative one, speaking to a revisionist reengagement with the "taken for granted." In the American context, it is especially the case that animation . . . has served to operate as a distorting and repositioning parallel genre both to established live-action films and television texts (and their predominantly conservative codes of representation), but more importantly, to society in general.[18]

As an example of this process, Wells presents the television version of *The Simpsons* (1989–) as "merely a variant on the American sitcom traditions . . . but it's very status as an animation asks an audience to reperceive supposedly everyday issues, themes, and knowledge."[19] While the television version of *South Park* (1997–) began and was perceived as a further regression into childhood irresponsibility and bad behavior, within its first two years, it began to morph into a "potentially radical art form" by its mockery of celebrities and social issues. It started rather naturally by making fun of such popular entertainment figures as Barbra Streisand, Mel Gibson, and Tom Cruise, mainly because they took themselves so seriously (a mortal sin in the world of animated comedy), with their respective crusades for feminist issues and liberal politics, conservative religious views, and promotion of Scientology. It then moved on to tackle such controversial issues as homosexuality with Cartman's "gay" dog and Big Gay Al; famine in Africa with the boys' African immigrant classmate, Starvin' Marvin; and even cartoon versions of Jesus, Muhammad, and Moses.

The filmmakers' interest in religion is one of the features of *South Park* that has received little attention (however, with the enormous success of their multiaward-winning Broadway musical *The Book of Mormon* [2011–], this is no longer the case). Like the reference to the founders of the three monotheistic religions in their television series, Parker's and Stone's religious references are not particularly satiric, falling much more into the taboo-breaking pattern of transgressive humor. In the opening number, Stan's mother compares her son to Jesus because he is "so tender and mild." As Stan gathers the boys to see *Asses of Fire*, Kenny's mother does not give her permission because he is supposed to be going to church. Instead, Kenny joins the boys for the movie, as his mother warns him that he will go to hell when he dies because of missing church— which, in fact, he does about a third of the way through the film. On their way to the movie, the boys ignore a homeless man, and they quickly pass by the church choir and the minister.

But all of this is nothing compared to the film's depiction of hell. After being rejected from heaven, Kenny is welcomed into hell by Satan himself. Kenny is immediately chained and stretched, in accordance with the traditional image of eternal punishment. Indeed, several of hell's inhabitants are eventually shown hanging upside down. It is not too surprising to find Saddam Hussein in hell, although in 1999 he had not yet died, or to find Hitler there as well, but the presence of Gandhi and Burns might raise a few eyebrows. Satan, the sensitive partner in a gay relationship with Saddam Hussein, "gets all biblical" when he realizes that the execution of Terrance and Phillip could bring about the Apocalypse. The French leader of the boys' revolution is an atheist. In the film's finale, Kenny finally goes to heaven, where he is greeted by naked female angels. Indeed, religion plays a part in the worldview of everyone in the movie, with the exception of the existential atheist who leads La Resistance. In none of these sequences is religion seriously criticized, only played with for shock effect.

Some reflexive humor about the role of the media in society occurs in the presentation of the nightly news and the newsreel about the war with Canada, but the primary joke is that this is a naughty movie about another naughty movie and its effect on children. The boys have their own opinion about the role of movies in their lives as they sing, "Movies teach us what the parents don't have time to say."

When even the mainstream animated films could be controversial, a more subversive film can be counted on to provide much more offensive material. In her listing of the distinguishing features of such nontraditional fare, Furniss includes the "tendency to reflect alternative lifestyles, challenge dominant beliefs, and represent the concerns and attitudes of marginalized social groups."[20] The portrayal of Big Gay Al, the sexual relationship of Satan and Saddam Hussein, the sexual frankness of Chef, the suggestion that Cartman's mother may have made a pornographic movie, and the reaction of the African American soldiers when they realize that they have been assigned to the front lines as cannon fodder in the war against Canada provide plenty of depictions of alternative behavior and attitudes.

Even with its critical acclaim and huge box-office numbers, *South Park: Bigger, Longer & Uncut* did not inspire much imitation in the Hollywood film industry. Instead, the presentation of subversive material has proceeded much further on television, with boundaries constantly being broken on the small-screen counterpart by the continued popularity of *South Park*, the television series, as well as on *Family Guy* (1999–), *King of the Hill* (1997–2010), *Futurama* (1999–), *American Dad* (2005–), *The Cleveland Show* (2009–), and other animated sitcoms. Meanwhile, Hollywood keeps turning out Disney and Pixar creations year after year that manage to entertain children, as well as their parents.

Coincidentally, *The Simpsons Movie* (2007), the big-screen version of the longest-running animated television show in history, with its milder violations of social norms, proved to be much more popular, earning more than ten times more than *South Park: Bigger, Longer & Uncut* at the box office. Much of Hollywood's transgressive comedy in the twenty-first century has shown up in films associated with Judd Apatow and Adam McKay. In such films as *Knocked Up* (2007), *Superbad* (2007), and *The Hangover* (2009), crude dialogue and bad behavior have led to major box-office success. As things stand, *South Park* remains something of an anomaly. Alone in its transgressive glory, it just might be a true classic.

Comedy is a many-headed Halloween monster, a shape-shifter that continues to surprise and delight us even when we don't know what to call it. After all is said and done, while it can be fun to analyze and categorize the wealth of comedy our filmmakers have produced, all we really need to do is sit back, relax, and have a good laugh. See you at the movies!

A Sampling of Recent Animated Comedy

Toy Story (1995)
Antz (1998)
Shrek (2001)
Monsters, Inc. (2001)
Finding Nemo (2003)
The Incredibles (2004)
Cars (2006)
Happy Feet (2006)
Ratatouille (2007)
Up (2009)

Notes

1. Stefan Kanfer, *Serious Business: The Art and Commerce of Animation in America from Betty Boop to "Toy Story"* (New York: Scribner Press, 1997), 42.

2. Kanfer, *Serious Business*, 43–44.

3. Kanfer, *Serious Business*, 59.

4. Kanfer, *Serious Business*, 65.

5. Kanfer, *Serious Business*, 73.

6. Karl Cohen, "Racism and Resistance: Black Stereotypes in Animation." *Animation Journal*, vol. 4, no. 2 (Spring 1996): 43.

7. Maureen Furniss, *Art in Motion: Animation Aesthetics* (Sydney, Australia: John Libbey & Company, 1998), 232.

8. Roger Ebert, "*South Park: Bigger, Longer & Uncut*," *Chicago Sun-Times*, June 30, 1999, p. 19.

9. Stephen Holden, "Film Review: *South Park: Bigger, Longer & Uncut*." *New York Times*, June 30, 1999, p. 30.

10. Mick LaSalle, "It's Crude, Dude: *South Park*, Shockingly Vulgar—and Hilarious South Story." *San Francisco Chronicle*, June 30, 1999, p. E-1.

11. Wesley Morris, "It's a Gas, Dude! *South Park* Is Crass, Crude—and Scathingly Funny." *San Francisco Examiner*, June 30, 1999, p. C.

12. Please refer to the treatment of satire in chapter 6, "Satire: *Dr. Strangelove*."

13. Paul Wells, *Animation and America* (Piscataway, N.J.: Rutgers University Press, 2002), 1.

14. Wells, *Animation and America*, 12.

15. Morris, "It's a Gas, Dude!," p. C.

16. Holden, "Film Review: *South Park: Bigger, Longer & Uncut*," p. 30.

17. Wells, *Animation and America*, 16.

18. Wells, *Animation and America*, 5.

19. Wells, *Animation and America*, 6.

20. Furniss, *Art in Motion*, 30.

Bibliography

Books

Allen, Woody. *Four Films of Woody Allen*. New York: Random House, 1982.
———. *Woody Allen on Woody Allen*. New York: Grove Press, 1993.
Altman, Rick. *The American Film Musical*. Bloomington: Indiana University Press, 1987.
Ames, Christopher. *Movies about the Movies*. Lexington: University Press of Kentucky, 1997.
Bailey, Peter J. *The Reluctant Film Art of Woody Allen*. Lexington: University Press of Kentucky, 2001.
Behlmer, Rudy. *America's Favorite Movies: Behind the Scenes*. London: Samuel French, 1990.
Bergman, Andrew. *We're in the Money: Depression America and Its Films*. New York: Harper & Row, 1972.
Bergson, Henri. *Laughter: An Essay on the Meaning of the Comic*, trans. Cloudesley Brereton and Fred Rothwell. New York: MacMillan, 1924.
Bernheimer, Kathryn. *The 50 Funniest Movies of All Time: A Critic's Ranking*. Secaucus, N.J.: Carol Publishing Group, 1999.
Blake, Richard. *Woody Allen: Profane and Sacred*. Lanham, Md.: Scarecrow Press, 1995.
Chandler, Charlotte. *Nobody's Perfect: Willy Wilder, a Personal Biography*. New York: Simon & Schuster, 2002.
Charney, Maurice. *The Comic World of the Marx Brothers' Movies*. Teaneck, N.J.: Fairleigh Dickinson University Press, 2007.
Cohan, Steve. *Hollywood Musicals: The Film Reader*. New York: Routledge, 2002.
Conklin, John E. *Campus Life in the Movies*. Jefferson, N.C., and London: McFarland & Co., 2008.
Cornford, Francis MacDonald. *The Origin of Attic Comedy*. Ann Arbor: University of Michigan Press, 1993.
Crick, Robert Alan. *The Big Screen Comedies of Mel Brooks*. Jefferson, N.C., and London: McFarland & Co., 2002.

de Seife, Ethan. *This Is Spinal Tap*. New York: Wallflower Press, 2001.

Detith, Simon. *Parody*. London: Routledge, 2000.

di Battista, Maria. *Fast-Talking Dames*. New Haven, Conn.: Yale University Press, 2001.

Dunne, Michael. *American Film Musical Themes and Forms*. Jefferson, N.C., and London: McFarland & Co., 2004.

Eyles, Allan. *The Marx Brothers: Their World of Comedy*. New York: Paperback Library, 1969.

Feuer, Jane. *The Hollywood Musical*. Bloomington: Indiana University Press, 1982.

Fordin, Hugh. *M-G-M's Greatest Musicals: The Arthur Freed Unit*. New York: DaCapo Press, 1996.

Fox, Julian. *Movies from Manhattan*. Woodstock, N.Y.: Overlook Press, 1996.

Frye, Northrop. *Anatomy of Criticism: Four Essays*. Princeton, N.J.: Princeton University Press, 1957.

Furniss, Maureen. *Art in Motion: Animation Aesthetics*. Sydney, Australia: John Libbey & Company, 1998.

Gehring, Wes D. *Parody as Film Genre*. Westport, Conn.: Greenwood Press, 1999.

———. *Romantic vs. Screwball Comedy: Charting the Difference*. Lanham, Md.: Scarecrow Press, 2002.

———. *Screwball Comedy: A Genre of Madcap Romance*. New York: Greenwood Press, 1986.

———. *The World of Comedy: Five Takes on Funny*. Davenport, Iowa: Robin Vincent Publishing, 2001.

Gelmis, Joseph. *The Film Director as Superstar*. New York: Doubleday, 1970.

Gemunden, Gerd. *A Foreign Affair: Billy Wilder's American Films*. New York: Berghan Books, 2008.

Girgus, Sam B. *The Films of Woody Allen*, 2nd ed. Cambridge, UK: Cambridge University Press, 2002.

Glitre, Kathrina. *Hollywood Romantic Comedy: States of the Union, 1934–1965*. Manchester, UK, and New York: Manchester University Press, 2006.

Harris, Dan. *Film Parody*. London: BFI Publishing, 2000.

Harris, Warren G. *Clark Gable*. New York: Harmony Books, 2002.

Hirsch, Foster. *Love, Sex, Death, and the Meaning of Life: The Films of Woody Allen*. Cambridge, Mass.: DaCapo Press, 2001.

Hughes, David. *The Complete Kubrick*, rev. ed. London: Virgin Publishing, Ltd., 2001.

Jones, Frederick. *Juvenal and the Satiric Genre*. London: Gerald Duckwork & Co., Ltd., 2007.

Juster, A. M., ed. *The Satires of Horace*. Philadelphia: University of Pennsylvania Press, 2008.

Juvenal. *The Satires of Juvenal*, trans. Rolfe Humphries. Bloomington: Indiana University Press, 1970.

Kagan, Norman. *The Cinema of Stanley Kubrick*, 3rd ed. New York: Continuum, 2000.

Kanfer, Stefan. *Serious Business: The Art and Commerce of Animation in America from Betty Boop to "Toy Story."* New York: Scribner, 1997.

Karnick, Kristine Brunovska, and Henry Jenkins, eds. *Classical Hollywood Comedy*. New York: Routledge, 1995.

Kendall, Elizabeth. *The Runaway Bride: Hollywood Romantic Comedy of the 1930s.* New York: Doubleday, 1991.

Lee, Sander H. *Eighteen Woody Allen Films Analyzed: Anguish, God, and Existentialism.* Jefferson, N.C., and London: McFarland & Co., 2002.

Louvish, Simon. *Monkey Business: The Lives and Legends of the Marx Brothers.* New York: St. Martin's Press, 1999.

Marmorstein, Gary. *Hollywood Rhapsody: Movie Music and Its Makers, 1900–1975.* New York: Schirmer Books, 1997.

Martin, A. S. *On Parody.* New York: Henry Holt and Company, 1896.

Mast, Gerald. *The Comic Mind: Comedy and the Movies,* 2nd ed. Chicago: University of Chicago Press, 1979.

McCann, Graham. *Woody Allen.* Cambridge, UK: Polity Press, 1990.

McDonald, Tamar Jeffers. *Romantic Comedy: Boy Meets Girl Meets Genre.* London and New York: Wallflower Press, 2007.

Muir, John Kenneth. *Best in Show: The Films of Christopher Guest and Company.* New York: Applause Books, 2004.

———. *Singing a New Tune: The Rebirth of the American Musical from* Evita *to* De-Lovely *and Beyond.* New York: Applause Books, 2005.

Nelson, Thomas Allen. *Kubrick: Inside a Film Artist's Maze.* Bloomington: Indiana University Press, 2000.

Nichols, Mary. *Reconstructing Woody.* Oxford, UK, and Lanham, Md.: Rowman & Littlefield, 1998.

Nietzsche, Friedrich. *The Birth of Tragedy and the Genealogy of Morals.* New York: Doubleday, 1956.

Parish, James Robert. *It's Good to Be the King: The Seriously Funny Life of Mel Brooks.* Hoboken, N.J.: John Wiley & Sons, 2002.

Rasmussen, Randy. *Stanley Kubrick: Seven Films Analyzed.* Jefferson, N.C., and London: McFarland & Co., 2001.

Roscoe, Jane, and Craig Hight. *Faking It: Mock-Documentary and the Subversion of Factuality.* Manchester, UK, and New York: Manchester University Press, 2001.

Rosenblum, Ralph, and Robert Karen. *When the Shooting Stops.* New York: Viking Press, 1980.

Rowe, Kathleen. *The Unruly Woman: Gender and the Genres of Laughter.* Austin: University of Texas Press, 1995.

Schwarz, Richard A. *Woody, from* Antz *to* Zelig: *A Reference Guide to Woody Allen's Creative Work, 1964–1998.* Westport, Conn., and London: Greenwood Press, 2000.

Sennett, Ted. *Lunatics and Lovers.* New Rochelle, N.Y.: Arlington House, 1973.

Sinyard, Neil, and Adrian Tucker. *Journey down Sunset Boulevard: The Films of Billy Wilder.* Ryed, Isle of Wight: BCW Publishing, 1979.

Small, Christopher. *Mary Shelley's* Frankenstein: *Tracing the Myth.* Pittsburgh, Pa.: University of Pittsburgh Press, 1973.

Sperb, Jason. *The Kubrick Façade.* Lanham, Md.: Scarecrow Press, 2006.

Stam, Robert. *Subversive Pleasures: Bakhtin, Cultural Criticism, and Film.* Baltimore, Md.: Johns Hopkins University Press, 1989.

Umphlett, Wiley Lee. *The Movies Go to College*. Teaneck, N.J.: Fairleigh Dickinson University Press, 1984.

Walker, Alexander. *Stanley Kubrick, Director*. New York and London: W. W. Norton & Company, 1999.

Wartenberg, Thomas E. *Unlikely Couples: Movie Romance as Social Criticism*. Boulder, Colo.: Westview Press, 1999.

Wells, Paul. *Animation and America*. Piscataway, N.J.: Rutgers University Press, 2002.

Wernblad, Annette. *Brooklyn Is Not Expanding: Woody Allen's Comic Universe*. Cranbury, N.J.: Associated University Press, 1992.

Wiley, Mason, and Damien Bona. *Inside Oscar: The Unofficial History of the Academy Awards*. New York: Ballantine Books, 1996.

Wollen, Peter. *Singin' in the Rain*. London: British Film Institute, 1992.

Yacowar, Maurice. *Loser Takes All: The Comic Art of Woody Allen*. New York: Frederick Ungar Publishing Co., 1979.

———. *Method in Madness: The Comic Art of Mel Brooks*. New York: St. Martin's Press, 1981.

Articles

Ansen, David. "Gross Out." *Newsweek*, August 7, 1978, p. 85.

———. "*Waiting for Guffman*." *Newsweek*, February 10, 1997, p. 66.

Brustein, Robert. "Out of This World." In *Perspectives on Stanley Kubrick*, Mario Falsetto, ed., pp. 136–40. New York: G. K. Hall & Co., 1996.

Canby, Vincent. "*Young Frankenstein*." *New York Times*, December 16, 1974, p. 48.

Cohen, Karl. "Racism and Resistance: Black Stereotypes in Animation." *Animation Journal*, vol. 4, no. 2 (Spring 1996): 43–68.

Corliss, Richard. "*This Is Spinal Tap*." *Time*, March 5, 1984, p. 35.

"Current Cinema: *Animal House*." *Christian Century*, December 6, 1978, p. 1,186.

Ebert, Roger. "*National Lampoon's Animal House*." *Chicago Sun-Times*, January 1, 1978, p. 53.

———. "*South Park: Bigger, Longer & Uncut*," *Chicago Sun-Times*, June 30, 1999, p. 19.

———. "*This Is Spinal Tap*." *Chicago Sun-Times*, March 1, 1985, p. 57.

Holden, Stephen. "Film Review: *South Park: Bigger, Longer & Uncut*." *New York Times*, June 30, 1999, p. 30.

Kael, Pauline. "The Man from Dream City." *New Yorker*, July 14, 1975, pp. 52–59.

Krutnik, Frank. "Genre, Narrative, and the Hollywood Comedian." In *Classical Hollywood Comedy*, Kristine Brunovska Karnick and Henry Jenkins, eds., pp. 17–38. New York: Routledge, 1995.

Lane, Anthony. "Boys Will Be Girls." *New Yorker*, October 22, 2001, pp. 72–77.

LaSalle, Mick. "It's Crude, Dude: *South Park*, Shockingly Vulgar—and Hilarious South Story." *San Francisco Chronicle*, June 30, 1999, p. E-1.

Leach, Jim. "The Screwball Comedy." In *Film Genre: Theory and Criticism*, Barry K. Grant, ed., pp. 75–89. Metuchen, N.J.: Scarecrow Press, 1977.

Lent, Tina Olsin. "Romantic Love and Friendship: The Redefinition of Gender Relations in Screwball Comedy." In *Classical Hollywood Comedy*, Kristine Brunovska Karnick and Henry Jenkins, eds., pp. 314–31. New York and London: Routledge, 1995.

Lieberfeld, Daniel, and Judith Sanders. "Comedy and Identity in *Some Like It Hot.*" *Journal of Popular Film and Television*, vol. 26, no. 3 (Fall 1998): 128–35.

Mariani, John. "Come on with the Rain." *Journal of Popular Film and Television*, vol. 14, no. 3 (May–June 1978): 6–23.

Maslin, Janet. "Movie Review: *This Is Spinal Tap.*" *New York Times*, March 2, 1984, p. 14.

Morris, Wesley. "It's a Gas, Dude! *South Park* Is Crass, Crude—and Scathingly Funny." *San Francisco Examiner*, June 30, 1999, p. C.

Moskowitz, Gary. "*What Would Jesus Buy?*" *Mother Jones*, November 22, 2007, n.p.

Petro, Patrice. "Legacies of Weimar Cinema." In *Cinema and Modernity*, Murray Pomerance, ed., pp. 235–52. Piscataway, N.J.: Rutgers University Press, 2006.

Reaves, Jessica. "Movie Review: *What Would Jesus Buy?*" *Chicago Tribune*, November 29, 2007, pp. 22

Rich, Frank. "Cinema: *School Days.*" *Time*, August 14, 1978, p. 87.

Schatz, Thomas. "*Annie Hall* and the Issue of Modernism." In *The Films of Woody Allen*, Charles L. P. Silet, ed., pp. 123–32. Lanham, Md.: Scarecrow Press, 2006.

Schwartz, Tony. "College Humor Comes Back." *Newsweek*, October 23, 1978, pp. 88–89.

"Screen Queen." *Advocate*, March 18, 1997, n.p.

Index

About the Author

Michael V. Tueth, S.J., is associate professor of communication and media studies at Fordham University in New York, where he has also served as associate chair for several years. He received his doctorate in American studies from New York University, where he focused his research on the image of the family in popular American theater of the post–World War II era. He has also taught at Regis University in Denver, Colorado; Georgetown University in Washington, D.C.; Loyola University Chicago; and the University of Maryland. He is the author of *Laughter in the Living Room: Television Comedy and the American Home Audience* (2005). He has conducted numerous courses and workshops on comedy and its relationship to changes in social attitudes. Having taught many courses on the role of television in American culture, he now devotes his study and teaching to courses in film criticism.